Portraits and Portents

W. R. INGE, D.D., C.V.O.

Portraits and Portents

By
Alfred G. Gardiner

Essay Index Reprint Series

 BOOKS FOR LIBRARIES PRESS
FREEPORT, NEW YORK

Library of Congress Cataloging in Publication Data

Gardiner, Alfred George, 1865-1946.
    Portraits and portents.
    (Essay index reprint series)
    1. Gt. Brit.--Biography. 2. Biography--20th
century. I. Title.
DA566.9.A1G26 1971   920.042   79-167344
ISBN 0-8369-2499-1

PRINTED IN THE UNITED STATES OF AMERICA
BY
NEW WORLD BOOK MANUFACTURING CO., INC.
HALLANDALE, FLORIDA 33009

Preface

IN the following sketches I have attempted to present some of the salient aspects of the time in the terms of the personalities which embody those aspects. The studies include not only portraits, but portents. They sum up, successfully or otherwise, movements as well as characters. A comparison of the book with similar collections from the same pen written before the war will indicate, roughly, the significant changes which have come over society as the result of the convulsion of 1914-18. With the world-wide collapse of the monarchical idea, the place which was filled in the previous volumes by the European dynasts is taken by the dictators, whether reactionary or revolutionary, who have emerged to power from the welter of the war and the peace. The widespread challenge to the parliamentary idea brings into prominence a new type of politician who aims at governance, here according to the gospel of Marx and there according to the gospel of Cæsarism, but in both cases in contemptuous repudiation of that tradition of liberalism which was the prevailing motive on both sides of the Atlantic in the years before the war. If America has escaped the revolutionary blast, it has not been unaffected by it, and if President Coolidge is the representative man in the United States in the post-war years, it is only because the peril of change has struck America with a cold fit that has frozen the warm currents that were released by the

Preface

war. In England organized liberalism has been shattered and the Labour party, negligible in 1914, has emerged as the new political power in the state. But, in emerging, it is itself split in twain by the contrary ideas of parliamentary government and government by the "proletariat." Since the sketches were written the general strike in England has thrown that collision into clear outline, without deciding in which direction the main current of Labour will go. In the world of religion, thought, and amusement the years of disruption have left an equally vivid mark upon the new time. Dean Inge, with his mordant pen and destructive wit, has displaced the whole bench of bishops as the representative man in the realm of theology, and the new medium of the screen drama has made Mr. Charles Chaplin the master of the world's revel. With the trumpets of the war, the feminist movement reached the goal of complete political emancipation, and Lady Astor, as the first woman to sit in the British House of Commons, enters the gallery as the representative woman of the time. The great Irish drama blazed to its culmination during and after the war, and the puck-like spirit of Mr. Timothy Healy, softened and mellowed by the years, embodies the close of one long chapter in Anglo-Irish history and the beginning of another. But though the portents have been kept in mind, they are subsidiary to the main purpose of the book, which stands or falls as a collection of studies of some of the outstanding personalities of the time. Most of the sketches have appeared in the *Daily News* and in certain American journals.

A. G. G.

Contents

Illustrations

Portraits and Portents

1. Mr. Stanley Baldwin

THE emergence of Mr. Baldwin will furnish the historian with an attractive theme. Was he an accident or was he the architect of events? If an accident, was he a happy accident? If the architect of events, was he a good architect? The questions are as baffling to his own party as to his opponents. There are times when he seems to be a prophet coming with a message hot from Sinai, and there are times when he suggests that Alice has wandered, round-eyed and innocent, into the Wonderland of Westminster. Lord Birkenhead is frankly puzzled by the phenomenon, Mr. Churchill is equally perplexed, and Mr. Lloyd George can make nothing of it.

Their perplexity is shared by the rank-and-file of the parties. "Why, this is the veritable simple Simon himself," declare the Liberals, as Mr. Baldwin leads his party down a steep place into the Protectionist abyss in a sort of absent-minded "View halloo!" "On the contrary," they say, a little later, as he leads his party out—"on the contrary, here is a very Moses of a man, talking our own language as if he had been used to it from the cradle." "At last," cried the Die-hards, after the fateful Carlton Club meeting, at which he broke up the Coalition, "at last we have found a hero." "No hero at all," they say, as later, they sit gloomily silent while he ascends the pulpit and talks to them of peace and good-will when they are hot on the trail of blood—"no hero at all, but little better than a psalm-singing Puritan."

And his qualities of character are as equivocal as his policies. In one connection he seems the complacent instrument of more energetic spirits, almost a marionette dancing to the tune set by the Amerys and Cunliffe-Listers. In another he acts with a decision and an initiative that surprise all the more because they come from so seemingly naïve and childlike a character. Nor is the tendency of the conventional politician to dismiss him summarily as an incredible accident of circumstances due simply to the apparent incoherence of his actions. It is due in no small measure also to his modest and unassertive address.

If on the memorable afternoon of August 3, 1914, anyone, looking down on the crowded benches of the House of Commons, had sought to pick out the man who would be at the helm when the storm that was about to engulf Europe was over he would not have given a thought to the member for Bewdley. Mr. Baldwin had been in the House six years without creating a ripple on the surface of the waters. He passed for a typical back-bencher, who voted as he was expected to vote and went home to dinner. A plain, undemonstrative Englishman, prosperous and unambitious, with a pleasant, humourous face, bright and rather bucolic colouring, walking with a quick, long stride that suggested one accustomed to tramping much over ploughed fields with a gun under his arm, and smoking a pipe with unremitting enjoyment. If you had been moved to inquire about him you would have learned little beyond that he was the head of an old-established business of ironmasters and that he was a cousin of Rudyard Kipling, his mother being one of the remarkable daughters of the well-known Wesleyan minister, G. D. Macdonald, whose three sisters married Burne-Jones, Poynter, the President of the Royal

Academy, and Lockwood Kipling. To the great dignitaries of politics he seemed little more important than the door-keeper of the House of Commons.

Then one astonishing afternoon in October, 1922, he went to the Carlton Club and sprang a mine that blew the most powerful combination of politicians to fragments. There had not been anything like it since David went out with his sling and pebble and slew the Philistine. The Coalition fell with a resounding crash, and in the ruins were the most formidable chieftains of politics—men who, had they been asked the day before about Mr. Baldwin, would have said "Mr. Baldwin! Mr. Baldwin! Who is Mr. Baldwin?" What was to become of a nation that sacrificed its "first-class brains" for so pitiful a substitute? And in the interval of waiting for some sign of divine displeasure Lord Birkenhead wrote a book foretelling the woes that must befall the unhappy country and party that had succumbed to the worship of such a wooden idol.

To-day Mr. Chamberlain, Lord Birkenhead and Mr. Churchill sit obediently round the Cabinet table presided over by Mr. Baldwin's second-class brains. The mystery of the rise of this inferior orb to dominion over them is still dark and unfathomable, but office is sweet, humility is a Christian virtue and the service of one's country is a duty that transcends all private feelings. The truth is that Mr. Baldwin is unintelligible to the politician because he is the least politically minded person who has ever reached great office. The political mind has many manifestations. It may be philosophical with Lord Balfour, an exercise in strategy with Mr. Lloyd George, a passion for order and constitutional forms of government with Lord Oxford, a secular instrument of religious orthodoxy with Lord Hugh

Cecil, or a lively adventure with Lord Birkenhead and Mr. Churchill.

But Mr. Baldwin does not come within any of the categories of the political mind. When he said that he would prefer a decent life in the country where he could read his books and keep his pigs he was not uttering a conventional lie, but stating a fact. Like Diocletian, he would be happier among his cabbages than in Parliament. He has not the Parliamentary manner nor the Parliamentary habit of thought. He has trained himself to speak easily and well, but he is neither a debater nor a rhetorician. He loathes rhetoric, which he calls "the harlot of the arts." Nor has he any of the arts and crafts of the Parliamentarian. His mind, like his appearance, is a little bucolic and slow, and he is indifferent to, perhaps unconscious of, the Parliamentary play. He comes on to the stage with something of Lord Grey's air of detachment, and talks like one who has been for a long walk in the country, has been turning the subject over in his own mind, and approaches it from that independent attitude rather than from the debating points that have been discussed. He imports as little personal animus into discussion as Mr. Asquith used to do, but gives the impression of a friendly, good-natured mind that follows the argument wherever it leads him without thinking too much of the consequences to himself or others. He himself has spoken of what he owes to his Quaker and Wesleyan traditions, and his habit of self-communing, whether on those solitary country tramps which are his chief form of recreation, or walking rapidly to and fro on the Terrace with head thrust forward, pipe between his teeth, and hands clasped behind his back, is a reminiscence of that Quaker reliance on the "inner light" which makes his thought and action so informal and individual.

It does not help to make him calculable and coherent. His mind works with extraordinary freedom and candour, but it is apt to be loose and unstitched, to use the phrase of the Abbé Sieyès. He thinks hard, but he thinks in patches and does not connect up the immediate theme with the large circumference of things. Hence, the lack of continuity that characterises him. In March, 1922, he was the most stalwart defender of the Coalition and Mr. Lloyd George against the Die-hards. "There are a large number of Tories in the House of Commons to-day," he said, "who would never have been there if they had not had the Lloyd George token in 1918. It sits badly on these men to indulge in that kind of criticism." Within six months he was the leader of the Die-hard attack on the Coalition, and his speech at the Carlton Club dismissed Mr. Lloyd George forever from the company of the Tories.

But still more illustrative of this tendency to repudiate himself was the extraordinary incident of 1923. When he was chosen to succeed Mr. Bonar Law as Prime Minister, he selected as his Chancellor of the Exchequer, Mr. Reginald McKenna, who, whatever other changes had taken place in his views, was still, first and foremost, an uncompromising Free Trader. It was a courageous, almost defiant act. It did not mean that he was a Free Trader, but it did mean that he had definitely put Protection into cold storage. It strained the loyalty of the Die-hards, of whom he had become the idol, to the breaking point. Sir Frederick Banbury refused to make way for Mr. McKenna in the City, even though he was offered a peerage as the reward, and Mr. Baldwin's hot fit having passed, he gave way instead. And within two months he plunged "over the top" under the banner of Protection, leading his magnificent majority to a catastrophe that would have closed his career as leader but for the handsome amends Mr. Ramsay MacDonald made to him a year later when he restored him to office with an even larger majority than before. And, as if to add a note of comedy to the fantastic story, he gave a peerage to Sir Frederick Banbury, whose refusal to surrender his seat had prevented Mr. Baldwin having a Free Trade Chancellor instead of a Protectionist crusade.

It was all in that spirit of amiable irrelevance that pervades so much of his public activities. If he could not have a Free Trade Chancellor, he could at least give the Protectionists some fun. If he could not have his way, they could at least have theirs.

When, in the midst of the election, a Cabinet colleague of Mr. Baldwin was asked to explain the true inwardness of his leader's sudden and inexplicable plunge into Protection, he replied: "Baldwin turned the tap on and then found that he could not turn it off." He is always turning taps on and finding that he does not know how to stop them. And when the bath overflows he goes outside, lights his pipe, and rejoices that he has such a fine head of water on his premises. Consequences have no terror for him, for they do not occur to him until they happen, and when they happen he has forgotten the cause of them; and even if he does not forget the cause, his self-complacency saves him from any disquiets.

He belongs to the pulpit rather than to the forum, and raises grave issues in the spirit of the preacher rather than of the statesman. He forgets that a statesman must not turn on taps unless he means them to run and that his pious opinions have to be implemented in policies. Hence the inconsequence of his actions. In a mood of Christian charity it occurred to him that he would like to summon Lord Birkenhead back to the Government of 1923. As usual he turned on the tap without a thought of what it involved. He made his overtures, and then found that, as in the McKenna case, he had aroused the angry passions of his own Die-hard followers. His under-secretaries revolted at such a meek turning of the cheek to the most truculent of his assailants, and he promptly withdrew his offer, rather in the spirit of Mr. Toots: "It was of no consequence—no consequence whatever."

And it was much the same in the strange episode of the Paris *communiqué*. Lord Curzon, his Foreign Minister, had just issued a flaming arraignment of M. Poincaré's policy in the Ruhr and Mr. Baldwin had duly endorsed it. Then he went to the continent, paid a formal call on M. Poincaré, and issued a *communiqué* in which he expressed the fullest agreement with the French policy. Nobody knows to this day the true facts about the extraordinary incident. Mr. Baldwin has never referred to it in public: but I understand that in private the explanation is that when the *communiqué*, having been drawn up by secretaries, was brought to him, he did not realise that it did not say what it ought to have said. Some words that should have been in were left out, but he did not notice that they were left out. It was unfortunate, but we have to remember that though he is honest he is not a politician. He means well, but he is not always clear as to what he means. It was so in the case of the singular remark in the House that the mistake we had made was in thinking too much about our exports. Even his Protectionist followers felt that this was going too far. "Imports," they cried, "imports." "No, I mean exports," he said. We had thought too much of trifles like the cotton trade and the ship-building trade, of clothing the mild Hindoo and the heathen Chinee, of exporting rails and engines to the remote places of the earth, and of sending our coal to drive trains across the pampas. What we needed was not trade with the foreigner, but taxes on ourselves. Let the producer only have full liberty to exploit the home consumer behind tariff walls, and we should be able to ignore the foreigner and cultivate prosperity in our right little, tight little island by providing each other with motorcars. That was how it seemed to him; but if his Lancashire followers insisted on being Free Traders and having Free Trade candidates, he gave them his cheerful "God bless you," and wished them well. He remembered that he thought as they did a few weeks ago, and bore no malice.

It has been assumed from this that Mr. Baldwin is a feather weight blown before stronger minds, now this way, now that, according to the breeze that catches him. That is not my reading of him. He has disconnected modes of thought, and is apt to rush a little heedlessly in pursuit of any hare that crosses his mental horizon, unimpeded by the calculations which give pause to more instructed politicians. His artlessness is indeed bewildering. He seems unconscious of the gravity of his own acts, and the indiscretions of his interviews with the Press, as in the case of that on his return from America, and still more that with the "People," in which his private opinions of Mr. Churchill, Lord Birkenhead and Lord Beaverbrook were discussed with surprising freedom, reveal a guileless mind.

His merits are of the heart rather than the head. His good nature and his good humour are invulnerable, and no man ever came to supreme office in public life with so few enemies. You cannot dislike him if you "try with both hands," as Humpty-Dumpty would say. He exhales an atmosphere of friendliness that warms the general air, and when he speaks he lifts the argument to the plane of moral ideas without unction and without rhetoric. You may doubt whether he is a great man, but you cannot doubt that he is a good man, who wants nothing for himself that all may not share in common with him. It is said, and I do not question the report, though he is the last person to give currency to it himself, that he sacrificed a third of his fortune at the beginning of the war and handed it over to the Treasury, and I can conceive him suffering any reverse of fortune, not merely with fortitude and without complaint, but without the sense of the loss of anything that was truly valuable. I like to see him taking his week-end tramps among the woods and hills about Chequers, always alone, except for two stalwart figures that follow at a discreet distance, his hat off, his cherry-wood pipe in full blast—he once confessed that he had never given more than a shilling for a pipe— and his long strides devouring the miles with an air of lusty exhilaration. He is English to the core and loves his country for the right things, in proof of which let me quote one passage from his published speeches which I give not only to illustrate that feeling, but also to show that he gathers "the harvest of a quiet eye" and knows how to garner it in moving utterance:

And when I ask myself what I mean by England, when I think of England when I am abroad, England comes to me through my various senses—through the ear, through the eye, and through certain imperishable scents. I will tell you what they are, and there may be those among you who feel as I do. The sounds of England—the tinkle of the ham-

mer on the anvil in the country smithy, the corncrake on a dewy morning, the sound of the scythe against the whetstone, and the sight of a
plough team coming over the brow of a hill, the sight that has been seen
in England since England was a land, and may be seen in England long
after the Empire has perished, and every works in England has ceased to
function, for centuries the one eternal sight of England. The wild
anemones in the woods in April, the last load at night of hay being
drawn down a lane as the twilight comes on, when you can scarcely distinguish the figures of the horses as they take it home to the farm, and,
above all, most subtle, most penetrating and most moving, the smell of
wood smoke coming up in an autumn evening, or the smell of the scutch
fires: that wood smoke that our ancestors, tens of thousands of years ago,
must have caught on the air when they were coming home with the
result of the day's forage, when they were still nomads, and when they
were still roaming the forests and the plains of the Continent of Europe.
These things strike down into the very depths of our nature, and touch
chords that go back to the beginning of time and the human race, but
they are chords that with every year of our life sound a deeper note in
our innermost being.

He has none of the attributes so common to the politician
Envy, jealousy and ambition are wholly absent from his
character, and he cherishes so little animosity that he will
give his most inveterate opponent a seat at the high table.
He took Lord Birkenhead's gibes at his "second-class brains"
with good-humoured indifference and then invited him into
his Cabinet. He might have feared so turbulent and wilful
a rival as Mr. Churchill; but he received him at the penitent
form amid the indignation of his Die-hards and seated him
at the place of honour at the Exchequer, regardless of the
fact that he, like Mr. McKenna, was a Free Trader.

In all this he proclaims a disinterested and dispassionate
mind, concerned not with his own career but with the public
well-being. He will never, as others have done, risk great
things from mean or personal motives or from vain ideas

of political strategy. If his intellectual powers were as remarkable as his public instincts, he would be equal to the greatest task of political navigation that has ever confronted a pilot. He may be equal to that task even as it is. He threw down a challenge to the nation to join him in a great adventure, to help him to fashion a world nearer the heart's desire, and for the moment he created the atmosphere in which it seemed that vision might be translated into reality. He called himself a revivalist, and the world needs the ministrations of the revivalist. But revivalism is not a policy, and a fine emotion is not an achievement.

And his handling of the tragic conflict in the coal trade leaves one without the confident assurance that behind the revivalist and the preacher of social reconciliation there is the constructive statesmanship that can turn fine dreams to enduring realities.

II. President Coolidge

PRESIDENT COOLIDGE lives in the White House to-day by grace of a phrase. Six years ago he uttered twenty words which made him famous from the Atlantic to the Pacific, between the rising and the setting of the sun. In the morning he was unknown: at night there was hardly a tongue in the United States that had not uttered his name. Such is the magic of a phrase. The world, especially the modern world, is governed by phrases. The prairie of the public mind may be as dry as tinder, but until the spark of a phrase is dropped there is no blaze and the wind blows in vain. Protectionism had been dormant with us for a generation. Then Joseph Chamberlain said "Tax the foreigner," and it flared like a bonfire from John o' Groats to Land's End. No country has been more hypnotised by phrases than America. In politics and business alike the slogan is everything. "Keep Cool with Coolidge" sets millions marching to the poll, and "No Oil on Al." (Alfred Smith) is the antistrophe from the opposition. It is doubtful whether Lincoln himself would have emerged if it had not been for that sentence—"No nation can long continue to exist half slave, half free"—which suddenly illuminated the whole slavery issue, and made him at once the champion of the North and the abhorrence of the South.

The phrase and the occasion must of course synchronise. In the case of Calvin Coolidge, as in the case of Lincoln, the words he uttered would have passed unnoticed in normal times. But they fell on a world seething with vague fears and alarms, apprehensive to the verge of panic, ready to mobilise itself under anyone who could condense its emotions into a phrase. No one who was in the United States, as I chanced to be, in the autumn of 1919, will forget the feverish condition of the public mind at that time. It was hagridden by the spectre of Bolshevism. It was like a sleeper in a nightmare, enveloped by a thousand phantoms of destruction. Property was in an agony of fear, and the horrid name "Radical" covered the most innocent departure from conventional thought with a suspicion of desperate purpose. "America," as a wit of the time said, "is the land of liberty —liberty to keep in step." In the midst of this panic an incident occurred in Boston which attracted alarmed attention all over the States. The police of the city of Boston went out on strike. All the formless fears that agitated the public mind were epitomised in a struggle that involved the whole conception of social order and security. If the police were honeycombed with Bolshevism, what could save the State? *Quis custodiet?* The answer came from the Governor of Massachusetts, a lawyer, still in the early forties, named Calvin Coolidge. He brought in the military, he organised a voluntary force, he broke the strike, he refused to reinstate the strikers, and he made a speech. And in that speech he said "There is no right to strike against the public safety by anybody, anywhere, any time."

I state the legend in its crude form. It is in some measure mythical, as is proper to the man, for President Coolidge is himself something of a myth, an exhalation of the Press, a rumour on the wind, an invention of the popular imagination to satisfy a mood and meet an occasion. Strict historical accuracy compels me to attune the heroic tale to a lower key. The plain fact is that Mr. Coolidge was away from Boston

at the time, that the Mayor, Mr. Peters, was the active
power, and that he was supported by an emergency committee of citizens, whose prompt formation and recommenda-
tions led to the calling out of the State Guard. Mr. Coolidge's one undoubted contribution was the slogan he coined
for the emergency which the Mayor duly released on the
world at the critical moment.

It was that phrase that made Calvin Coolidge in due time
President of the United States. "It struck fire from the
Americanism of the entire country," wrote a commentator
at the time. "Wires relayed it to the remotest regions, and
it thrilled the United States. Men breathed more freely.
At last a universal issue was defined. Either you stood for
public safety or you stood against it." Thenceforward Calvin Coolidge was in the centre of the great stage. He had
put it across, as they say in America. His name was a household word, and it symbolised a creed, a policy, a conception
of government. Two or three months afterwards he came
up for re-election as Governor of Massachusetts, and was
returned to office on a tidal wave of popular feeling, amid
the acclamations of the whole country, including even those
of President Wilson himself. His fame was secure. He
was a national figure, a national asset.

But great as his prestige was the White House still seemed
beyond his reach, for he was a New Englander, and since
J. Q. Adams, no New Englander had been elected to the
Presidency. The fact is due partly to the still smouldering
memories of the Civil War, but still more to the shift of
population, the political necessity of holding the Middle
West and the need of winning a large State or two. Thus
no Pennsylvania man can hope for a nomination, any more
than a Massachusetts man can, for Pennsylvania is Repub-

lican and cannot be lost to the party; while no Democrat could win it though he had the voice of an Archangel. The mere accident of birth alone therefore seemed to bar Mr. Coolidge's way to the Presidency. But he was nominated for the Vice-Presidency, an office sometimes reserved as consolation prize for men of high claims which cannot be disregarded, but who, for one reason or another, are not wanted at the White House. To all appearances Mr. Coolidge's career had ended in a back-water. But it chanced in his case, as in that of Theodore Roosevelt, that events decided his fate. President Harding died in the midst of his term of office, and according to practice the Vice-President automatically filled the vacancy. And when the new election drew near, fortune still favoured him. The Harding Administration had foundered in a sea of oil. The Teapot Dome scandals had left it a discredited by-word for corruption that ought and probably would have made the return of the Republicans to power impossible, but for the fact that no breath of suspicion in connection with the scandals had fallen upon Calvin Coolidge. It was his character alone that enabled his party to survive the disclosure of its monstrous malpractices, and thus it came about that, after sixty years, a New Englander once more entered the White House by right of election.

It will be apparent that the god of chance has played no small part in manœuvring Calvin Coolidge to the highest seat of power in the world. Had the Boston police not struck at a moment when the American mind was unhinged, and when Coolidge chanced to be in office, had Harding not died, had—— In a word, is Calvin Coolidge an accident at the White House, or is he there by the divine right of merit or by the decree of destiny? No one less resembles the type of the Man of Destiny, and yet the superstitious might be excused for seeing in this singularly commonplace man the instrument of fate. For events have always played the trump card for him and his luck is a legend. When the Harding ministry was formed, a distinguished American financier remarked to a friend of mine: "Something will happen to Harding. I have known Coolidge ever since my college days when we were students together at Amherst. He has never won the first place or won the first prize, but something has always happened after the event to put him on top. Something will happen now to put him in the White House." He is certainly not there, as Mussolini is in power in Italy, by virtue of his histrionic arts and his ruthless ambition. Nature and events never made a great man out of more homely material, or less spectacular qualities. Lincoln was homely too, but his natural wisdom was illimitable, his magnanimity sublime, and his humour touched every situation with its clarifying and humanising power. Mr. Coolidge has no hint of these great gifts.

In America they get out of the difficulty of explaining him by calling him an enigma. He is not that. Few men could be more obvious. If there is an enigma it relates to the mystery of his elevation to the Chief Magistracy of the greatest and wealthiest community the world has ever seen. I like to think that when he is sitting, silently gazing out of the White House at the tennis court below, he is himself puzzled to explain how this enormous thing came about. I imagine him giving the thing up in despair, as past all human unravelling.

For in his dour, unsmiling, New England nature there is no touch of vanity or sham. "I'm afraid we are just common, everyday people, regardless of my husband's office,"

Mrs. Coolidge is reported to have observed, and Mr. Coolidge himself is almost aggressively ordinary. He remains obstinately unchanged by circumstances from the Vermont farm boy who did his chores of wood, got a scholarship at Amherst College, married a teacher of the deaf and dumb, went into the law and practised at Northampton, Massachusetts, became Mayor of the town, and Governor of the State, all naturally, simply, unromantically. Neither his habits nor his outlook have been affected by his translation. He preserves the severe personal economies of his New England tradition, and his frugality in the matter of clothes is a national and good-humoured jest. When as President he travelled to Chicago he went by ordinary train at ordinary fare, refusing a "special," but agreeing to a private carriage until he found that twenty-five tickets were needed. "I will not pay extra fares when the extra tickets are not being used," he said. He is entirely unfashionable in his tastes, does not play golf, has only one luxury, a sailing boat, and finds his recreation in riding a mechanical horse and in walking in the streets, and standing reflectively in front of the shop windows.

Sometimes the frugality note is overdone by his publicity artists. For example, there was the story of his cheap suit which shook the Continent. Easter in America is the harvest time of the retail trade, and no good American fails to honour the festival with a new outfit. But some one at the White House outraged the sound tradition by announcing that the President, ever mindful of the toiling multitude, was having his soft felt hat electrically cleaned at a trifling cost and paying only sixty-five dollars for his new spring suit. A cry of horror went up from the retail trade at this shocking tale of frugality. The story was instantly contradicted and a different one put on the wires. The sixty-five dollar suit was a regrettable mistake. As a matter of fact the President had a dozen fine suits, not one of which could have been made at so inglorious a price as sixty-five dollars. And with this assurance the President was restored to his place in the retail heart of America.

He was named Calvin, and looks it. Meagre and sinewy of frame, his face bears the impress of that bleak philosophy with which Calvinism took the creases of laughter out of the human countenance. His lips are thin, horizontal, disciplined against idle speech, and his eyes, in the admirable New England phrase, are ever "looking between the horse's ears." He has neither oratorical power to move a crowd nor the personal animation that attracts the individual. Like that great New Englander, Thoreau, he says "No" much more easily than "Yes." He feels more comfortable, safer, in denying than in agreeing. He is as true to his Scotch origin as Shaw's jarvey was to the Irish temperament when he said "Shure, he'll say what will give your honour most pleasure and himself least trouble." Mr. Coolidge distrusts giving "his honour" the pleasure of agreement about anything. He will not commit himself on the weather or the crops.

His most conspicuous gift is negative. It is his power of silence. William the Silent owes his immortal sobriquet to one great exercise of silence in a critical situation; but "Silent Cal" is silent with the silence of a lifetime. It is not an uncommon characteristic in rural New England. The currents of speech were always a little frozen there, and readers of Mary E. Wilkins' admirable books will be familiar with the Coolidge type. But the legends of his capacity for saying nothing place him in a class by himself. "Mr. Coolidge," said the lady sitting by him at dinner, "I knew that I was to sit by you and I've made a wager that you would talk." "You've lost," said Mr. Coolidge. He allows people to talk and explain and persuade until they collapse before his impenetrable silence. Then, perhaps, he will say, as in one case when a fellow-lawyer had been arguing with him for an hour, "Sam, there's nothing in it."

Some of the stories of his penuriousness of speech have already become classics, like that of his coming home from church and being asked by his wife what the sermon was about. "Sin" said the President. A long pause. "And what did he say about sin?" "Against." It is probably an invention, but it is as true to the spirit of the man as the brief but boisterous address to the election of Roosevelt: "Boys, you have heard of the Ten Commandments. I stand for the Ten Commandments. They are bully."

Behind this stony, embattled front lurks the New England Puritan of the seventeenth century, with little taste for the arts or the sensuous life, no fiction in his library, but plenty of grave books and a well-thumbed Bible that opens at the Twenty-third Psalm and has a bookmark at the Sermon on the Mount. And there lurk tender feelings, too. When he first went to the White House, the hostesses of Washington entertained him, here at lunch, there at dinner. But whether it was lunch or whether it was dinner Calvin sat silent. Polite society was at its wit's end. How could social intercourse survive such an Arctic presence? Then one day all Washington was agog at the great news that at Mrs. So-and-So's the President had gossiped amiably all through lunch with his hostess. Mrs. So-and-So, a charming woman, who prided herself on her youthful appearance, was exalted by her success in thawing the President, but, meeting Mrs. Coolidge just after, the secret of that triumph was artlessly revealed. "The President so much enjoyed your lunch and the talk with you," said Mrs. Coolidge. "He said you reminded him so much of his mother." There is fragrance in that story.

And what quality of public significance is there in this sombre personality? Is the silence the silence of profound thought or merely of generations of self-absorbed habit? Is Calvin Coolidge as great as his office or only the accident of events? The answer of history will probably be that he was an accident. His character is high, his motives honest; but his outlook is narrow, his understanding limited. He has brought a certain bleakness into the atmosphere. The air is pure, but unsympathetic. He is at once timid and tenacious; shrinking from great ideas and bold actions, but clinging obstinately to petty and, as in the Warren case, indefensible legalities. He has neither the driving energy of a Roosevelt that would make Congress obedient to him, nor the rather flabby bonhomie of Harding that made Congress amiable to him. No President in history has suffered such humiliation from the Senate as he has borne.

And yet he is not wholly an accident. He represents the mind of America in reaction. It has swung back from the mood of chivalrous adventure to the mood of self-interest, from the rôle of world deliverer to the rôle of America first, last, and always. Of this transition Calvin Coolidge, with his rigid ideas of the sanctity of property, his respect for convention, and his parsimony of spirit, is representative. Himself the least avaricious of men, he has become the instrument of the ideas and aims of material wealth as the goal of Americanism. He is no enigma. If there is an enigma, it is the America that can pass so easily from a great emotion to a vision so poor and parochial as that which possesses it to-day.

III. Dean Inge

SYDNEY SMITH used to tell the story of a boy who, found scratching the shell of a tortoise and being asked why he did it, replied that he did it to "tickle the tortoise." "My dear boy," replied the famous wit, "you might as well scratch the dome of St. Paul's to tickle the Dean and Chapter." In spite of the implications of that reply, it is not irrelevant to remark that nobody became alarmed about the dome until Dean Inge went to the Deanery. I am far from suggesting any connection between the two facts; but it will be agreed that if the dome had any capacity for being shocked by a dean its present instability would be explained. For it is undeniable that the voice of Dean Inge is the most explosive sound that has ever echoed around the dome, and if the Dean has not shaken the Cathedral it is the only thing that he has not shaken.

I do not know what the relationship of a bishop is to a dean; but I am kept awake at nights wondering what the Bishop of London really thinks of the Dean of St. Paul's. I imagine Dr. Ingram tossing on his pillow in feverish anxiety as to what the Dean is saying or writing at the moment, and seizing the paper in the morning to know the worst. "What can he do," he asks, "to stem the torrent? What can the homely fowl do to clip the wings of the eagle that has been so miraculously hatched in the fowlhouse?" I don't wonder that he does not approve of deans any more than fowls approve of eagles, and that he regards the £70,000 spent on them as wasted money. "It's of no consequence," said the Dean gaily to a reporter who asked for his comments, "He can't do anything."

It is fortunate that he can't, for life without Dean Inge would be like lamb without mint sauce. Charles said of Prince George that he had tried him drunk and he had tried him sober, and "there was nothing in him either way." I do not suppose the Dean has ever been drunk, but every phase of his sobriety is delightful. When you agree with him he goes down like milk and when you disagree with him the ginger is gloriously hot in the mouth. His insults have a flavour that makes you lap them up with gusto, and before you have time to be angry with him for his savage assaults on your pet enthusiasms, you have forgiven him for some swashing blow that he has struck at your pet aversion. He is like a man who talks in his sleep, or like a visitor from some remote planet, or some Lazarus from the grave.

In thought and appearance alike he has the quality of loneliness and abstraction. He enters the pulpit and reads his sermon as if he were unaware of his surroundings, and of the rattle of his own shrapnel; he sits at the table as if he too had shot the albatross and was hag-ridden by the terrific memory; he walks the street like a man in a dream, twitching with the agonies of his own nightmare. His face is long, pallid, and sorrowful; his mouth thin lipped and whimsical; his eye fixed, lacklustre and melancholy. A rare, wistful smile plays across his features, but it flees incontinently like a ghost that has heard the cock crow. He is deaf, but I think it is the deafness of the mind rather than the sense, for I have noticed that in conversation he hears very well what he wants to hear. He does not suffer fools gladly, and like Reynolds—

When they talked of their Raphaels, Correggios and stuff
He shifted his trumpet and only took snuff.

In religion he passes for a mystic, but his mind is hard as
steel and as bright, and his tongue as sharp and biting as the
east wind. His genius for controversy is only matched by
that of Mr. Bernard Shaw, with whom he has much in
common in spite of the wide disparity in their views and
professions. Mr. Shaw is, of course, much nearer the accepted Christian ethic. He lashes us, but he loves us, toler-
ates us, in a way believes in us. He has pity and compassion.
In a word, he is a humanitarian.

Now there is no one who fills the Dean with so much
rage as a humanitarian, and nothing which infuriates him so
much as the sentimentalism of pity. "There is an increasing
orgy of sentimentalism and indiscipline over England," he
says, "due in part to the fact that board-school boys are not
caned. Thank God, the lads at Eton are still birched."
Like Nietzsche, of whom he is curiously reminiscent, he sees
society being destroyed by its care of the unfit, the diseased,
the weak, the inefficient. Hence his hatred of Rousseau,
whom he regards as the author of all this "mawkish travesty
of Christianity which transforms morality by basing it on
pity." He is preoccupied with one obsession—how to get
rid of the superfluous mob and stop its unrestrained propaga-
tion. The Houses of Convocation leave him cold, but a
Birth Control Commission touches his horizon with a bleak
ray of hope.

When Dr. Saleeby charged him with being the prophet
of the "Better Dead school," he retorted: "There is no such
school, but there is 'A Better-not-to-be-born school.' " And
he admits he is of it. But if he does not advocate the lethal
chamber openly, he comes very near doing so. He charges

medicine with keeping alive persons "whom Nature, with
perhaps greater wisdom, might have preferred to kill"; he
has no mercy for what Nietzsche called the "botched" and
he calls the parasites who suck the blood of the healthy, the
efficient, and the "heavily taxed"; and he looks forward, not
uncheerfully, to a time when "the State will take life mercifully, it is true, but more freely than now." For one who
confesses that he has never killed anything bigger than a
wasp, his speech is often singularly bloodthirsty. Of revolutionaries he says that we should "kill the infected like mad
dogs," and writing to Lieutenant-General Phelps, the President of the Anti-Vaccination League, he said:

I cannot imagine a more disgraceful or unpatriotic agitation than that
in which you are engaged. If I were at the head of affairs I should have
you shot summarily.

With these views, it follows that the idea of democracy
stirs him to uncontrolled wrath. His diatribes against the
late President Wilson were, I think, inspired by the phrase
about "making the world safe for democracy." It was to
him like talking about making the world safe for smallpox
or delirium tremens. He prefers Prussianism to Democracy, and in the midst of the war had the courage to describe
Germany "as in many ways the best-governed country in the
world." Democracy is the expression of that sentimentalism, that faith in the many headed, that is the disease from
which society is perishing. It is "the silliest of all fetishes
seriously worshipped among us," and the voice of the people
is "the old divine right of Kings standing on its head."
Labour and Socialism are anathema to him, and he denounces both with a reckless disregard of facts that lays him
open to serious attack. He talks of the "lazy miner who

extorts his thousands a year from the householders of England, and the bricklayer who battens on the rates and does about two and a half hours of honest work in the day"; he "imagines" that it is true that "the miners are receiving help from the enemies of the country in all parts of the world," and he speaks of Labour leaders who have "probably received tempting offers from unfriendly Powers." "Imagine"! "Probably"! This is not the language which a responsible mind uses in launching monstrous charges against vast masses of his fellow-citizens. Socialism and democracy are "looting the accumulations of Queen Victoria's reign and living on the rates and taxes." But there is a Nemesis in sight, "The Yellow man will make short work of the pampered trade unionist," and when the European labour movement has transferred industry and wealth to the Far East, Poplar and East Ham will be grazing farms.

For he is as fond as is Mr. H. G. Wells of forecasting the future, and his vision is always sombre. He sees the British Empire falling to decay and dissolution and leaving "not a wrack behind" and the great globe itself a cold, tenantless orb whirling meaninglessly round a dying sun. And the tale that is told was, so far as the secular life of man was concerned, a meaningless tale, for it led no whither. "We have fancied that there was an automatic law of progress. Of course there is nothing of the kind." That unconscionable creature man has no faculty of automatic progression. What he was he remains, the most savage and barbarous of created beings. If what "we are pleased to call the lower animals," he says somewhere, were to fashion a religion of their own, they would have some difficulty in imagining a beneficent God, but they would find their devil in a large *white* man.

He denies that he is a pessimist and accuses the "over-worked drudges of journalism" of misrepresenting him. "They bite to live not to hurt," he says of them, quoting Nietzsche. "They want our blood, not our pain." He would probably also deny that he is a misanthrope, but he certainly dislikes men in the mass. Like Pascal, he "prefers dogs." He talks touchingly of a canary in a cage, indignantly of fox-hunting, and when it was reported that an American lady had killed a gorilla he said it would give him pleasure to hear that a gorilla had killed her.

But in spite of the violence of his feelings in regard to democracy, he is no commonplace reactionary. If he believes in an aristocracy, it is an aristocracy of the intellect and of high living, not of blue blood, which, if it is not revitalised by plebeian but eugenic marriage, is stale blood. He is as scornful of Imperialism as he is of Socialism, is a good European, and never talks the cant of patriotism. The greatness of his country is not a material thing, and does not depend on painting the map red. It is a moral and a spiritual thing, that has been our noblest contribution to the world. During the war he kept his sanity as few of his order did, challenging the passions of the time with courageous speech. He loathes the garb that his calling imposes on him, but he never trotted about in khaki as so many of his episcopal brethren did, and I think that nothing on earth would have induced him to stoop to such folly.

And when the war was over, his was one of the few voices that urged wisdom. "We were all stark mad together," he said, in a sermon in St. Paul's. . . . "There is no abstract demon called Germany. . . . We cannot afford to have a humiliated, embittered, degenerate Germany any more than a triumphant militant Germany." His fellow-clerics fell on him in the *Times* as though he had impeached the doctrine of the Trinity, but he stood his ground against these "fatuous and insolent" attacks. And though he may refer to that "greasy instrument of party politics, the Nonconformist conscience," he is innocent of the vice of sectarianism, has no respect for ecclesiastical millinery, and likes to point out the similarity between St. Augustine and a good Quaker. But though free from theological partisanship, his sense of realities rejects reunion with Rome as a dream. "Rome would accept no terms short of submission, and Englishmen are no more likely to pay homage to an Italian priest than they are to pay taxes to an Italian King."

I have left myself little space to deal with the constructive thinker behind the destructive critic. Yet it is as a Christian philosopher that Dean Inge must ultimately be judged. In this sphere he pursues as individual and fearless a line as he does in public affairs. Into the company of timid clerics, nursing officially a pre-Copernican vision of the universe, and seeing the ground of faith visibly slipping from beneath them, he comes forward with a re-statement of Christianity which cuts across all the schools. It leaves the historicity of the miracles to science and rejects the verbal inspiration of the Scriptures. "Our Lord is recorded in the Gospels to have made predictions which have not been and cannot be fulfilled" (*e. g.*, the imminent Second Coming). He does not believe they were made. "A man must be a saint or a humbug to preach the Gospel in these days in a pure and unalloyed form." If miracles are incompatible with science, then so much the worse for miracles, and he has no respect for "the vulgar conception of miracles as the suspension of a lower law by a higher." He does not

with shadowed hints confuse
A life that leads melodious days.

Shadowed hints have no place in his armoury, and his impatience with melodious days whose melody rests in an effete orthodoxy is declared with ruthless directness. He sees an Infallible Church and an Infallible Book disestablished with grim acceptance, and will have no illusions about "mummified customs that have long outlasted their usefulness and otiose dogmas that have long lost their vitality." He will parody sentimental hymns with the levity of a Rationalist lecturer, and he dismisses the antiquated geographical conception of the universe "as a three-storied building consisting of heaven, the abode of God, the angels and beatified spirits; an earth; and the infernal regions." Religions were best when they were fresh from the mint, and "the future of Christianity as an institution. . . . is not a matter of supreme importance. It is even possible to speculate (though I should not go so far myself) whether the religion of Christ might not be a greater power in the world if its professional custodians were removed." In other words if bishops as well as deans came down from their high places and walked the streets without gaiters and broad-brimmed hats. He is as hostile to institutionalism and the religion of authority as any Quaker, and his "Religion of the Spirit" is the Quaker's doctrine of the "Inner Light" under another name. The visible Church, by becoming worldly and secularised, has compromised almost "irreparably its professed character as a spiritual force," becoming indeed "inwardly divorced from the whole spirit and temper of the Gospel."

Christ Himself, if He had returned to earth in the Middle Ages, would certainly have been burnt alive for denying the dogmas about His own nature. The hierarchy would have recognised in Him with more alacrity than Caiaphas did, the most deadly enemy of all that they meant by religion. For Christ was primarily concerned with awakening into activity the consciousness of God in the individual soul: His parting promise was that this consciousness should be an abiding possession of those who followed in His steps. He declared war against the orthodoxies and hierarchies of His time.

The path of life, as He showed it by precept and example, was superior to anything that either Greeks or Indians traced out, but the conception of salvation is essentially the same—a growth in the power of spiritual communion by a consecrated life of renunciation and discipline. His Kingdom of God was a spiritual fellowship of those who were "baptized with the Holy Ghost."

He finds no substitute for supernaturalism in the nature worship of Wordsworth, for nature only echoes back the mood of the spirit; nor in pantheism which leaves the world as we find it; nor in the revolt against intellectualism which takes refuge in ghosts, faith healing, and Christian Science. Religion is the search after the nature of God and Christianity is a standard of spiritual values and a way of life. The philosophy of Greece is as vital to this conception as the Incarnation, and Neoplatonism furnishes Christianity with its theology, its metaphysics, and its mysticism.

In this realm of speculation I leave him. In the Middle Ages he, too, would certainly have been burned alive, and a generation ago he would have been hounded out of any orthodox community as an heresiarch. Even in the latitudinarian atmosphere of to-day it is startling to find the most disruptive force in the Church pronouncing his philippics against dogmas and against organised ecclesiasticism from beneath the central dome of Anglicanism. But whether we agree with him or whether we differ from him, we cannot be indifferent to him. He compels us to think. He bursts into the spiritual stagnation and hedonism of to-day with defiant questionings—Why? What? Whence? Whither? He lashes us across the face with his whip. He calls us ugly names. But there is a flame in him, and he does not measure life by the things that perish. He, in his way, has as clear a vision of the City of Destruction as "the God-intoxicated" Calvinist of the seventeenth century had, and if the journey to Beulah is not so plain to him as it was to Christian he is, at least, desperately seeking to find it.

iv. Viscount Grey of Fallodon

THE world is surfeited with books about the war and cries, "Hold! Enough!" But Lord Grey's book on that inexhaustible but depressing theme cannot fail to live, not merely as one of the major documents of history, but as a literary achievement of quite exceptional power. It is easily the most impressive epic of the war, sombre as an Æschylean tragedy, in which the destinies of men are the sport of implacable fate. Incidentally, though not deliberately, it is the apologia of Lord Grey himself. Whether to friend or foe, he will live as the most significant English figure in the play of forces that ended in the catastrophe that shook the world and drenched Europe with the blood of millions. His part in that drama will be charged with a certain pathos which, I think, will distinguish him from all the other principals, with, possibly, the exception of Beth-mann-Hollweg. It is pathos of the kind which hangs about the memory of General Lee in the American Civil War—the pathos that belongs to a man who has become the vehicle of a tragedy he feared with the depth of feeling that only a singularly noble nature can sound.

When I think of him, I see a picture that embodies the emotion of which I speak. It is the Wednesday of that most tremendous week in the secular history of mankind—the first week in August, 1914, the first day of the war. In the House of Commons, Mr. Asquith is making his indictment of Germany and his defence of his own Government, and beside him sits Sir Edward Grey, his head flung back, his gaze fixed immovably, abstractedly, on the high windows of the Chamber, his whole aspect that of one who has passed through a prolonged agony only to find utter shipwreck, and who now sits looking bleakly into the terrific and incalculable future.

We shall not understand Lord Grey's part in the tragedy if we do not appreciate the poignancy of his feeling in the presence of that overwhelming failure. It is the custom of his critics, notably of Mr. Bernard Shaw, whose judgments of men are curiously perverse, to represent him as a typical "junker" and jingo, a sort of Palmerston rattling the sword with reckless and provocative levity. There could be no more complete misapprehension of the man. There were statesmen and politicians in all countries who did not regret the war, even enjoyed it for the power, the freedom, the excitement it provided, and the ambition to which it ministered; but if I were asked to name the English statesman who lamented it most deeply, I do not know anyone whose name would come before that of the man who led his country into it. Joseph Chamberlain said that the Boer War was "a feather in his cap," and he wore that feather throughout with defiant gaiety. But to Lord Grey the war was the defeat of all his hopes, and he entered into it more regretfully than any British statesman had engaged in war since Walpole saw his great record as the Peace Minister submerged in the absurd war about Jenkins's ear.

That is the truth which makes the element of pathos that will always be associated with the name of Lord Grey. He had more than any man in affairs the passion for world pacification, and he was, whether as the victim of events, or by the machinations of others, or by his own failure, or as a result of all these and many other causes, one of the chief instruments of Armageddon. It would not be easy to imagine a more tragic comment on a man's career. He had one supreme object in life, and he failed in it supremely. There is a moving passage in his book that dwells in the mind as revealing the emotions of his mind under the failure. It is the evening of the third of August, 1914. He is in his room at the Foreign Office and there enters a friend with whom he talks. They move to the window and stand gazing at the scene without. Dark is beginning to fall and in the space below the lamps are being lit. "The lamps are going out all over Europe," he says: "we shall not see them lit again in our life-time."

Whatever may be the final judgment, if there is ever a final judgment, as to the distribution of the blame, it is certain that Lord Grey's share in making us a party to the war was decisive. It may be true—I think it is true— that in the mood of the country at the time no power could have prevented our being caught in the vortex of the war ultimately; but the fact that we went in at once and that we went in with almost unprecedented unanimity was due to Sir Edward Grey.

The fact is a tribute to the power of his personality. Lord Grey has never been a popular figure of his time. He has none of the arts of the demagogue, and none of the ambitions of the adventurer. When he first entered office, in 1892, as Under-Secretary for Foreign Affairs he was by virtue of a certain distinction of mind and bearing universally acclaimed the man of the future. No one, it was said, could be quite so wise as Sir Edward Grey looked; but no one could doubt the gravity of his thought, the high and chivalrous note of his character, the simplicity and candour of his mind. He was a man after Gladstone's own

heart, and one of the rare and rather pedestrian exercises
in verse of that great man was an improvisation in his praise
on Rochester's lines to Charles II:

> Behold our Grey, the dry fly King,
>   Whose word the world relies on;
> Who never said a foolish thing,
>   Nor did he an unwise one.

When Harcourt welcomed him into the new Government,
he welcomed him as the man who had the world before him.
"Go on," he said. "You have the ball at your feet." "I
don't want the ball," was the reply, and, unlike most disclaimers of the sort, it was sincere. He went into public
life without enthusiasm and escaped from it with gratitude.
His spirit is that of the recluse and his thought is contempla-
tive rather than active. He is happier in throwing bait to
the fish than in throwing bouquets to the electorate, and he
has a greater passion for birds than for blue books. His
only contribution to literature is a book on the art of dry-fly
fishing, and he carries with him the atmosphere of White's
"Selborne," the "Compleat Angler," and the "Prelude,"
and the breath of the country-side. He came into Parliament like a visitor from another planet, who had strayed
inadvertently into the House, seemed lonely there, and was
only waiting a convenient opportunity to escape to the more
friendly solitude of a moorland stream. No one was less
avid of the plums of office nor more indifferent to popular
applause.

And in spite of all his aloofness from the game of politics—partly no doubt in consequence of this aloofness—he
carried more personal weight, not merely in Parliament,
but also in the country, than any single Parliamentarian
since Gladstone. There have been many more brilliant

speakers in the House of Commons in our time than Sir
Edward Grey; but if the test of a speech is the measure of
conviction it conveys there has been no one so effective. Its
strength was in its extraordinary simplicity, its entire freedom
from artifice and emotional appeal. In the rhetorical sense,
using the word rhetorical in its wider meaning, it was not
oratory at all. No ornament was used, no heat was gener-
ated, no gesture was employed, no play of voice disturbed
the grave current of his speech. He raised no laughter and
made no epigrams. He seemed entirely passionless and entirely disinterested, a man thinking aloud, unconscious of his
audience, emptying his mind of the facts, concealing nothing,
and leaving the judgment to the Court.

I do not say that he concealed nothing. He concealed
the nature of our "conversations" with the French for years,
whether wisely or unwisely is not to the present purpose. I
am speaking of the impression he conveyed. It was the impression of a character of high probity and flawless honour,
of a man who had no ambitions to serve and who was telling
the truth as he saw it without reserve and with a plain leaning to the understatement rather than the overstatement of
the case. Lord Birkenhead has described his oratory as
"pontifical." It is a curious misdescription of the least self-
regarding of men. Lord Grey is as innocent of vanity as
Lord Birkenhead is of modesty.

The secret of his power is apparent in the reference he
makes in his book to the feeling he experienced when he rose
to deliver his momentous speech in the House of Commons
on August 3, 1914. No one who heard that speech or
witnessed the scene will ever forget either. The afternoon
sun of a brilliant Bank Holiday filtered into the sombre and
crowded Chamber. From outside the rumble of the buses

passing over Westminster Bridge and the hum of the happy commonplace world that was about to be extinguished broke faintly upon the silence within. The last hope had gone. Europe was plunging into the abyss of war—war on a scale such as the world had never seen. Sir Edward Grey rose in a House shaken with the agony of an unprecedented occasion, torn with the bitterest dissensions, the bulk of his own supporters gloomily distrustful of the policy that was sweeping the nation into a catastrophe that, whatever the result, must ring down the curtain on the familiar landscape of things for ever. He sat down in a House, silent, sorrowful, but convinced. It was that speech and his personality that carried the nation into the war at once and with practical unanimity. "When I stood up," he says referring to this supreme moment in his life, "I don't recall feeling nervous. At such a moment there could be neither hope of personal success nor fear of personal failure. In a great crisis a man stands stripped and bare of choice. He has to do what it is in him to do; just this is what he will do and must do and he can do no other."

I do not think that the contemporary judgment of his character will ever be questioned, any more than I think that his disinterested pursuit of peace will be questioned. If he is criticised, it will not be on the score of his spirit and his intentions, which were alike noble, but on the score of his methods and his understanding. I can conceive him in that moment when, with Europe falling into the abyss, he sat by Mr. Asquith, looking sadly, unseeingly, at the high windows of the Chamber, asking himself questions that history will go on asking long after this generation has become a memory—questions to which there will never be an answer. And I can conceive that on the subject of his intelligence there will always be suspicion. If his understanding and knowledge had equalled his qualities of character his preeminence in our time would have been unchallenged.

But his intellectual limitations are severe. Within those limitations his mind works with remarkable truth and sureness, but outside the limits there is no free play of ideas and little of the imaginative understanding of things. He is apt to become wedded to a view and to move in an unchanging orbit. His mind is rigid, not plastic, and his loyalties, as in the case of Lee, do not discriminate between the great and the small. When his opinion is formed, he is liable to be inaccessible to new thought and new points of view, and his judgment of men is equally decisive and, not infrequently, equally mistaken. His failure to understand the deep wisdom that underlay the modest, almost rustic, surface of Campbell-Bannerman was a flagrant example of his misjudgment of men, and the Washington episode to which I shall refer later illustrated his tendency to subordinate great issues to lesser loyalties.

Like Wilson, he has "a single-track mind." That phrase is usually employed in a depreciatory sense, as meaning a narrowed outlook, an undue servitude to a fixed idea, a failure to allow for the play and complexity of things. This may be true; but it is equally true that it may imply a simplicity, concentration, force in the pursuit of the essential that constitutes supreme greatness. The verdict on the wisdom or unwisdom of the single-track mind depends on the quality of judgment exercised in the choice of the track. In the case of Lord Grey, that judgment offers a problem of unequalled interest. His public life ran parallel with one great world theme. With that theme he was exclusively preoccupied, and throughout the orbit of his course was never deflected. For twenty-five years he sat like a physician beside a patient tossing in high fever. The patient is Europe, and the fever lasts a generation before it culminates in the catastrophe. Sometimes the fever subsides, sometimes the patient is quiescent, sometimes the danger-point seems even to have passed, as in 1913, but always the high temperature returns, the peril reappears, and the agony is renewed. Was the disease too deep-seated to be beyond cure? Was the peril avoidable by the wisdom of men, or was the catastrophe inherent in the conditions?

Let us look at the progress of the fever as Sir Edward Grey saw it, and as he records it. His vigil by the bedside begins in 1892 when, the foremost figure among the younger politicians of the time, he became Under-Secretary to Lord Rosebery at the Foreign Office. The loom of fate had already begun to weave its pattern. The Triple Alliance of Germany, Austria, and Italy had called into being the counter-alliance of France and Russia. England stood aloof. It was the period of "splendid isolation" with its complementary aspiration for the Concert of Europe. In so far as England had sympathies, they were German sympathies, inspired in part by an unbroken historical amity, in part by the German sentiment of the Victorian court. They were expressed by successive Prime Ministers of unusual authority and of both parties—Gladstone, Salisbury, Rosebery. Throughout the 'nineties these sympathies prevailed. If there was fear, it was fear of France and Russia, and all the preparations for naval security were made on the Franco-Russian calculation. Twice we were on the brink of war with France, over the Bangkok incident, in 1893, and the Fashoda incident, in 1898. The pin pricks of France and the menace of the incalculable despotism of Russia were tending to strengthen the German sympathies of the country and pave the way, if "splendid isolation" had to be sacrificed, to an understanding with that country. This tendency, implicit in the policies of Salisbury and Rosebery alike, took form in 1899 when Chamberlain made his memorable speech suggesting an Anglo-Saxon-Teutonic understanding, which should cover not merely England and Germany, but, if she were disposed, America also.

That gesture, made under the impression that it would be welcomed, evoked no response from Germany. It evoked no response because throughout the 'nineties, while the hostility of France was open and flagrant, there was no compensating spirit of friendship from Germany. Bismarck had fallen, the young Kaiser was in the saddle, and the Bismarckian tradition of Continental dominance had given place to the dream of world power. That dream had changed the orientation of Germany. "Our future is on the sea," said the Kaiser at Stettin, in 1898, and there began that development of the sea power of Germany in which collision with the sea power of Britain was implicit. The significance of this change of attitude was not realised in England in the nineties in spite of such unfriendly incidents as the Kaiser's telegram to Kruger, and at the very time that Chamberlain was making his overture to Germany, Bülow, the Chancellor, was writing a private memorandum in which he said:

On the whole it is certain that opinion in England is far less anti-German than opinion in Germany is anti-English; therefore those Englishmen like Chirol and Saunders [the *Times'* correspondent who was subsequently banished from Berlin] are the most dangerous to us since they know from their own observations the depth and bitterness of German antipathy against England.

The practical rejection of the Chamberlain overture did

not sensibly increase suspicion in England and even as late as 1902 the disposition of the Government to work with Germany was illustrated, and most unfortunately illustrated, by the association with the Kaiser in the Venezuelan episode. It can hardly be doubted that the Kaiser's purpose in that affair was to challenge the Monroe doctrine and to involve England in the controversy. The peril was fortunately realised before events had gone too far, and when the cloud passed and it was seen how near the country had been brought to a grave rupture with the United States, public opinion was deeply aroused. From this incident sprang the widespread suspicion of Germany, and the definite impulse to sacrifice the doctrine of "splendid isolation." The doctrine was valid while it was believed that the feelings of Germany were friendly, but that belief seemed no longer tenable in view of the spirit of German relations and the now unconcealed challenge to the naval supremacy of England.

This change of mentality was the opportunity for Delcassé, whose mind had dominated French foreign policy for ten years, and who was the true author and begetter of the Entente. Sir Edward Grey, then out of office, welcomed the Anglo-French understanding. He had no personal enthusiasm for France, and no hostility to Germany, but he was alarmed by the drift of events and was seized with the conviction that England must have cordial relations with somebody. When he came into office as Foreign Secretary, in 1906, he had two motives, the first was to stop the drift of Europe to war, the other was to secure the position of his own country in the event of failure by an unfaltering attachment to France. "I re-entered office," he says, "*with the fixed resolve not to lose the one friendship we had*

made, not to slip back again into the friction of 1892-1895.
With Germany I wanted to be as friendly as I could be,
without sacrificing friendships already made."

The history of the next eight years was the history of
the failure of the one motive and the success of the other.
Perhaps they were irreconcilable. Perhaps "splendid isolation" still represented the true function of England in Continental affairs—we shall never know. But the pauseless
challenge of Germany at sea was the rock on which Sir
Edward Grey's major motive split. Gesture after gesture
was made to Germany without response. We stopped
building capital ships: Germany went on building more.
We offered a ten years' naval holiday: Tirpitz produced a
new and more formidable naval programme. We sent
Lord Haldane to negotiate privately with the Kaiser: he
returned with the confession of failure. Meanwhile Germany was testing the reality of the Entente. The first
Moroccan crisis in 1905, the Bosnia-Herzgovina crisis in
1908, the second Moroccan crisis in 1911 in turn aimed at
trying the ice. With each incident the universal tension increased. Then with the Balkan war in 1912, and the success of the London Conference, there came a momentary
lift of the cloud. It was Sir Edward Grey's hour of triumph. He seemed to have restored the Concert of Europe.
The Kaiser paid him a handsome tribute, and for a few
brief months the sky of Europe was clearer than it had been
for seven years. Then, almost out of the blue, came the
catastrophe. Grey acquits the Kaiser of a desire for war.
He wanted another "shining armour" victory of diplomacy,
but he had lost prestige with the military autocrats by the
compromise of 1911 and was swept into the current.

Lord Grey fairly emphasises the refusal by Germany to

accept a conference as the crucial test of responsibility for the war. Only a little more than a year before, the London Conference of Ambassadors had saved Europe. All the members of that conference were still in London. Their intervention might have checked the mad torrent of events, changed the atmosphere, perhaps averted the disaster. But Germany said "No," and in saying "No," willed war.

If, in the record of the events of the great drama which will give him a place in history not dissimilar to that of Pitt, criticism is directed against him, it will be on account of the tyrannical obsession indicated in the words I have italicised. He did not swim into the orbit of France because of any predilection for France. In 1894, his warning to France over her African policy had alarmed Morley and Harcourt, and had nearly brought about a Cabinet crisis. All through the 'nineties he had shared the prevailing leaning to Germany; but when that phase had passed and Delcassé's goal was reached, the whole force of his mind was canalised into the French channel. At last we had a friend. To cling to that friend at all costs became the motive to which every other consideration was subordinated. France was not slow to take advantage of the fact. Her most subtle diplomacy assumed a commanding influence in our affairs and both before and during the war that "fixed resolve" was the pivot around which Sir Edward Grey revolved. He was the static force, France the dynamic. His loyalty was splendid, but it paralysed initiative.

How much it was paralysed is illustrated by the incident of the House memorandum embodying President Wilson's peace overture in February, 1916. Colonel House was despatched to England to tell Sir Edward that the President, on hearing from France and England that the moment was opportune, would propose a conference to put an end to the war. Should the Allies accept this proposal and should Germany refuse it, the United States would probably enter into the war on the side of the Allies. As to the conditions of peace, Colonel House, speaking for the President, expressed an opinion favourable to the restoration and indemnification of Belgium, the transference of Alsace-Lorraine to France, the acquisition of an outlet to the sea by Russia, with certain compensations to Germany outside Europe. At that time we were straining every nerve and offering every inducement to bring Italy, Bulgaria, Roumania, any ally into our system. And here was a proposal from the greatest power in the world, the power without whose resources the war, as events showed, could not have been won by anybody, that Germany should be challenged to confess defeat as the alternative to seeing America numbered among her enemies. Of course at that time—before Verdun and the Somme—she would no have accepted the President's terms, and American intervention would have been antedated by more than a year.

In any circumstances, the proposal was of momentous consequence. It was entirely disregarded. Beyond being forwarded without comment through the French Ambassador in London to M. Briand, it might as well have been dropped in the waste-paper basket. No word was ever uttered by Sir Edward to M. Briand on the subject, and no pressure was applied to get the proposal discussed. This was not because Sir Edward undervalued the importance of America in the struggle. Nothing in his record is more praiseworthy than his success in preventing our necessary interference with American commerce at sea developing into a conflict with America like that of 1812. It was because he feared, by mentioning the word "peace," to give France the impression that we were weakening. He left the initiative, if initiative there was to be, to M. Briand. He did not ask him to consider the proposal: he waited to see if M. Briand would ask him to consider it.

It was not until nine months later, with Russia rocking to its fall, and when the Asquith Government was near its end, that Sir Edward remembered the memorandum, and cautiously suggested that in certain circumstances—the possible defection of Russia was obviously in his mind—the Wilson overture should be considered. But the moment had gone by, the "knock-out blow" policy was in the ascendant, and two years of bloodshed followed.

The same rigid mentality is illustrated in the Washington episode to which I have alluded. The facts are more familiar in America than here, and have been given in great detail in the columns of the *New York World*. It is the story of the clash of two minds, curiously alike in their strength and their weakness, each sacrificing great things to a matter of etiquette. When, after the peace conference, Lord Reading was at Washington and President Wilson had returned from Paris, a rumour reached the White House that a member of the Embassy staff had been gossiping with great indiscretion about Mrs. Wilson. The President indicated that the presence of this person in Washington was no longer agreeable. Lord Reading pointed out that he was leaving shortly and that he would take the person in question with him, and it was agreed that that would meet the case. Lord Grey duly arrived to succeed Lord Reading, and great things were hoped from the intercourse of two men so profoundly in sympathy as the President and Lord Grey in regard to the future of human society. They never met. It is true the President was ill, but that was not the reason. The reason was that on the staff that accompanied Lord Grey from England was the man who had incurred the President's displeasure. Lord Grey, of course, knew nothing of the original incident, but he was loyal to his staff, did not sacrifice his man, and after some months came back to England with his mission unfulfilled.

But whatever his faults of method or of understanding, Lord Grey will live in the story of these days as "the noblest Roman of them all." If he made mistakes, he made them for no personal or ignoble ends. If he has any share in the responsibility for the tragedy, it was a share imposed on him by events and necessities and not by any vulgar ambition or will to power. He came into politics when the great storm was brewing, and he strove valiantly to avert it. He had the vision of the good European, and he sought to build up a dam that would retain the insurgent waters. If his method was force, it was not because he believed in force, but because he inherited a situation that left no other alternative. After the crisis of 1911 it seemed that he had won, and in welcoming President Taft's arbitration proposals he looked forward to a time when the nations "would discover, as individuals have discovered, that all the time they have been in bondage the prison door has been locked on the inside." But the dam burst and the flood swept the earth. The waters still heave and from the midst of the wreck he utters to the world the lesson of the vast tragedy in which his own life is so peculiarly involved—"Learn or Perish."

v. Lord Beaverbrook

AMONG my letters one morning was one from a share-
broker who seems to take a kindly interest in my welfare
and sends me frequent hints of how to make my fortune.
On this occasion he was very urgent (of course for my own
good) that I should buy shares in the *Daily Mail* Trust Ltd.
presided over by Lord Rothermere, and he enclosed a document showing the possessions of that corporation. And
among those possessions I found included 49 per cent. of the
shares in the *Daily Express*, and 49 per cent. of the shares in
the *Evening Standard*. It was a reminder of the pleasant
relations that exist between those twin potentates, Lord
Rothermere and Lord Beaverbrook, who, instead of cutting
each other's throats, divide their empire of the Press in a
spirit of brotherly love, and who, while preserving a decorous air of independenc in public, wink, like the augurs, com-
panionably behind the scenes.

In that mutual exchange, Lord Beaverbrook's is the more
knowing wink. There are no hinterlands in the colourless
mind of Lord Rothermere; but Lord Beaverbrook is as engaging as a cross-word puzzle. He keeps you guessing and
keeps you amused. You feel that he is always "up to some
game," and that behind that debonair frankness with which
he disarms your distrust he is laying mines and counter-
mines which you are not invited to inspect. He encourages
you to think that he is a simple-minded young man from the
backwoods, full of beautiful enthusiasms, trustful and innocent, and most singularly in agreement with your point of

view. He will unbosom himself. He will take you to his heart. He will apologise for his past and throw himself on your mercy. His modesty verges on humility, his trans-Atlantic accent breathes the fine flavour of democracy, and his smile, which is enormous and frequent, is almost childlike and bland. And as in the case of another smile that was childlike and bland, you know it is not a smile to presume on, and, if you examined his sleeve, it would not surprise you to find that it was stuffed with aces. I do not mean illicit aces. I have no doubt that they would be quite honour-ably there, as the reward of the calculations of one of the astutest minds that ever played the game of life.

Nature equipped him for that game with an ingenuous manner, a pair of mischievous, laughing eyes, a friendliness that gets behind all defences, and a swift, fertile brain adapted to exploit the position to which his engaging quali-ties have given him access. He is, before everything else, a manipulator of men, of situations, and of occasions. Perhaps he would claim as his greatest achievement the overthrow of the Asquith administration, in 1916. It is certainly as representative of his methods as any of his feats.

The situation was complex. For months the Government has been assailed from within and from without by ceaseless intrigue; but it had survived every attack and seemed invul-nerable. It rested on the foundation of the alliance between Mr. Asquith and Mr. Bonar Law, who commanded the sup-port of the most numerous and most reputable elements of both the dominant parties. While that alliance remained, the fabric of the Government was invincible against the as-saults of the sensational Press inspired from within the Government. It was Sir Max Aitken's ingenuity which en-

gineered the downfall, and his cunning and diplomacy succeeded where the noise and fury of Northcliffe had failed.

The elements with which he worked were simple. Mr.
Lloyd George's dissatisfaction with the leadership of Mr.
Asquith was notorious, and his relations with Northcliffe,
who was daily pouring obloquy on his leader, were a commonplace. On the Conservative side, Sir Edward Carson
had left the Government and was inaugurating a parallel
assault on the position of Mr. Bonar Law. The two movements seemed to be coalescing with a common purpose which,
if it brought down the Government, would leave Mr. Lloyd
George and Sir Edward Carson in and Mr. Asquith and Mr.
Bonar Law out.

Sir Max Aitken, moved by his personal friendship for
Mr. Bonar Law, conceived the idea of diverting the plot
into another channel. His scheme was to unite Mr. Lloyd
George, Sir Edward Carson, and Mr. Bonar Law, and
eliminate Mr. Asquith. He first patched up the differences
between Sir Edward Carson and Mr. Law, and then brought
Mr. Lloyd George, without, I imagine, any great resistance,
into the conversations. Once begun on this promising tack,
the loom of events worked rapidly. There were, as the
author of "Lloyd George and the War" observes, almost
daily meetings between the members of the triple alliance,
with their plenipotentiary, Max Aitken, as their host or go-
between, sending out feelers and acting as intelligence officer.
There were breakfasts, dinners, suppers, numerous conclaves,
and when the moment had come to explode the mine, it was
Max Aitken who applied the match. One day the streets
were aflame with placards announcing that Mr. Lloyd
George was "packing up" at the War Office, which was the
signal for the assault. Forty-eight hours later Mr. Asquith

had resigned, and one of Mr. Lloyd George's first acts on taking his office was to convert Sir Max Aitken into Lord Beaverbrook. It is not true that there is no gratitude in politics.

This art of manipulating men and circumstances had been acquired in youth. Born and brought up in a remote Presbyterian manse in Nova Scotia, Max Aitken went to Halifax with nothing but his wits and his bonhomie by way of fortune. They were quite sufficient. Before he was twenty-five he was immersed in big business, dabbling in finance, manœuvring combines, founding trusts and banks, controlling the cast-iron trade in Canada, concerned in paper mills, in car building, in anything and everything that came within his enterprising grasp. His best known exploit was the cement merger of Canada. Eleven cement companies were bought out by the Bond and Share Company—of which our hero was chairman, and, according to the "Grain Growers' Guide," the practical proprietor—for $16,592,250, and were disposed of to the Canada Cement Company for shares and mortgage to the total value of $28,993,400. The result, as not uncommonly happens, was less agreeable for the consumers than the financiers, for, according to the authority I have just quoted, "the price of cement at the factories instantly jumped on the completion of the merger from $1 to $1.50 per barrel." Sir Sandford Fleming, the honorary president of the purchasing company, took the view that $12,000,000 was rather much to pay for promotion expenses, resigned his position, and even applied to Sir Wilfrid Laurier for a Government inquiry into the transaction. I do not find that Mr. Max Aitken ever disputed the accuracy of the figures, though he denied that he had received one-fortieth of the amount. In any case, he did very well out

[Photo Central News

LORD BEAVERBROOK

of his activities, for he was reputed to be a millionaire at thirty, by which time he felt that Canada was too limited a stage for his gifts, and sought new worlds to conquer.

It was in 1910 that he descended on Ashton-under-Lyne, as the apostle of Empire and Protection. His candidature was something of a joke, for he knew nothing about politics, talked jerkily and badly, proclaimed his origin by sometimes discussing money in the terms of dollars and cents, and filled up the gaps by such assurances as, "If I could make you men of Ashton realise what this Empire of ours means, there would not be a Radical left in the place"; but he discovered a genius for organisation, won the seat, and began the second phase of his career. It was not, however, until the war that his peculiar genius found its opportunity. His gifts are not the gifts of public debate, but of private wire-pulling, and in the settled world of pre-war days the scope for the wire-puller was limited. The slight splash which the young Canadian had made in the home waters in 1910 had long been forgotten, and it seemed that Max Aitken had become submerged in the depths of Parliamentary obscurity and that he would have done better to stay at home.

But when the convulsion came and all the ordered public life of the nation became a swirl of confused currents and anyone who had the ear of the mob and an adventurous temperament might hope for anything, Sir Max Aitken found the perfect medium for the exercise of his genius. With a true instinct for strategy, he established himself as the representative Canadian on this side of the Atlantic, and with equal astuteness got into the heart of things by securing appointment as the Canadian "Eye Witness" at the front. In this position his talent for manœuvring had free play, and the fall of General Alderson from the command of the

Canadian division in France was, I have reason to know, not unconnected with his activities, though his attempt to impose his own nominee as successor on Sir Douglas Haig was less successful. But most astonishing was his campaign on this side on behalf of Sir Sam Hughes, when, in connection with the investigation into Canadian War Contracts, Sir Sam had been instructed by the Canadian Premier to return at once to Canada. Sir Max Aitken organised a great Press boom of his friend in this country to impress opinion in Canada. Sir Sam passed through the land like a hero. Bands blared in his honour, mayors welcomed him, banquets awaited him. It was magnificent and it was all manufactured for Canadian consumption. The details of that episode threw a flood of light not only on the secret history of the war, but on the skill with which public opinion and great matters of policy may be influenced without the hand that pulls the strings ever being visible to the world.

It was not until the war had shown him the real source of power in the modern community that Lord Beaverbrook found his feet in this country. He had failed egregiously as a Parliamentarian, but he saw that there was a short cut to a throne by way of Fleet Street. Get control of public opinion, and the politicians who rose and fell by public opinion would feed out of your hand. Lord Northcliffe had anticipated him in the discovery, but Lord Beaverbrook was swift to take up the running, and, being supple and quick-witted where Lord Northcliffe was only a heavy-footed blunderer, he quickly insinuated himself into the centre of the intrigues, plots and ambuscades of the post-war years. He himself has told us, with his naïve and childlike egotism, of the roaring time he had in that rather squalid world.

Now he is deep in the Lloyd George strategy; now he is
plotting against him with Bonar Law as his chief instrument.
Back to Mr. George and out with Mr. Churchill. In with
Mr. Churchill and out with Mr. George. In with both and
momentarily out with both. To Lord Birkenhead and Sir
Robert Horne alone he is constant; to Mr. Baldwin alone
he is consistently hostile. His vanity is beyond belief, and
no sense of humour checks the wild comedy of his self-
revelation. He is as proud of the number of successful
"tips" that the sporting prophets of his newspapers have
offered to a grateful public as he is of dictating policies and
blowing up ministries. Governments fall at the blast of his
trumpet and even the finances of Europe tremble at his nod.
He goes to Berlin and from thence sends a series of des-
patches to his papers with catastrophic consequences:

These prophecies proved correct. The mark broke instantly and
rushed down into the abyss. Whether this was in some part the consequence of the prediction, or whether prophecy and fulfillment syn-
chronised naturally, I cannot say; but the fact remained that by a
dramatic stroke the *Sunday Express* and the *Daily Express* had shown
themselves a powerful force in the world of European commerce and
industry.

If the gifts of Lord Beaverbrook for manipulating men
and events had been accompanied by any considered view of
life or any moral purpose, he would have been one of the
most considerable figures of his time. But it is impossible
to discover any purpose in his activities except the satisfaction
of being active. He pulls strings, not because he has any
particular object in view, but for the love of pulling them.
He represents the new spirit in the Press which aims, not at
influencing statesmen by giving them an instructed and en-

lightened public opinion, but at making them subservient
to a power which will exalt them or hound them out of office
according to whether they will or will not accept its dictates
and its terms.   Mr. Asquith fell during the war because he
would not bargain with this new tyranny of an irresponsible
power, and it is not the least of the claims which Mr. Baldwin has established upon the gratitude of the country that he
has set his face resolutely against the insolent pretensions of
newspaper owners to reduce Downing Street to the position
of an annex of Fleet Street.

It is the claim of Lord Beaverbrook that following in the
breach made by Lord Northcliffe he has invented something
better than our old-fashioned system of Parliamentary
Government.   It is government by the Press—by stunts and
headlines, supplemented by deals between the newspaper
magnates and a certain type of politician.   In the old be-
nighted days before Lord Beaverbrook made his momentous incursion into Europe, the Press was a very stupid affair.
It did not know its business.   It was hitched to dull old
parties, mumbled the party jargon, and danced to the party
tune.

Now all is changed.   Fleet Street is emancipated.   Fleet
Street pulls the strings and sets the tune.   It makes Ministries and unmakes them.   The tenant of 10, Downing Street,
no longer looks to Parliament as his master.   He goes down
to Lord Beaverbrook's country place to hear what Lord
Beaverbrook thinks, to make terms with him, to arrange what
tune shall be played to the public on the various instruments
that Lord Beaverbrook and his friend Lord Rothermere
control.

Now, with all respect to Lord Beaverbrook, I think that

the revolution he rejoices to have helped the late Lord Northcliffe to accomplish is bad for politics, bad for the country, bad for the Press. Parliamentary government is our greatest contribution to the affairs of the world. The people elect the Parliament, the Parliament controls the Executive. If the Executive ceases to command the support of Parliament it resigns, goes to the country, and the country delivers its verdict by electing a new Parliament, with a new mandate from the people. That is representative government, and human ingenuity has discovered no other system of government so stable, so wise, so responsive to considered public opinion.

What is the function of the Press in the system? It is to report the facts, argue the case, inform the public. Its relations with politicians should be consistent with the maintenance of the authority of Parliament. Its client is the public. Its business is to help the public to come to an instructed decision and not to exploit its influence for personal power.

Lord Melbourne used to complain of the John Walter of the *Times* of his day that there was "nothing that the d——d fellow wanted," in other words that there was no bribe he would take to influence his conduct of his paper. That was the handsomest tribute ever paid to a great journalist. We have lived to see a time when Ministers of the Crown have bargained away honours and offices to the magnates of the Press as the price of their support. Both statesmanship and journalism have been degraded by the intercourse, and in breaking with that evil practice Mr. Baldwin has done something to restore the better traditions of public life and to cleanse the atmosphere both of Downing Street and Fleet Street. Lord Beaverbrook does not like the change and does not approve of Mr. Baldwin. But in this difficult world it is impossible to please everybody. And, after all, he has had a great lark over here. I wish I knew what it was about.

vi. Mr. Winston Churchill

I T IS not true that a rolling stone gathers no moss. Mr.
Churchill has gathered a great deal of moss. Not that a
stone, whether stationary or rolling, is a suitable symbol for
this extraordinary man. He is like a rocket that intermit-
tently dazzles the night sky, disappears, and dazzles it again;
flashes now from this quarter, now from that; is always
meteoric but never extinguished. The principal difference
between Mr. Churchill and a cat, as Mark Twain might say,
is that a cat has only nine lives. By all the laws of mortality,
Mr. Churchill should have perished a score of times, sometimes in laughter, sometimes in anger, sometimes in contempt; but the funeral has always been premature, the grave
always empty. You may scotch him for a moment, but you
cannot kill him, and we grow weary of pronouncing his
obsequies.

What is the use of insisting that he is dead when you
know that to-morrow he will be so flagrantly, so impudently
alive? "In war you can be killed but once," he has said,
"but in politics many times." It is not always so. His
father was killed by one self-inflicted wound. He died
almost from the prick of a pin, but the tough fibre of the
son, due to his American mother, survives as many arrows
as legend plants in the body of St. Sebastian. Like the camo-
mile, the more he is trodden on, the more he flourishes. His
failures are monumental, but the energy of his mind and
the sheer impetus of his personality make his failures more
brilliant than other men's successes.

At fifty, at an age when most public men are only beginning to catch the limelight, when Mr. Baldwin was unknown
and Mr. Bonar Law had not held office, he looks back on
thirty years of romantic adventure that would provide material for a dozen normal lives which would find a place in the
Dictionary of National Biography; on experiences of war
in more continents than Napoleon fought in; on a library of
books that would not do injustice to a life spent in literature;
on journalism, lecturing, painting; on a political career more
full of vicissitudes than any since that of Bolingbroke; and
on the tenure of more great offices in the State, not merely
than any contemporary statesman, but, I believe, than any
man in our political history.   In spite of his ups and downs,
I doubt whether anyone since Pitt has spent so large a proportion of his Parliamentary life in office.   It is twenty-five
years since, hot from his escape from the Boers as a prisoner
of war, he entered Parliament on the "Khaki" tide, and
seventeen of those years have been passed on the Treasury
Bench.

He came into the world booted and spurred to ride, and
he rides at the gallop all the time.   Do the citizens of Dundee cast him out of Parliament, and leave him apparently
and, this time, finally dead under the load of his transgres-
sions?   He sits down, like a Cæsar, to write a history of the
war, as brilliant as it is brazen, and leaves soldiers and statesmen gasping at his boundless effrontery, at a nerve, a cheek,
an audacity that reduces them to amazed helplessness.   "I
will not go back to the Admiralty," said Lord Fisher to me
in the midst of the Ministerial crisis of 1915.   "I will not
go back to the Admiralty if Churchill reappears in the Cabinet.   How can I fight Tirpitz if every moment has to be
spent in watching Churchill?"   He is like an embodied fury

in a Rugby pack. He twists and turns and wriggles and lunges; but always he emerges from the scrum with the ball racing for the goal. He obeys no one, fears no one, reverences no one. He is his own superman, and is so absorbed in himself and in his own fiery purposes that he does not pay others the compliment even of being aware of them.

His isolation is unprecedented. He has personal friends, the chief being that other kindred spirit, Lord Birkenhead, and his loyalty to them is notorious; but he is an Ishmael in public life, loathed by the Tories whom he left and has now returned to; distrusted by the Liberals, on whose backs he first mounted to power; hated by Labour, whom he scorns and insults, and who see in him the potential Mussolini of a wave of reaction. His genius is the genius of action, and he loathes "the canker of a long peace and a calm world." He sees life in terms of war, and his high and turbulent spirit is only entirely happy when politics and war are merged in one theme. The grotesque incident of the Sidney Street bombardment revealed the whole temper of a mind that has never outgrown the boyish love of soldiers; and when, as Home Secretary, he was confronted with a national strike, John Burns entered his room one day and found him poring over a large scale map of the country on which he was marking the disposition of troops at strategic points. "What do you think of my military arrangements, John?" asked the young Napoleon. "I think you are mistaking a coffee-stall row for the social revolution," said Burns, leaving the room with a resounding bang of the door. There is a passage in Mrs. Asquith's (Lady Oxford's) Autobiography which sticks in the mind as illuminating the Churchill landscape. It is the night of the fatal fourth of August, 1914. In a room at Downing Street Mr. Asquith and three of his colleagues are awaiting the German reply to the British ultimatum on Belgium. If there is no satisfactory answer by midnight, war, with all its incalculable consequences, engulfs the land. The minutes pass in tense silence, and at last the clock strikes. "As I was passing at the foot of the staircase," writes Mrs. Asquith, "I saw Winston Churchill with a happy face striding towards the double doors of the Cabinet Room."

When someone told Harcourt that Randolph Churchill was practically an "uneducated man," Harcourt replied: "If he was educated he would be spoiled." In the academic sense, Mr. Churchill is as uneducated as his father. He was an indifferent scholar at school, and of formal learning he would still be outclassed by Macaulay's fabulous schoolboy. It is said that Randolph Churchill, on his mournful visit to South Africa after his sun had set, sought to find a career there for a lad who had to earn his living and gave no promise of a career at home. Perhaps if Winston had been educated, he, too, would have been "spoiled" in the sense Harcourt meant. He would not have been the Churchill we know, the Churchill who flings himself into life with the uncalculating vehemence and passion of the boy in the school playground. "There are times," says Mr. Wells in speaking of him, "when the evil spirit comes upon him, and then I can think of him only as an intractable little boy, a mischievous, dangerous little boy, a knee-worthy little boy. Only by thinking of him in that way can I go on liking him."

His appearance supports the impression. In spite of the bowed shoulders, the thinning hair, and the portentous gravity of bearing, there is still the sense of the intractable, unschooled boy, the terror of the playground, the despair of the master. The pouting, petulant lips give a note of child-ish wilfulness to the face, and the smile, which borders on a grin, has a hint of boyish mischief that has not been dis-covered. But if he is uneducated in the school sense, and if he is rudimentary in the moral sense, his intelligence is extraordinary, his understanding powerful, his intellectual activity unrivalled, his will despotic. He has little contact with ideas or ideals, but he sees the play of life and the clash of material forces vividly and imaginatively, and leaps at his conclusions and convictions with an assurance and imperi-ousness that impose them on those who doubt and hesitate. One man with a conviction will overwhelm a hundred who have only opinions, and Mr. Churchill always bursts into the fray with a conviction so clear, so decisive, so burning, that opposition is stampeded.

That is the explanation of the astonishing part he was allowed to play in the war, from the Antwerp fiasco to the Russian fiasco. He triumphed by the sheer energy of his mind. He swept his colleagues by the fervour and passion of his vision. He could not be repressed; he could not be denied. If his wisdom had been equal to his force, he would have been the towering figure of the war. But, as I think Lord Oxford once said of him, "He has genius without judgment." He sees only one aspect of a situation at a time, and the ardour of his vision exercises a maniacal and perilous spell. His inspirations, which sometimes have a touch of genius, should have been listened to, and then he should have been stood in a corner and forbidden to speak while wiser men examined them and decided. For unless Mr. Churchill is silenced he will win in a dialectical "war of attrition." He will fight his foes to a standstill. He will wear them down by his tireless attack, by the intensity of his feeling, the versatility of his proof. For he knows his case as he knows his speeches—word and letter perfect. He leaves nothing to chance. He works at the documents like a navvy; he recites his arguments with ceaseless industry. He practises on everybody. His life is one long speech. He does not talk: he orates. He will address you at break- fast as though you were an audience at the Free Trade Hall, and at dinner you find the performance still running. If you meet him in the intervals, he will give you more frag- ments of the discourse, walking up and down the room with the absorbed, self-engaged, Napoleonic portentousness that makes his high seriousness tremble on the verge of the comic. He does not want to hear your views. He does not want to disturb the beautiful clarity of his thought by tiresome re- minders of the other side. What has he to do with the other side when his side is the right side?   He is not arguing with you: he is telling you.

This method of self-saturation with his theme gives him an enormous power in council and on the platform. His arguments are always ready; his periods always perfectly rounded; his rhetoric has passed the test of innumerable listeners. And it is good rhetoric, occasionally, it is true, bordering on the "penny plain twopence coloured," as in such sentences as these from his book on the war:

> Son of the Stone Age, vanquisher of nature with all her trials and monsters, he met the awful and self-inflicted agony with new reserves of fortitude.
>
> A world of monstrous shadows, moving in convulsive combinations, through vistas of fathomless catastrophe:

But generally his sense of language is sound and masculine and his feeling for form hardly rivalled among contem- porary speakers. And it is bare justice to him to say that, though he has few principles and few scruples, he has the courage always to be himself and to carry his political life in his hand. He possesses that honesty of speech which enabled him to say during his first candidature in the midst of the "Khaki" election: "If I were a Boer, I should be fighting with them in the field." He is neither a demagogue nor a sycophant, and if he changes his party with the facility of partners at a dance, he has always been true to the only party he really believes in—that which is assembled under the hat of Mr. Winston Churchill.

To-day, in the prime of life, with the dangerous "forties" navigated, with the most plentiful crop of political wild oats ever sown or ever survived, reunited to his traditional party, miraculously translated to the office from which his father fell never to rise again, he is easily the foremost figure in Parliament, with a past that would have extinguished any-one ordinarily destructible, and nevertheless with a future that is the most interesting subject of speculation in politics. He emerges to-day from No. 11, Downing Street, and such is his buoyancy and tenacity of grip upon the lifeboat of office that I see no reason why he should not one day emerge from No. 10. But before that happens, I hope he will have given evidence that he has judgment as well as genius and that he has ceased to be "an intractable little boy, a mischievous and dangerous little boy, a knee-worthy little boy."

vii. Lady Oxford

ONE spring day, some forty-odd years ago, that Nimrod of the chase, the late Duke of Beaufort, was hunting with the Beaufort hounds in Wiltshire, when he came across a girl seated upon the wettest of wet ground, having been flung from her horse, Storm, in her first hunting exploit. She was whistling unconcernedly, and the Duke, in admiration of her pluck and her riding, promised her the blue habit of the hunt and a top hat to save the neck of a young lady who, in ducal language, bade fair to "ride like the devil."

"Good gracious!" said the girl, "I hope I have said nothing to offend you. Do you always do this when you meet anyone like me for the first time?"

"Just as it is the first time you have ever hunted," replied the Duke, "so it is the first time I have ever met anyone like you."

And for forty years the world has been saying the same thing. For the girl was Margot Tennant, who, as the Countess of Oxford and Asquith, is still so unlike anybody else that you meet upon earth that she seems to belong to another planet. W. S. Gilbert once told his wife that he was "too good to be true," and it might be said of Margot that she would be too incredible to be believed, if she had not existed. She has gone through the life of her time like a wind that bloweth where it listeth, a sort of natural element untamed and untameable.

When the historian of the future sets out to tell the story of these thrilling years, he will find two figures who will baffle him. The Earl of Oxford will baffle him by his reticence; the Countess will baffle him by her candour. Mr. Asquith's public utterances and public bearing have the impersonal quality of a Blue Book. He has been one of the most conspicuous figures in the public life of this country and of Europe for nearly forty years, but he has never touched, nor sought to touch, the popular imagination by the revelation of his intimate life and feelings. He is as shy as the late Lord Salisbury, without the habit of that remarkable man of throwing the flashlight of a phrase upon the deeper currents of life.

Mrs. Asquith (if I may call her by the more familiar name), on the other hand, is as expansive, as frank, and as palpable as a child. She pours out "all as plain as downright Shippen or as old Montaigne." There is not a concealment about her, no privacies, secrecies, self-repressions. She is open as the day, and lives in a blaze of light. She tells you everything that comes into her head, about herself, about her children, about her friends, about her enemies. The tears she sheds, the prayers she utters, the secret emotions she experiences, the slights she gets, and the retorts she gives, the moments of triumph and the moments of humiliation— all are revealed with the disarming candour of childhood.

When she wrote her astonishing "Autobiography," she tells us, she intended to use as a motto, "As well be hanged for a sheep as a lamb," but she changed her mind, and on the title page appears instead Blake's aphorism, "Prudence is a rich, ugly old maid wooed by incapacity." And under that bold banner she burst upon the public, as she bursts in upon the drawing-room, or as she used to burst into the nursery at Glen, with a defiant, challenging "Here's me!" She laid bare her life, her thoughts, her friends, with a prodi-

gality as boundless as her wit, her gaiety, and her high
spirits. It was like one of those gallops across country that
she describes with such life and zest. No hedge so high, no
stream so wide, but she will put her horse at it with fearless
intrepidity. She pays the penalty, but she is undaunted.
"I have broken both my collar bones, my nose, my ribs, and
my knee-cap; dislocated my jaw; fractured my skull; and
had five concussions of the brain; but though my horses are
to be sold next week (June 11, 1906)—I have not lost my
nerve."

And so with the adventure of life. She plunges into it
with the uncalculating momentum of a child of nature.
She has her falls in circumstance, but her spirit is always in
the saddle again and away like the wind. She belongs to
the wild and has more than a hint of the Romany in her
high temperament and her passion for the colour, the movement, the tang of life. There are no social fences in her
landscape, and her instinct for human comradeship makes
her at home with anybody who has nature in him. She sees
the fine things of character beneath the disguises of circumstance, and responds to them with a certain noble kinship.
There are few finer things in books than the record of her
accidental meeting with General Booth, and her shepherds
and tramps and factory girls live in the memory, much as
Velasquez made his beggars live, by the appeal of the eternal humanity of things. Take an example at random:

After my first great sorrow, the death of my sister Laura (the first wife
of Alfred Lyttelton)—I was suffocated in the house, and felt I had to
be out of doors from morning to night. One day I saw an old shepherd
named Gowanlock, coming up to me, holding my pony by the rein. I
had never noticed that it had strayed away, and, after thanking him, I
observed him looking at me quietly—he knew something of the rage

and anguish that Laura's death had brought into my heart—and putting his hand on my shoulder, he said:

"My child, there's no contending. . . . Ay . . . ay." Shaking his beautiful old head. "*That is so*, there's no contending. . . ."

With this fearless and uncalculating spirit and intense contact with life she couples a terrifying truthfulness that is the more formidable from the swift wit in which it is clothed:

Sir William: Margy, would you rather marry me or break your leg?
Margot: Break both, Sir William.

Her tongue and her pen are like that. They are not anxious to wound, but they must strike. They must out with the truth, though the heavens fall. The edge of her sword may descend on herself, on her family, on her nearest and dearest, but it must fall. Thus, one day at lunch, while the discussion turns on the relative merits of the public schools, she suddenly cuts in: "This is all nonsense. It doesn't matter what school a boy goes to. All that matters is the brains he takes there. Look at the Asquiths. You can send them where you like and they always come out on top. Look at Freddy here (and she turns to her neighbour, one of her own blood). He went to Eton, and he can hardly write his name." "Come, come, Margot," says Freddy, "that's going a bit too far."

She does "go a bit too far," for, not being touchy or impenitent herself, she takes adverse criticism very well, and does not understand why the truth should hurt others. She sees everything objectively, including her family, whom she discusses in their presence as one might discuss one's next-door neighbours or the pictures on the wall. And she sees herself with the same detachment and candour, as if she

were a fellow-mortal. She admires Margot in certain of
her aspects with the dispassionate enthusiasm with which she
would admire anything of beauty, from a horse to a woman's
hair, or from a flash of wit to an act of sacrifice; but she has
an acute eye for Margot's abundant failings, and through all
the gallop of self-expression there runs a vein of disarming
humility that makes her personality at once so bewildering
and iridescent.

She loves everything that has nature in it, everything
that comes up warm and glowing from the heart, whether
it is her own or another's, and though she has said many hard
things I do not think she ever did a mean thing, for next to
what I have called her terrifying truthfulness the most
marked feature of her character is her compassion and her
sense of justice. She will go through fire and water for a
friend, and a tale of wrong makes her a flame of indignation.
Rumour has played more havoc with her than with any personality of our time, and it is fair to say that her breathless
gallop through life has given rumour abundant encourage-
ment. One cannot break through the social fences without
scratches, and Margot has been breaking new ground ever
since, as a girl just out of short frocks, she was the most discussed woman in society; taking the town by her wit and
audacity; discussing the ethics of divorce with Gladstone
and reminding that great man, when he spoke of the
Fathers, that their authority in England was not sanctioned
by Act of Parliament; bursting into the solemnities of golf
—hitherto a game only for men—with an "Halloo" of the
hunting field, "It is a game, not a sacrament," she once told
Mr. Balfour; and discoursing on time and eternity with
the mighty Jowett. One of Gladstone's rare excursions into
verse was a panegyric of the amazing damsel, though his love

of old-fashioned ways in women was expressed in the remark: "Margot is charming; the fascinating opposite of everything I wish my granddaughter Dorothy to become."

Her genius is the genius of temperament rather than of intellect. She is not a learned woman in the academic sense, and her mental processes have little to do with formal logic. But her intuitions are swift, searching, and sometimes uncanny, and in more superstitious days she would have been worshipped as a seeress, or, perhaps, burned as a sorceress. Her interest is less in ideas than in emotions, and I would take her opinion about character rather than about policy. She has sense, but more sensibility. In a word, she is an artist rather than a thinker, and if her instincts do not give her a conviction she has none. But within the orbit of her faculties, she has one of the most brilliant and illuminating minds of her time, sudden as lightning and cutting to the quick of things like a sword. Her manner of speech is brief and epigrammatic, and she has probably said more witty things in fewer words than any person of her time. Her vocabulary is as fresh, vivid, nervous, as her husband's is formal and bookish, and she can make a word sparkle with sudden meanings. Take one or two examples of her gift for the illuminating phrase.

Of Rhodes in the midst of a party of admiring ladies:

He sat like a great bronze god among them; and I had not the spirit to disturb their worship.

He gave a circulating smile, finishing on my turban.

Had Lady Randolph Churchill been like her face she could have governed the world.

If I am hasty in making friends, and skip the preface, I always read it afterwards.

Of Alfred Lyttelton:

His mentality was brittle and he was as quick tempered in argument as he was sunny and serene in games.

Of Sir William Harcourt:

He was a man to whom life had added nothing; he was perverse, unreasonable, brilliant, boisterous, and kind when I knew him; but he must have been all these in the nursery.

Of Lord Rosebery:

He was not self-swayed like Gladstone, but he was self-enfolded.

Of the late Duke of Devonshire:

He had the figure and appearance of an artisan, with the brevity of a peasant, the courtesy of a king, and the noisy sense of humour of a Falstaff. He gave a great wheezy guffaw at all the right things and was possessed of endless wisdom.

Of Lord Curzon:

He had appearance more than looks, a keen, lively face, and an expression of enamelled self-assurance.

Lord Morley once wrote to her protesting against the "impertinents" who wished her to improve. "I very respectfully wish nothing of the sort," he said. "Few qualities are better worth leaving as they are than vivacity, wit, freshness of mind, gaiety, and pluck. Pray keep them all. Don't improve by an atom." She hasn't. She retains her dauntless youth and her indomitable self. She will live in history as a legend and as the most brilliant woman who ever dwelt in 10, Downing Street. Perhaps she was too brilliant for a part which was subordinate, for a personality so incisive and romantic could not escape the limelight. The ideal partner of a Prime Minister is one who has no place in the public eye, no coruscations of her own with which to dazzle the sky of affairs. We think of Mrs. Gladstone in connection with Mr. Gladstone's slippers and the mysterious julep she used to prepare for the due functioning of his vocal chords on great oratorical occasions. Mrs. Disraeli would command Dizzy to tie up his shoe lace on a public staircase, but her quaint personality never had more than a comedy interest to the public. Of Lady Salisbury the world knew nothing, and Mrs. Baldwin is known only as a lady who pays periodical tributes to the surprising worthiness of her husband in whose accession to power she sees the visible hand of destiny. But Lady Oxford was born to dazzle and astonish, not by the reflected lights of circumstance, but by her own intense incandescence. It may have been this thought which prompted the reply of Mr. Balfour, recorded in the "Autobiography." The gossips of the Press had been busy with his name and that of Miss Tennant.

"I hear you are going to marry Margot Tennant," someone said to him.

"No, that is not so," he replied. "I rather think of having a career of my own."

VIII. The Prince of Wales

WHEN the Prince of Wales came home again from the latest of his many wanderings, there was one question in the public mind in regard to him—"What next?" He had completed his education. What part was he to play in the State? The Prince would be less than human if he did not occasionally feel that this public curiosity is irksome, and if he did not wish that he could enjoy the liberty of any private citizen to do what he pleases and go where he likes without let or hindrance or discussion. But that is not possible. He has the good or ill fortune to be a public institution, and we can no more be indifferent to his future than we can be indifferent to the future of St. Paul's. It is a hard fate—perhaps the hardest fate allotted to man. The legends of the nursery have bred in us a notion to the contrary, but we know it to be an illusion. The two most precious things in life are liberty and privacy, and the prince enjoys neither. He is a prisoner of State, and though we gild his cage we never allow him to escape observation from the day he comes into the world to the day he leaves it. Hence, having followed the movements of the Prince of Wales in two continents with the relentless vigilance of a policeman's bull's-eye, we now ask—"What next?"

It would be idle to pretend that there is not an increasing note of anxiety in the question. In it is involved concern for the future of the great institution the continuity of which the Prince embodies. That institution has passed unscathed through the greatest storm that has ever swept the world—

a storm that scattered the mightiest monarchies of Europe like leaves blown by an autumnal gale. To-day the monarchical idea has less hold on the world than has been the case for a thousand years. Leaving Canada aside, no Crown survives on the whole American continent. Leaving India and Japan aside no crown survives in the continent of Asia. All the great monarchies of the European continent have gone. You may draw a line from the Straits of Dover to the Sea of Japan without passing through the territory of King or Emperor. There is a fringe of minor Kingships around Europe, and the Mikado still rules in Japan; but broadly speaking there is only one of the great historic thrones of the earth left, and that is the one of which the Prince of Wales is the inheritor.

It has survived for two reasons, because, stripped of all despotic, personal power, it has become an integral part of our self-governing system, and because the successive holders of the office have had the wisdom to recognise that, though they reign, they do not govern, and that their functions are strictly defined within the limits of an entirely democratic constitution. And the result is that while the war almost destroyed Kingship on the Continent and entirely destroyed the last remnants of despotic Kingship, it left the British throne, if any thing, more secure and certainly not less respected than it has ever been. Republicanism, which was a real issue fifty years ago, finds no place in the program of any party, except perhaps that of the Communists, and is rarely discussed as a practical question even by those who endorse it. The test of a governing machine is whether it functions wisely and efficiently, and while the Monarchy does that, and while the royal line conforms to certain well-understood codes of conduct, the principle of Monarchism in this country will not be disturbed.

The interest taken in the Prince of Wales, therefore, is not a matter of mere idle curiosity, but arises from very weighty considerations that deeply concern the well-being of the nation. If we are anxious about his future, it is mainly because we are anxious about our own future. He was born to what may be said to be the greatest position the world has to offer; and if our desire is that he should fill it worthily, it is not a wholly disinterested desire. We do not ask for a brilliant King, and we should not tolerate an ambitious King, but we need a King whose character we can respect, whose loyalty to his office is above suspicion, and whose capacity is adequate. We have such a King to-day, and it is because we hope the country will have such a King in the future that we scrutinise a little closely the promise of the Prince.

He has now passed through that phase in which it was sufficient to regard him as the Prince Charming of romance, a sort of visitor out of a fairy tale, whose engaging ways won all hearts, and from whom nothing was asked except that he should appear and be acclaimed. The light of common day visits princes as it visits the rest of us. It is falling upon the Prince of Wales. He is now a man of thirty-two. He has served his apprenticeship, and has reached an age when the character is formed and when responsibilities must be assumed. He has undergone an education as free and liberal as that of his grandfather was harsh and despotic. He has moved freely among all classes, and has been given the run of the estate. He is probably the most widely travelled man of his time, and has certainly seen more of the kingdoms of the earth than any previous heir to the throne.

Nature has equipped him abundantly, almost too abundantly, with many of the qualities of democratic Kingship. His presence and his address are both attractive. Slight of figure—he weighs only 9.2 stone—he keeps himself in perfect physical condition by rigorous exercises, and watches any tendency to increase in weight with the anxiety of a jockey. His spirits are high, his smile instant and responsive, and his manner boyish and impulsive and entirely free from any calculated restraints. He is hail-fellow-well-met to anyone who has crossed his path and is indifferent to the niceties of formal etiquette. His courage amounts to bravado, and his passion for horsemanship led him systematically to ride horses far too powerful for a man of his weight, with the result that he sustained a long series of accidents at steeple-chasing and in the racing field, which only ended when the matter had become a subject of such serious political concern that the Government was asked to intervene.

The years of the war were the formative period of his life. He went into it a boy, extraordinarily young even for his nineteen years; he emerged from it, still boyish in appearance, but with his habits formed and his manner marked by the ease and freedom of camp life. If his intellectual gifts are not remarkable, they are sufficient. He has the natural bonhomie which warms the ceremonial air, and he can deliver a speech as gallantly as he can ride a horse. If he is checked with a good-natured interruption, he is ready with a good-natured retort, as when at some fox-hunting dinner he spoke of taking the hedges, to which some voice rather cruelly observed, "Not all of them." "Well, then, through them," said the Prince. Not much, perhaps, but evidence of a good-natured readiness to take what some people would feel to be a "check" in a gay and lively spirit.

In all these respects the Prince's equipment is fitted for the high task that awaits him. It has been excellently tested in the prolonged round of world visits which has been his chief occupation since the war ended. Without straining language, it may be said that wherever he has been he has left behind him a pleasant impression and an atmosphere of good will. He has in a high degree the gift of friendliness, and no better commodity could be desired in the representative of one people to another.

But is the catalogue of virtues I have recited enough for the heir to the throne? The danger with princes is that they do not enjoy the chastening criticism to which the rest of us, and most of all, public men, are mercifully subject. It is assumed that princes are beyond any comment except that of flattery, eulogy, and adulation. This attitude of servility, curiously enough, has strengthened as the throne has become more democratic in spirit and more restricted in function, and as the Press has become more free. It is not a healthy state of things that any man born or raised to great office should be deprived of the salutary breath of public opinion. It is especially mischievous in the case of one who is compelled to live in an artificial world in which private criticism is equally dumb.

In breaking through this foolish conspiracy of silence the *Spectator* performed a conspicuous service not only to the public but in the highest interests of the Prince himself. Nothing can be more prejudicial to him than that he should not know frankly what the world is saying and thinking about a subject which is of deep and mutual concern. All that has been said about the Prince's charm of manner, friendliness of spirit, and good nature is gladly and universally recognised, but behind this ground for satisfaction is a widespread and growing doubt as to whether other qualities no less necessary to the great place he holds and the still greater place which he will in all human probability one day hold, are being cultivated with equal zeal.

There is a feeling that there is a lack of seriousness which, excusable and even natural to healthy youth, is disquieting in the mature man. This implies no disapproval of the Prince's love of sport, of fun, and of innocent amusement. Nor does it imply a demand that the heir to a throne should have intellectual tastes that nature has not endowed him with. Least of all does it imply that the qualities of a snob would be a desirable exchange for the Prince's high spirits and companionable temper. But it does mean that the public would be relieved to read a little less in the encomiums of the Press about the jazz drum and the banjo side of the Prince's life. "We are not amused"—to recall a famous phrase of his great-grandmother in a not dissimilar connection—when we see the newspapers splashed with photographs of the heir to the throne disporting himself as a girl in farcical situations. These things are amusing in the youth: they are not quite in accord with the man.

Above all, the public would welcome the evidence that these frivolities are mixed with more serious interests than is at present apparent, and that the general and admirable friendliness of the Prince is combined with a trifle more discrimination in the matter of his particular friendships. The easy path is not necessarily the wise path, and popularity of a sort may be purchased at too high a price. It is difficult to avoid the conclusion that the unfortunate oversight in the Argentine to which the *Spectator* referred, and which has been much commented on in the Argentine Press, would not have occurred if the entourage of the Prince had been as efficient as it should have been.

These things are said because it seems the clear duty to say them and to say them now. The Prince's future is not a personal affair only, but an affair of the nation and of the world. His apprenticeship to life is over. His career is henceforth in his own hands. He commands an affection and good will on the part of the nation that cannot be overstated and that a man of his genuine kindliness of heart must wish to repay. He can repay it by emulating the admirable example which is offered by his parents of how a modern democratic throne should be filled. It is the general wish, now that his travels are over, that he should take up some task which will reflect his interest in the weightier matters of the national life and that will prepare him for the heavy responsibilities which will one day fall upon him. And finally, it is proper to say that the nation would be gratified and relieved to find that the heir to the throne, like Dame Marjorie in the song, was "settled in life."

ix. Lord Balfour

Mr. "TIM" HEALY once complained that Mr. Balfour treated the Nationalists as if they were black beetles. It was the one insult they could not endure. They could bear his blows, but they could not bear his disdain. They enjoyed his anger, because anger flatters our pride. It is a tribute to our prowess, and gives us the spiritual satisfaction of equality. But disdain hurts our self-respect. Six months in Kilmainham was six months of heroic seclusion, of splendid isolation, but a slight, a tone of voice, an air of weary indifference, as of one who was tired of the impertinence of grasshoppers, rankled like a wound.

It was Disraeli who said that if you would govern men you must be superior to them or despise them. Lord Balfour has succeeded in being and doing both. He has accomplished it without effort or striving. Nature and circumstance combined to give him the signature of the Eminent Person, and he can no more help filling the part than a black beetle can help being a black beetle, or a man of six-feet-two can help being conspicuous in a crowd of five-feet-eights. If he is superior, he is not so by deliberation, and if he despises us, there is no element of egotism in the attitude.

In this he differs from another Eminent Person of his own time. Lord Curzon's superiority was aggressive and self-conscious. It was not merely implicit; it was explicit. It hit you in the face. He could not forget Lord Curzon, and he moved through life as if it were a Roman triumph arranged to celebrate his magnificent transit through time.

He was a man of extraordinary gifts, but he could not let them speak for themselves and he missed the crown by over-insistence on the fact that it was his by divine right.

Lord Balfour has no touch of this infirmity. He is abstract and impersonal. If you see him in the street, coming up to Pall Mall from Carlton House Terrace, or crossing Parliament Street to the House, in his soft hat and loose, careless, Cecilian clothes, your eye is arrested, and you have something of the agreeable emotion with which you see a picture from the brush of an Old Master. The note of distinction is there, but it is not stressed or conscious. He is not aware of you, as with hands clasped behind, head flung a little back, eyes fixed far away in the blue, he strides along; but neither is he aware of Lord Balfour. Pride which is self-admiration and vanity which suns itself in the admiration of others are not among his traits. He is probably navigating, as he moves through the phantom shapes of the moment, the limitless seas of speculation where Berkeley's idealism, Spencer's external reality, and the new realism of the modern school flicker like uncertain beacons over the vastness.

But whatever he is thinking about, he is pleasant to look upon. He suggests the fine and delicate flavours of life, the adventures of the mind, the quest of unsearchable things. His philosophy may leave you only more perplexed about the great mystery, but you like to think that these spiritual explorations are being made, and you have a reflected pride in the adventure. If we have an aristocracy, this is the sort of preoccupation it should have, and this the type of character it should produce. His interests give us a sense of contact with ultimate problems, just as his strain supplies us with a feeling of the historic continuity of things. He was dandled in the arms of the Iron Duke, his godfather, and these lives of two Prime Ministers carry the mind back more than 150 years, to the days when Chatham's eloquence still echoed in the halls of Westminster, and when the United States of America were still unformed. And his Cecil blood links him, through a chain of not ignoble tradition, with Elizabeth's England and the mighty Burghley.

It has been said of him—not in jest but with professional gravity—that "had he devoted himself to philosophy instead of politics he might have had a really distinguished career," and it is undoubtedly true that it is in the realm of philosophy that his life has been really lived. But I doubt whether, even if he had not stooped to the lower world of temporal activities, his sceptical and critical genius would have reached any more determinate conclusion than he has reached on the practical issues of life. In one of his Gifford lectures at Glasgow University, after a devastating examination of the philosophy of materialism, he paused with that ingenuousness which sometimes irradiates his subtlety and said: "You may ask if I have nothing positive to suggest. Frankly, I am much more certain that the particular doctrine I have been trying to examine is wrong than I am that any of its rivals is right."

There, in an illuminating aside, you have the key to Lord Balfour's career. He leans to the doctrine of "guidance" as against "blind chance" in the great argument of existence, but the verdict is as muffled and equivocal as the accents of his thoughts on "Insular Free Trade." He would deny that he is a sceptic. "The barren sceptic," he says, "is a gentleman who surveys the world and finds therein nothing worth doing, nothing worth admiring, nothing worth knowing. Scepticism of that type is, after all, but a pretentious expression of bored satiety." In that extreme sense, it is true, he is not a sceptic, for he has done much, enjoyed much, and admired much.

But if in a more limited sense he is not a sceptic, I do not know into what category we can place him. He follows with interest the life and thoughts of men, but he rejects their enthusiasms, and doubts the utility of their strivings and their passionate struggles for emancipation. He sees the perils of change: not the perils of stagnation. Whatever is is right, because to disturb it is to invite the unforeseen and the incalculable. He has pity, but no indignation against wrong, because indignation must issue in action and action cannot be limited in results. You must take the evil with the good, lest in correcting the one you jeopardize the other.

Hence that strange indifference which he has often shown to the agonies of stricken peoples; that readiness to ally himself with interests and persons from whom his own fine and sensitive nature must have shrunk; that tendency to do shabby things, such as leaving his friends—Wyndham, Hugh Cecil, Edward Clarke—to be mauled by the mad dogs of his party. On the eve of the overthrow of Mr. Asquith's Government in the war, he was the momentary target of the changing appetite of the gutter Press for a victim. So savage was the pursuit that he offered his resignation to his chief. It was refused, and I think he was much moved by such a demonstration of loyalty. But when, a week or two later, Mr. Asquith resigned, it was Mr. Balfour's transfer to the combination that had overthrown him that made the new Government possible.

These nonhuman traits do not mean an insatiable passion for office. They spring from a philosophy of making the best of whatever is, no matter who suffers or what tradition is sacrificed; but they do not encourage collaboration in a tiger-hunting adventure. They do not breed confidence. His smile is childlike, almost seraphic, and his charm of manner is irresistible, but it is a feline charm, a manner whose graciousness, as someone has said, conceals the absence of a heart; and the smile has no deep cordiality in it. It is illusive, a delicate shimmer upon the surface. You feel that he would give you the same smile in sending you to the scaffold as he would in passing you the salt. He does not easily inspire deep attachments, and his estimates of men are wayward, and often shallow, being governed by love of their intellectual adroitness rather than by respect for their character. A witty, insincere speech, even though attacking him, will make him not merely love the speech, but love the speaker; but plain honesty, like that of Campbell-Bannerman, merely bores him, and his misjudgment of and open contempt for that great man laid him open in the end to as shattering a rebuke as the House of Commons has ever heard. It was only three words—"Cease this fooling"—but they were final because everyone felt that they expressed the truth.

The distrust of change and experiment, beyond slight adaptations to circumstances, which makes Lord Balfour the greatest living representative of the Conservative idea, in the end destroyed him as the Conservative leader. For he was as hostile to reaction as to revolution, and his immortal duel with Chamberlain's coarse pushfulness, though it defeated Protection, dethroned him. Whether he believed in Free Trade or Protection no one to this day knows; but he did not believe in change. He wanted property to be strong and to resist Radical and Socialistic encroachments on it; but he knew that to tamper with real wages would bring its revenge, and through the mists of the argument with which he bewildered his followers that wise fear was plainly visible.

With this outlook, the whole force of his mind in affairs is destructive of challenging ideas. I doubt whether the House of Commons has ever heard so brilliant a debater, one who could riddle a case or tear a proposal to rags and tatters with such triumphant ease as he could. But on the platform, where the constructive motive must be assumed and heard, his bleak philosophy of negation left his audience cold.

He dislikes action, not because he is a dreamer, but because he is a doubter, and he perplexes the minds of others with doubts to paralyse their will to act. Campbell-Bannerman once described to me an occasion of national emergency in which he was called into conference by Lord Salisbury. "I soon saw," he said, "how that Government functioned. Salisbury explained that there was nothing to be done, and that if there was anything to be done, it had better not be done. Then Arthur Balfour's head ascended to the clouds, and he discussed every possible course of action, and left the matter in the clouds with his head. At last Joe rose, keen, clear, decisive, with everything cut and dried, and determined to have his way. But on this occasion I took care that Master Joe did not have his way." This habit of leaving the issue *en l'air* is illustrated by the comment attributed to Clemenceau, who, after Mr. Balfour had been expressing himself with admirable impartiality for twenty minutes on a point under discussion, looked at him perplexedly and said: *"C'est fini? Mais*—are you for, or are you against?" It might be the epitaph on this fascinating figure that has played so illustrious a part on the stage of the world for fifty years. "Was he for or was he against?"

And yet it would not do to leave it there. In moments of great crisis and on the larger stage of things, he has been rapid, ruthless, and able. He has the world mind, free, elastic and capacious. He would have made the greatest and I think the wisest Foreign Secretary of our time, for the larger the scale of things the more powerfully and luminously does his mind work. His appearance at the Geneva Conference of the League of Nations revealed his intellectual stature as few things have done, and his domination of the Washington Conference, with his courageous yet exquisitely discreet warning to France of the dangers of her submarine policy, made a deep and lasting impression on America of British statesmanship at its highest and best.

Whatever we may think of his philosophy, or of his theory of domestic government, he is in the great argument of the world on the side of the angels, not merely by the teaching of the war but by virtue of the large enlightenment of his understanding. He said truly at Geneva that he was a League of Nations man long before the League of Nations, and I recall as one of the memorable utterances of our time a speech following the first Venezuelan conflict with America, in 1896, in which he foreshadowed a world accommodation to which we may hope the world is at last moving. And among the influences which will make for that movement I count none more sincere nor more instructed than the Lord President of the Council.

x. Mussolini

"WE HAVE tamed Parliamentarism," said Mussolini to the fifth Facist Congress. In that phrase he summed up his policy and stated the issue that confronts not Italy only but Europe. Dictatorship or Democracy, the black (or the red) shirt or the ballot paper; the authority of force or the authority of reason; the will of a despot or the consent of a people—these are the alternatives that have emerged from the war. We thought the choice had been settled forever. We thought that Parliamentarism, which had been our greatest contribution to the solution of the problem of human government, was established beyond all risk of challenge. But the war that shook the Kings from their thrones made the Parliaments rock too. Four years of bloodshed had created the habit of violence, and the loss of faith in ourselves had awakened the demand for a hero. The world was in the mood for super-men, those strong, silent, grim fellows whose gospel is a word and a blow, "and t' blow fost," as they say in Lancashire.

And it cannot be denied that Benito Mussolini fills the part magnificently. He is incomparably the finest actor on the world's stage. He sees life as a terrific film drama, played before a gaping mob of rather childlike people who want someone to worship, someone to follow, someone to obey. And he sees himself as the hero of the drama, sublimely self-sufficient and all-powerful, despising the mob, dominating it by his own volcanic energy, thrilling it with the emotions of the stage. Nature equipped him for the rôle of the super-man with extraordinary completeness, and consummate art has supplied any deficiencies of nature. Poor Mr. Laszlo, who went to paint him, has put on record the tremendous nature of the experience. "When he speaks to you, you feel that an electric current is running through your veins." One can almost hear the chatter of the artist's teeth in his head as he prepares to commit this fearsome presence to the canvas.

It is a presence reminiscent, of course, of Napoleon; and Mussolini is not the man to forget that. Every trick of the actor is employed to emphasise the reminder. The dark, piercing eyes set under the straight, black eyebrows glare at you with a terrible, implacable scrutiny; the thick, sensual lips are thrust out with a sense of suppressed passion; the formidable chin is pushed forward to add to the effect of a merciless resolution. He comes on to the platform with the pomp of a Roman conqueror returning from a triumphant campaign against the Parthians or the Gauls. The trumpeters herald his approach. He enters with the famous chin thrust out, his face stern and unsmiling, his hand plunged, Napoleon fashion, in his shirt front, his air that of a god absorbed in god-like contemplation. No vulgar shouting or hand-clapping desecrates the terrific moment. The Fascisti rise and salute him in silence, with outstretched arm, according to the old Roman fashion. He receives the salutation as the Sphinx might receive a bouquet.

Or see him at a public reception—such as that of the International Chambers of Commerce. Around the walls of the brilliantly lit hall are the refreshment tables. In the centre of the hall the visitors from many nations are gathered awaiting the coming of the Dictator. Presently the door opens and Mussolini is seen advancing into the hall.

His head is half turned, his face is fixed in a mask-like in-difference to the scene, from his raised right hand a flower droops to his nostrils. Around him as he advances a group of Fascisti, each with arm outstretched towards the divinity, revolve in measured step like satellites round a sun. No word is uttered. Twice the great luminary with his attend-ant planets promenades round the room, the head still half turned, the face still fixed in a monumental glare. Then the luminary stops and the planets cease to revolve. The god is athirst. Flunkeys rush forward with champagne. The Dictator tosses off a glass—two glasses. His revolving suite obediently follow his example. Then, the function over, the planetary motion is resumed, the door is flung open and the Dictator disappears from the sight of his aston-ished guests.

I have dwelt upon these trifles because unless we realise that Mussolini is a very great master of stagecraft we shall miss the clue to the most astonishing performance that has been played on the European stage since Napoleon trod the boards. I do not suggest that Mussolini is as absurd as his own tomfoolery. In the privacy of his chamber, no doubt, he laughs at it as heartily as his European guests laughed at it. He would say that the Latins love these things and that when you set out to be a hero you must dress the part, look the part, and play the part. If he, the blacksmith's son of Forli in Romagna, is not a legendary being endowed with attributes that place him outside the common terms of humanity, he is nothing but an ordinary politician who has to argue with his foes and bargain for his place.

And as Mussolini hates arguing about anything or bar-gaining with anybody, he has made himself into a popular legend of the super-man who must be obeyed, whose very

BENITO MUSSOLINI

inkpot is a skull and crossbones, whose paper weight is a dagger, whose eyes send "an electric current running through your veins," whose pets are lion cubs that would eat anybody less heroic, and who goes into the lion cage at the Zoological Gardens in Rome and plays with the formidable "Italia" as if it were a kitten, while the other lions circulate round him as if willing to wound and yet afraid to strike so visibly anointed a head.

But it would be absurd to suppose that he has accomplished the greatest *coup de théâtre* of our time simply by the arts of the theatre. He was, of course, the creature of events. In a very real sense it was Lenin in Russia who made Mussolini dictator at Rome. Nowhere did the ideas which Lenin had brought to power in Russia germinate more menacingly than in Italy. In 1919, immediately after the war, a Leninist experiment seemed imminent there. Much of the responsibility for the emergence of Fascism must be borne by the Socialists, and the lesson of that startling episode needs to be remembered here. If the more moderate leaders of the Socialists, Turati, Treves, Modigliani, and the rest had broken with the disciples of Lenin, there would have been no Mussolini dictatorship and no Mussolini tyranny to-day. But the moderates hesitated, while the extremists seized the metallurgical plants, prepared to occupy the banks, and brought the whole structure of Italian life to the brink of catastrophe.

In this crisis all the moderating influences in the State were paralysed, and Parliamentary government and the Liberal idea were crushed between the clash of the revolutionary and the reactionary forces. The latter had their focus in Benito Mussolini at Milan, who had begun life as a passionate advocate of Socialism and internationalism, whose activities had got him into trouble which led him to take refuge in Switzerland and Austria, where he worked as a labourer, begged for his bread, got into prison for this, that, and the other, and finally had to leave as an undesirable alien. He returned to Italy and started "Class Warfare," becoming later the editor of the Italian *Forward*. He denounced patriotism. "The proletariat must no more shed its blood for the Moloch of patriotism," he said. He savagely attacked the Socialist deputies who had congratulated the King of Italy on his escape from an attempted assassination. "Why this hysterical sensitiveness to the fate of crowned heads?" he asked. "There are peoples who have sent their Kings on permanent holiday if they have not taken the further precaution of sending them to the guillotine. Such peoples are in the van of progress."

That was the Mussolini of a dozen years ago. It was the Mussolini down to the eve of the war, for one of his panegyrists, Signora Sarfatti, tells how, preaching revolution in the market place in June, 1914, "heedless of cavalry charges, he was to be seen in the most conspicuous place, erect, motionless, his arms folded, hurling forth his invectives with eyes ablaze." But when the war came, a new Mussolini appeared, who fulminated so violently against neutrality in the *Avanti* that his Socialist colleagues summoned him to defend himself. He marched into their midst, hands in pockets, with unconcealed contempt, was refused a hearing and then, lifting a glass amid the uproar, crashed it on the table, cutting his hand. Then, lifting the bleeding limb above him, he commanded silence, got it, and, with his blood dripping on the floor, launched his bolts at his comrades. "You hate me," he cried, "because the masses love me and will always love me. You hound me out of the party now because you are jealous, but a time will come when I, in turn, at the head of the masses, will drive you from the country."

With that characteristic touch of melodrama, he burned his Socialistic boats and started on his career as the patriot leader, the enemy of internationalism, the heroic Italian. He founded a newspaper, fought in the war as a corporal in the Bersaglieri, and when peace came and the domestic convulsion followed, became the idol of the Fascisti, and while still under forty the dictator of Italy and the most powerful personal ruler in Europe. There had been no such sudden leap to power since the young artillery officer of Ajaccio rode Europe like a whirlwind a century and a quarter ago.

It cannot be fairly denied that up to this point his action had been defensible and beneficial to the interests of the country. The machine of government had almost ceased to function, and the social fabric was crumbling visibly to ruin. Only some such drastic surgical operation as this could underpin the system, check the rush into the abyss, and restore the equilibrium of things. All the evidence goes to show that the immediate effect was good. It stopped the rot, restored confidence, enabled the activities of life to go on, gave the nation a breathing space. As an episode it was magnificent: as a policy it was as intolerable as any other tyranny.

If Mussolini had been a great man of the Cavour tradition, he would have used his *coup d'état* to tide the country over its time of peril and, having reached smooth water, to re-establish the authority of Parliament and the reign of constitutionalism. But the terrific egotism of the man forbade such a sacrifice of self. It takes a very great man in such circumstances to resist the temptation to play Napoleon, and Mussolini is not a very great man, but a very great actor. Italy had become his by right of conquest, and his principles being of the sort that adjusted themselves to his personal interests he proceeded to establish his dictatorship on the black-shirt basis.

The King, humiliated, ignored, reduced to a puppet of the palace, was allowed to remain as a harmless symbol of Mussolini's Roman triumph. Parliament, no longer freely elected, but the creation of Mussolini's own decrees, was left as a mere registrar of the dictator, that could be summoned at a word from the potentate of the Palazzo Chigi to ratify any monstrous invasion of the public liberties. The Press was put in chains, the Civil Service converted into an instrument of the despotism. The whole power in the State passed from Parliament to an armed minority who cudgel and purge with castor-oil anyone suspected of activities hostile to the dictator. Rossi, the former secretary of Mussolini and himself accused of complicity in the Matteoti murder, has published a statement in which he charges Mussolini with issuing orders for the cudgelling of public men like Amendola, who has since died in exile from the brutalities he suffered, Misuri and Forni; with decreeing the destruction of Catholic clubs and the "purging and cudgelling" of subscribers to the *Avanti*—the journal he edited in his Socialist days—and with even darker crimes.

If it is the Imperialism of Caesar and the histrionics of Napoleon that Mussolini most consciously has in mind, he does not forbid the comparison of himself with Lenin. It is a just comparison in one sense, for Mussolini and Lenin are the most remarkable portents thrown up by the war, and they are remarkable primarily for a similarity of aim. Both repudiated the idea of democracy, embodied in representative government working through a Parliamentary system, and aimed at government vested in a dictatorship and resting on the tyranny of an organised and armed minority. In a word, they were both, before everything else, rebels against the conception of government which is expressed by the idea of liberalism. "In Russia and in Italy," says Mussolini, "it has been proved that it is possible to govern outside, above, and against all liberal ideology." (Observe the adoption of Napoleon's favourite term of contempt for the liberals: "Necker is an ideologist," "Lafayette is an ideologist.") "We do not bother ourselves one whit about public opinion." Liberty is a dead creed and Mazzini and Cavour poor ghosts of the Risorgimento. "Fascism has already trodden," he writes, "and if necessary will calmly tread again, on the more or less decaying corpse of the Goddess of Liberty."

But though in this sense of hostility to liberalism Mussolini and Lenin were at one, no two men could be more dissimilar in character and temper. Lenin was a bleak abstraction of a man. His theory was his divinity and he worshipped it with a single-minded passion. His life in exile had been spent in formulating his theory into a system or a religion, and the apotheosis he sought was not of himself, but of his fanatical faith. He had no ambition for power except as the instrument of his doctrine, and his whole personality was subordinate to his cause. He was as ruthless and unscrupulous as Mussolini, but his ruthlessness and unscrupulousness were the servants of a tyrannical idea, never of personal ambition.

But Mussolini is a colossal egotist to whom personal ascendency is everything and principles and theories mere counters on the table.   He sees himself, like Napoleon, as the "Man of Destiny," and though his rhetoric has none of the keen, and often profound, wisdom of Napoleon's, it has the same quality of self-exaltation.   He does not appeal to men to die for a cause.   He appeals to them to die for a hero—for himself.   "If I advance, follow me," he cries; "if I retreat, kill me; if I die, avenge me."   His most extravagant eulogist, Signora Sarfatti, says that "ambition is the only trouble that gnaws at his vitals," and gives as the clue to his career the passion for power—"power over other men, power for its own sake, not as a means to an end, but as the conquerors of history have always loved it."   His talk often sounds like the ravings of the insane, imagined by Nietzsche on the threshold of the madhouse.   It is not so much an imitation of Napoleon as a grotesque travesty of Napoleon.   Every student of Napoleon will recall the terrific passage in which he poured scorn on the idea of love and friendship and declared that he had never had a friend nor had cared for anyone, except "perhaps a little for Joseph because he was his elder brother," and for Duroc because of the cold mercilessness of his spirit—"the fellow never shed a tear."   It is a terrifying picture, but there is in it a severity of form and a simple veracity that make it singularly impressive.   Compare it with this utterance of Mussolini (I quote from the Sarfatti life):

If the Eternal Father were to say to me "I am your friend," I would put up my fists to Him. . . . If my own father were to come back to the world I would not place my trust in him . . . I am obsessed by this wild desire—it consumes my whole being.   I want to make a mark on my era with my will, like a lion with its claw. A mark like this! (scratching the cover of a chairback from end to end).

and we see the cold realism of Napoleon turned into the terms of delirium. Or rather they would be the terms of delirium if they were not the terms of melodrama. For it is necessary to repeat that Mussolini is before everything else an actor who adapts his accents to his audience. It is that fact that should qualify our judgment of his volcanic artistry. We are a humdrum people, who are accustomed to confine our histrionics to the theatre and our lions to the Zoo and would doubt Mr. Baldwin's sanity if he began scratching furniture to show what a deadly claw he possessed. But the Italians have a different taste in public conduct, and Mussolini is probably correct in believing that they are not yet ripe for the tradition of self-government and that undramatic demeanour in statesmanship to which we have become habituated.

But though he is primarily an actor, it would be idle to deny that Mussolini has many of the characters of greatness. Whatever infamies have been associated with his rule, it is obvious that something more than charlatanry and the judicious administration of castor-oil have enabled him to establish for so long the most unequivocal dictatorship that has been introduced in Europe for a hundred years. He was, of course, the creature of events; but though it was the events that gave him his opportunity it was his own intrepid spirit that enabled him to harness those events to his imperious ambition. And it is the force of his personality that has kept him in the saddle and made him the most formidable problem that engages the minds and awakens the fears of European statesmen. For like all usurpers of power, he cannot afford to stand still. "My power would fall were I not to support it by new achievements," said Napoleon. "Conquest has made me what I am, and conquest must maintain me." And in the effort to maintain his power Mussolini, who models himself so ostentatiously on the Napoleonic formulæ, casts his eye abroad for the adventures which will preserve his authority at home. He must provide his people with sport and give them "circuses" if he is to keep their idolatry, and so his language in Europe assumes the godlike accents of the ex-Kaiser. He talks of the Mediterranean as if it were an Italian lake and he summons up visions of a Roman Empire that shall rival the dominion of the Caesars.

The urge of personal ambition, unrelated to any philosophy of affairs, drives him on and makes him the more dangerous. He knows that he is an incident, not an institution. And being an incident, self-exploitation is unfettered by considerations of past or future. He is not engaged in building up a system that has its roots in the past or any permanence in the time to come. He is engaged in a great adventure whose splendours will be exhausted in his own person. He knows the frail tenure of his power, and his star must be kept in the ascendent by all the artifices at his command. "I must dazzle and astonish. If I were to give the liberty to the press, my power could not last three days." How perfectly the Napoleonic *obiter dicta* express the whole Mussolini philosophy of action. He has followed in the wake of one convulsion as his prototype followed in the wake of another, and he will disappear as completely. He will remain in history a self-contained episode, contributing something, perhaps, to solve a temporary crisis in the affairs of a nation, but contributing nothing to unravelling the problem of human government. Napoleon had a fifteen years' run in the dictatorship of Europe before the world, both within France and without, cried with one voice, *"Assez de Bonaparte!"* He would be a daring prophet who would forecast so long a tenure for the brilliant actor who dwells with his lion cubs in the Palazzo Chigi.

XI. Mr. Arnold Bennett

THE first significant fact about Mr. Arnold Bennett is
that his front name is Enoch. The next most significant fact
is that he has shed the Enoch and chooses to be known only
by his second name of Arnold. I call these facts significant,
because unless we realise that there is an Enoch Bennett we
shall not understand Arnold Bennett. It does not follow,
because Mr. Enoch Bennett has dropped out of the title of
the firm, that he no longer exists. It does not even follow
that he is a sleeping partner in the concern of which his
junior, Mr. Arnold Bennett, is the brilliant and spectacular
head. Mr. Enoch is not in the least spectacular, but Mr.
Arnold would be the last to deny that he is active, and that
his part in the affairs of the firm is important.

Mr. Enoch is the patient, industrious artisan who brings
the raw material out of which his artist brother fashions his
masterpieces. He is the unassuming partner who supplies
the homely virtues without which the other's genius would
lose much of its steady luminance and power. And he is
the invincible provincial whom the great world has never
conquered, and who looks askance and critically at the Vanity Fair in which Mr. Arnold has plunged with such insatiable appetite and zest. If there had been no Enoch,
of whose quiet, solid, and modest parts only his intimates
have a clear view, there would have been no dazzling Arnold with his inexhaustible delight in all the glamour of life,
and his engaging swagger.

For it is the incurable homeliness and naïveté that lie at

the roots of his character that give Mr. Bennett his freshness of vision and his childlike astonishment at the wonderful thing that has happened to him. He set out as a boy from the provinces to conquer the great world and live spaciously in its Grand Babylon hotels, and having done it, he retains the fervour of the adventure, the youthful vividness of his impressions, the intense curiosity about life that make everything he does so alive.

He interests us because he is so amazingly interested himself. He recites the contents of a drapery shop with such enthusiasm that the picture becomes a vivid personal experience of our own. We may have seen a hundred drapery shops ourselves without emotion and without interest; but here is a drapery shop called up out of the past that, by some magic, is as fascinating as a fairy tale. He does not achieve this miracle as Dickens achieved it, by personifying inanimate things, by making them fantastically alive: he achieves it by the medium of his own unfailing interest in his theme, whatever it happens to be, and by the incomparable simplicity and directness of the relation.

It is the ordinary things of life that he makes so extraordinary. He does not say with Byron, "I want a hero"; still less does he want sensational action. The movement of his narrative—I speak of his great novels, not of his potboiling "Lilians" and "Pretty Ladies," or of his gay fantasies—is almost as uneventful as that of Jane Austen, and I recall only one heroic figure in all his work—that of Elsie, the poor "slavey" in "Riceyman Steps." It is the commonplaces of life, and the commonplace men and women that journey through life, that he translates in the alembic of his imagination. The people are often unpleasant people whom you would loathe to meet in life. "You feel as if they were your relatives and you disliked them," as "Punch" observed of the "Clayhanger" family. Mr. Bennett neither likes them nor dislikes them. He is only profoundly interested in them, as Fabre is interested in wasps and spiders, and he fills us with the contagion of his curiosity.

He is like a child at a fair, passing from booth to booth with devouring appetite to see and experience. He not only wants to know how things are done: he must know how to do them. It is not enough to admire pictures: he must paint them. He must provide his own music, sail his own boat, engross his own conveyance (for, the son of a solicitor, he began life in a lawyer's office and won the esteem of his employers by his ingenuity in drawing up bills of costs), write his own criticism. He will explain the art of the barber to you and tell you wherein the Italian barber surpasses the Dutch barber. He has as precise notions on the making of tea as he has on the writing of plays, and, with him, it is never too late to learn anything or everything. I met him not long ago and mentioned that I wanted a subject for an article. "I'll give you one," he said. "I am fifty-seven and a half years; I am thirteen stone; and I have just come from a dancing lesson."

In conversation he does not argue: he delivers judgments from the bench, generally in words of one syllable, and, aided by an inimitable stammer, he delivers them very well. His vanity would be staggering if the modesty of Enoch did not pull him by the sleeve, laugh at him, and leave you wondering whether this challenging, Cyrano bearing is not after all the pose of a shy and diffident man. He cultivates an almost truculent veracity, and will not be assumed to be what he is not or to know what he does not. For though he is vain, he is the least affected of men. Monsieur Jourdain said that of course he knew Latin, but asked his companion to translate as if he did not know. Mr. Bennett indulges in no make-believe of that sort. That is because, although Arnold does all the shop-window business, it is Enoch who has the last word. Arnold would have you know that he is a person who has nothing whatever to learn, but Enoch pricks the bubble of imposture with his incurable and obstinate candour. Take an illustration of how the partnership works. In an essay on Shelley in "More Things That Have Interested Me," Mr. Bennett says:

> Considered as a study in the essential frivolity of self-complacent theorists, M. Maurois' book [on Shelley] is masterly, ruthless, side splitting, absorbing. . . . I count his book as an antidote to Dowden (not that I have read Dowden, or ever shall, but one has one's notion of Dowden).

The omniscient Mr. Arnold pronounces a pontifical judgment on his subject and, by way of sustaining and enriching that judgment with an air of large reserves of knowledge, he compares the book with Dowden whom he dismisses with a cavalier wave of his hand. "But you haven't read Dowden," says Enoch stubbornly. "You have only heard his name. This sham jewellery won't do, brother. It must come out." Mr. Arnold pleads to be allowed to keep his flourish in. "Well, if you keep it in I shall tell the truth about it," says Enoch, and accordingly he inserts, "not that I have read Dowden, or ever shall," to which, when Enoch's back is turned the unblushing Arnold appends, "but one has one's notion of Dowden."

The world of his perceptions is the only world that engages Mr. Bennett's mind. In this respect he is wholly unlike his contemporaries, H. G. Wells and Bernard Shaw, whose main interests are not in people but in ideas. Mr.

Wells is always busy with his broom, sweeping the cobwebs out of the sky of a fatuous world. He is satisfied with nothing, and if he is not inventing a new God, he is growing apoplectic over the endowment of motherhood or the virtues of proportional representation as the latest short-cut to his matter-of-fact New Jerusalem. We grow breathless in the attempt to keep pace with the new editions of his Book of Revelation.

Mr. Bennett has none of this feverish unrest and discontent. He is neither a teacher nor a missionary nor a philosopher, but an artist recording the pageant of life as it passes before him. The function of literature, in his view, is to interpret life as it is, not as it ought to be, and its highest achievement is the enlargement of our vision of reality. If he has a "message" at all, it is the modest one expressed in his remark that, "What I am always wanting to make people see is that the world is a jolly fine place." He is frankly, almost arrogantly, of the earth earthy. He must see and touch, taste and smell, before his mind is engaged, and the atmosphere of dreams and speculation has no attraction for him. Why worry about the inscrutable, when there is this tumultuous, many-coloured world to be seen, enjoyed, and painted? The question of a future life is one of those questions which do not interest him, "for you cannot settle them," and his defiant realism will take no refuge in what baffles proof and reason. "I was an absolutely irreligious person, and still am," he has said, when referring to the experiences of his childhood and youth, passed in that severe Nonconformist setting of which he has given such vivid pictures.

And with this dogmatic realism goes a calculated rejection of sentimentalism and even sentiment. I have said that he is not a philosopher, but by that I do not mean that he has not a personal philosophy of life. I do not know anyone who strikes me as having a more precise code of conduct. It is a mixture of Epicurism and Stoicism. He has an inordinate delight in life, but he steels himself against its agonies. He takes its joy, but refuses its terrors. If there are tears in things, let others shed them. His work is coldly, remorselessly objective, and his own personal carriage is indifferent to the blows of fate. He not only bears the misfortunes of others with fortitude: he bears his own with the same stiff lip and untroubled front. He has never worn the white feather. He can stand failure that would crush others without the quiver of a muscle, and though he loves the Grand Babylon Hotel, I am sure that if he were taken thence to the stake in Trafalgar Square, he would go without asking pity from others or conceding it to himself. "Well, this is what life is," he would say with his own Constance Povey on her death bed.

There is a passage in "The Matador of the Five Towns" which expresses this aloofness from the incidental, this vision of life as an enormous, mysterious, but thrilling, show. The narrator has been waiting in the parlour of the Foaming Quart, while upstairs his friend, Dr. Stirling, has been officiating at a confinement. Twins are born, but the mother dies, and the doctor drives back in the early morning to Bursley with his friend, who describes the descent into the valley, the frost on the trees, the sound of the many bells (it is Sunday), the children going to Sunday school, and all the drab colour and movement of the new day:

I enjoyed all this. All this seemed to me to be fine, seemed to throw off the true, fine, romantic savour of life. I would have altered nothing in it. Mean, harsh, ugly, squalid, crude, barbaric—yes, but what an in-

toxicating sense in it of the organised vitality of a vast community unconscious of itself! I would have altered nothing even in the events of
the night. I thought of the rooms at the top of the staircase of the
Foaming Quart—mysterious rooms which I had not seen and never should
see, recondite rooms from which a soul had slipped away and into which
two others had come, scenes of anguish and frustrated effort! Historical
rooms, surely! And yet not a house of the hundreds of houses past
which we slid but possessed rooms ennobled and made august by happenings exactly as impressive in their tremendous inexplicableness.

It is time to return to Enoch. If it is Arnold who has
gone out like "The Card" to beard the world and possess the
Grand Babylon Hotel, it is plain Enoch who has done the
donkey work of the adventure. For Mr. Bennett's genius
is conspicuously that which consists of the capacity for taking infinite pains. That is the true secret of Mr. Bennett's
achievement. I have known more brilliant men—many men
who have struck me as having greater natural gifts. I have
never known anyone who seemed to me to have done so
much by patient labour to enhance his natural parts. His
cockiness is a pose: behind that delightful swagger is the
most sincere and deliberate of craftsmen, incessantly industrious, distressingly orderly, distributing his time with rigorous economy; his eye, with the drooping lid and considering
glance, taking in the play around him; his notebook ever
handy to receive his impressions while they are fresh; a
hedonist by taste but a martinet by will, hating sloppiness in
others, but still more in himself; working with undeviating
loyalty to the limited but rigorous code by which he lives.

There is nothing shoddy or sham about his singularly
English nature. He is as plain as his own beautiful pencraft,
and I know no one who would pass better that crucial test of
(I think) Whately: "It makes all the difference in life
whether we put truth in the first place or the second." Mr.

Bennett never puts truth as he sees it in the second place. His judgments are often wrong and his opinions often questionable, but no one ever doubted his word, and falsity shrivels in his presence. In spite of his external hardness, he is one of those rare men to whom you would go, not when you had a mere grievance against fate, for he hates weakness, but when the pillars of your firmament were falling, and to whom you would not go in vain. For though he disowns the faith of his childhood, he still carries the signature of its stern moralities, and draws, like his own Sophia Baines in her desperate plight, upon the "accumulated strength of generations of honest living."

And so, while I delight in Arnold, "The Card," it is Enoch whom I really love. And it is with pleasure that I restore his name to the shop front of the firm.

XII. Sir Austen Chamberlain

IT IS the pleasant custom of descriptive writers when they wish to say something complimentary about Sir Austen Chamberlain to trace the resemblance he bears to his famous father. The truth of course is that in all essential particulars two men more dissimilar could hardly be found in a day's march. Joseph wore an eyeglass and an orchid and Sir Austen wears an eyeglass and an orchid, and that is about the beginning and the end of the likeness. As Fluellen would say, there is an M in Monmouth and an M in Macedon. That is all.

When Joseph Chamberlain came into the House of Commons, with his long arms hanging loosely from his forward-sloping shoulders, his head cocked up with that foxy alertness that seemed to take in the whole landscape of things at a glance, the adventurous nose almost visibly scenting his prey, his cold, calculating, disdainful eye shooting its lightnings around the Chamber, he brought an air charged with electricity with him. You might hate him, or fear him, or admire him. But you could not ignore him. You watched his motions. You wondered what game he was up to now. He kept you expectant, mystified, waiting for the bolt that would be hurled you knew not where or how. When he spoke, he spoke in a soft, velvety voice that gave a curiously sinister effect to the cold steel of his words. No man said harsher things about his opponents, or stated more questionable facts, but he never withdrew and he never apologised. Right or wrong, "What I have said I have said." Let it stand. He disowned every policy and principle he had once held, but he never said that he had been in the wrong or admitted that he had changed his mind. The facts had changed, experiences had changed, principles had lost their validity; he had not changed. He would not tolerate a superior or suffer a rival near the throne. If he could not rule, he would not serve, and the whole record of his life is that of a powerful disintegrating, explosive force that broke parties and policies and men with a scornful indifference to consequences.

Now in all these respects there could not be a greater contrast than that presented by Sir Austen Chamberlain. He comes or goes and the calm of the House is equally unruffled. Even in externals he is, in spite of a certain facial resemblance, singularly unlike his father. He stands square shouldered and erect as a grenadier. His voice has no hint of that soft sibilant hiss which added sting to Joseph's most merciless thrusts. It is ponderous and a little muffled. The movements of his mind are ponderous too. One may almost hear the creaking of the machinery. So far from being a disturber of the peace or a reckless adventurer, he is the mirror of good form and the respecter of tradition. He is the last reminiscence of Victorian correctitude left in the House of Commons. He perspires respectability, and he would as soon think of surrendering his silk hat as he would of outraging the Union Jack. One feels that he regards the silk hat as a piilar of the constitution, a symbol of that dignity of things which is the essence of statesmanship. It is not inappropriate that his first recorded achievement in the House was associated with silk hats—lots of silk hats. He had just entered Parliament thirty-four years ago and was Junior Whip to the

Liberal Unionists. They were stormy days, the House was crowded, the Liberal Unionists insisted on sitting on the Liberal benches, and the difficulty of securing places was great. He invented a device for the emergency. It is recorded that he arrived early at the House in a four-wheeler full of silk hats, which he duly deposited on the Government side.

His deportment in all respects errs on the side of perfection. It makes the air just a trifle stifling, and an interruption from Will Thorne or David Kirkwood, even a rude interruption, a welcome relief. The normal man cannot be always on his best behaviour. He must occasionally unbend. But Sir Austen Chamberlain never unbends. When I see him sitting side by side with Mr. Amery on the Treasury bench, I am incontinently reminded of a famous picture of Landseer's, with Mr. Chamberlain in the rôle of "Dignity," and I am bound to confess that he fills it with distinction.

I have stressed this point of bearing somewhat because it helps to explain Sir Austen's part in the public life of his time. But I do not wish to overstress it. O'Connell said that an Englishman had all the qualities of a poker—except its occasional warmth. That would not be true of Sir Austen. He is stiff and formal; but he has warmth and he has kindness. If it is true of his father that he said more vindictive things than any man of his time, it is no less true to say that he himself has said as few unkind and unfair things as any man who has been in public life so long. I do not think he has the gift for saying them. I am sure he has not the taste for saying them. He is scrupulously fair. He is truthful, not only in form, but in intention. I have never known him consciously to mislead the

House. And what is even more rare I have never known him deliberately to cultivate a comfortable deception.

These are great and honourable attributes. They explain much. And there is another feature of his philosophy of conduct still more admirable. His father had the courage to refuse to withdraw, confess, apologise. Sir Austen has the higher courage to say, "Peccavi." He has said it not furtively and half-heartedly, but stoutly, firmly. And he has said it in circumstances in which he could have remained silent, which means that he felt that it ought to be said, even though it reflected not only on his own past, but on that of his father, his devotion to whom is notorious.

And his confessions have not been on side issues; but on the major issues of his career. Three events have dominated his political life—Home Rule, the Boér War, Tariff Reform. On all these issues he frankly followed his father's lead. Filial piety is an excellent thing, but filial servitude is a bad thing. I once knew a man who said: "In all the difficulties of life, I take my father for my guide. I consider what he would have done—*and then do the opposite.* In that way I keep fairly straight." Sir Austen's record would have been better if he had had the same independence. On the two great questions which filled the first half of his Parliamentary life he has publicly recanted by word and deed. He was one of the Cabinet that gave Home Rule to Ireland. He was, I believe the member of that Cabinet who most decisively revolted against the Black-and-Tan shame, and whose revolt turned the current of policy into the Home Rule channel. And on that noblest achievement of modern statesmanship, the grant of self-government to South Africa, he has pronounced his own judgment upon himself:

There came a change of Government, and by a great act of daring faith they conferred upon our recent enemies . . . full self-government. I voted against them. That is the vote I would undo if I could undo a vote once given.

That was finely said, and the two incidents make a fairly complete repudiation of his own past and of his father's statesmanship. There remains Tariff Reform, and here his record is more equivocal. In 1922, he seemed to have emancipated himself from his last rag of thraldom to his father's imperious but mistaken judgment. He said:

In a world where what you want is not to defend yourself against competition, but to find anyone who is in a position to purchase your goods and to place orders with you . . . to go out with the old program of Tariff Reform . . . seems to me perfect madness.

But a year later, when Mr. Baldwin made his memorable plunge into Protection, he retracted his retraction:

In the face of the existing situation, I agree with the Prime Minister that our first duty and the essential duty is to protect our home market.

There is one other incident of his career which reflects credit on his attitude to public life. When the exposure of the maladministration of the Mesopotamian campaign during the war was made, he resigned his post as Secretary for India, not because he was personally responsible for the maladministration, but because he was the official head of the department which was culpable. And finally, before we come to what all this signifies, it has to be put on record that his loyalty to his colleagues—no mean part of statesmanship if it is duly subservient to the still higher loyalty to the public interest—is above reproach. He has never played for his own hand. When Mr. Balfour was hooted out of the Conservative leadership by the Press, he might have regarded the reversion as his own, but Mr. Walter Long wanted it, and he yielded to a *tertium quid* solution in the person of Mr. Bonar Law without a murmur and with perfect good temper. And again, when the Coalition fell he stood by Mr. Lloyd George, and once more saw the leadership of his party pass from him, first to Mr. Bonar Law, and then to Mr. Baldwin. He is not a self-seeker. And if he were, his mental operations are too slow and his political strategy too negligible to enable him to succeed.

What valuation are we to put upon the personality that emerges from this survey? It would obviously be unjust to regard him as being wholly responsible for the mistakes of the first half of his career. He had the misfortune to be the son of a famous man who had an unrivalled power of imposing his will on others. Until that other vanished from the scene, Sir Austen was only the obedient echo of his voice. When the father preached "ransom," the son preached ransom too. While Joseph was raising the waters against the Lords in the country with, "They toil not neither do they spin," the son at the Cambridge Union was boldly declaiming: "Sweep them away. Why cumber they the ground?" And twenty years later, under the same sway, he was denouncing the Parliament Act's modest discipline of the cumberers as "this revolution, nurtured in lies," to which he would not "submit now or hereafter."

It was not until 1914 that he may be said to have been emancipated from leading strings, and to have lived a sep- arate political existence. Since then the most illuminating incident in his career has been that associated with the Locarno agreement. In that matter his reputation rose and fell with unexampled suddenness. It rose in virtue of the simple honesty of his character and it fell by the failure of his intelligence. In the negotiations at Locarno his influence was wise, his motives were trusted, and his success undeniable. He played the rôle of honest broker between France and Germany with a candour and good will that cleared the air of suspicion and paved the way to the admission of Germany to the League of Nations on a basis that, while laying a heavy liability on this country, provided France with a sense of security without giving Germany a sense of distrust. The reconciliation on which the reconstruction of Europe depended seemed established, and Sir Austen returned with the laurels of a diplomatic triumph more conspicuous than any similar occurrence in recent history. And four months later, at Geneva, when the undertakings of Locarno were to be formally implemented by the League, the world was presented with a humiliating exhibition of intrigue and political knavery that left all the hopes born at Locarno eclipsed. Most humiliating of all to Englishmen was the fact that Sir Austen himself was involved, not because he had been guilty of bad faith, but because he had failed to understand the significance of his own actions. He had been inveigled by astuter minds into moral acquiescence in proposals that Germany was bound to resent, and which she could only regard as a calculated abandonment of the spirit and letter of Locarno. His confidence in the integrity of his own motives blinded him to the plain meaning of things, and when the meaning was made clear, and the whole feeling of the country was mobilised against the course to which he had practically committed his Government, his solemn sense of the dignity inherent in one of his name still sustained him in a policy which could not be wrong since it was his own. Even when he came back from Geneva he seemed still quite honestly unaware that anything he had done had had anything to do with the catastrophe, and naïvely crowned himself with a wreath, proclaiming to an astonished House of Commons that he had raised the prestige of his country in Europe to a higher level than it had enjoyed—I think—since the days of Pitt. Against such panoplied self-complacency the lance of criticism breaks in vain.

It is just to him to say that he has earned respect of men for his character rather than their admiration for his powers. His industry is great, his sense of public duty is high, his word is respected, his honour is above reproach. He speaks competently, if a little cumbrously, as one who has learned the art against the grain, but has learned it. He reverences the House of Commons and the wisdom of the past, and he has neither an adventurous nose nor a gambling spirit.

But he is commonplace, uninspired, and uninspiring. He does not say foolish things, but he does say platitudes with aggravating solemnity, and he is one of those people who talk of "cheery optimism." He is not happy with new ideas and realises them slowly and a little painfully. And, lacking originality and force, and numbed by fifty years of subjection to a despotic mind, he gives the sense of a timorous spirit that takes refuge in the bureaucracy and disguises its dependence on the permanent official under the mask of a stiff and unyielding public bearing. He has the hauteur of conscious weakness, and works timidly within the limits of departmental sanction. His contribution to public life is that of a conscientious and painstaking rectitude, but he belongs to the past, and has no vision of the future. He was born under the shadow of a great name, and from that shadow he will not emerge.

XIII. Mr. Ramsay MacDonald

THE best way of approaching Mr. James Ramsay Mac-
Donald is by the ravine of Killiecrankie, where the Garry
goes sparkling and tumbling down to the lowlands. On
that tremendous July day, in 1689, when the wild clansmen
of the Highlands, the MacDonalds, the Macleans and the
Camerons, swept down the glen in their tartans and bare
feet, threw away their firelocks, drew their broadswords and
rushed to battle "with a fearful yell," there must have been
many a forbear of the ex-Prime Minister among them—
fierce, sombre men, big boned and strong jawed, with deep,
booming voices that filled the ravine with the sound of angry
thunder.

When I see Mr. MacDonald, I always see him in that
setting, rushing fast on the heels of Dundee, his eye lit
with gloomy fires and his claymore very busy among the
stricken foe. His actual descent to the battlefield was more
pacific, but not less resolute, and his victory will be at least
as historic as that day at Killiecrankie. For Dundee's triumph only carried the MacDonalds of 240 years ago as far
as the baggage waggons of the enemy, but Ramsay Mac-
Donald's great adventure swept the lonely Highland boy
from his remote fishing village to the highest seat of power
in the world, made him the equal of kings and potentates,
the dictator of policies, and one of the makers of world
history.

With what unction the late Samuel Smiles would dwell
upon that adventure. How he would take us to gaze rev-

erently at that dingy block of tenement dwellings called Duncan Buildings in a narrow turning off Gray's Inn Road, where forty years or so ago his hero, now a clerk in a London warehouse on 15s. a week, sat nightly over his books, studying, with the help of the Birkbeck Institute, for a science mastership. He would tell us how illness diverted him into other channels, politics and journalism, a private secretaryship to Mr. Thomas Lough, then Liberal member for one of the Islington seats; how he got caught in the Fabian movement, turned from it to the I.L.P., and became the chief creator and inspiration of the Labour Representation Committee, from which the giant growth of the Parliamentary Labour Party of to-day has sprung; how he married, travelled far and wide studying all the time, and got into Parliament; how during the war he sank into almost universal opprobrium, lost his seat in Parliament, was howled down here, there and everywhere; and how five years after the war he rose astonishingly, almost miraculously, to the seat that Walpole, Pitt, Peel, Gladstone, Disraeli, Salisbury had filled and a thousand illustrious men had aspired in vain to fill.

Thus Samuel Smiles, with suitable reminders to indigent youth that they, too, can "make their lives sublime." It is a story that needs to be remembered before we can do justice to this very obscure personality. That Highland ancestry, with the flashlight of Killiecrankie upon it, and that hard-featured youth, with its dour struggle for a place in the sun helps to explain much in Mr. MacDonald's career and bearing. Like Hal o' th' Wynd, he has "fought for his own hand" all through, neither asking nor giving quarter. Adopting Malvolio's categories—"some are born great, some achieve greatness, and some have greatness thrust upon them"—he belongs indisputably to the most worthy class. Whatever he has done he has achieved by his own determined spirit, hacking his way through with his claymore without seeking friends or placating enemies.

Few men have reached such eminence with so aloof a bearing and so lonely a spirit. He is at once shy and proud, with the shyness of the raw Highland youth who can never be quite at ease in the world he has conquered, and the sombre pride of the Highland clansman which nurses itself in secret, and feels a slight as if it were an insult to the Most High. Of the *savoir faire* of the Welsh Celt—the supple gaiety of Lloyd George and the breezy, winking gaiety of J. H. Thomas—he has no trace, and Mr. Babbitt would call him a poor "mixer." He is heavyfooted and squaretoed, and the sound of his tread is as the sound of armed legions.

His humour has more specific gravity than humour ought to have, and his speech is unduly garnished with "balderdash," "knocking things to smithereens" and similar weighty but somewhat effete missiles. Mr. G. N. Barnes once complained of the "vein of insufferable superiority which had become almost habitual with Mr. MacDonald," and it is undeniable that no Prime Minister was ever more inaccessible to his colleagues, with the possible exception of Salisbury, who did not always know his own Cabinet colleagues when he met them in the lobby. Even the admirer who has devoted two books to revealing him complains of his "secretiveness," of the increasing number of "I's" in his speeches, of the "familiar references to the Almighty, culminating in the famous sentence about 'having somewhat of the powers of the Creator,'" of a tendency to convey the impression that he was "one who, in his own mind, is not as others are," of his incapacity to communicate or delegate, his inaptitude for direct statement, and his mysterious reserve.

How much his solitariness is the effect of his shyness and lack of ease with others, and how much it is due to an inordinate self-sufficiency and pride is doubtful, but I think that, like the late President Wilson, he has a weakness for the companion who says "Yea" to his "Yea" and "Nay" to his "Nay," and that he does not easily forgive those who have done him the dishonour of disagreeing with him. There are moments when his actions and his accents have in them the echo of an immortal utterance—"What is Ter-ewth? My friends, I am Ter-ewth."

This august faith in himself leads him to plunge and hit out with a certain blind passion when he is thwarted. When he brought about the catastrophe to his Government in November 1924, he did it in a surge of imperious anger, like Samson pulling down the pillars of the temple. Every powerful voice in his own party was against him, imploring him to save his Government, imploring him to accept the olive branch that Mr. Asquith had held out to him. The anguish was open, undisguised. "There are 614 members of this House who do not want an election, and one man who does, and means to have it," said one of his Cabinet colleagues to a friend of mine in the Lobby on that fateful night. His best friends admit that in those closing days he had lost the anchor of himself and was like a giant striking blindly in the dark, reckless of the consequences to the wise policy he had done so much to inaugurate in Europe, consumed with only one burning thought—the consummation of the object that had been gathering impetus all through the summer.

The causes of the peculiar wrath that inspired him towards the Liberal Party are obscure and personal, like so much else in that secretive nature. They were not connected with a violent divergence from Liberal opinion, for he is a bourgeois Radical, as far removed from the thought of Clydeside as Lord Oxford or Mr. Baldwin, and much more of an orthodox Constitutionalist than Mr. Lloyd George. He took to Court dress as joyfully as Mr. John Burns had done before him, and when attacked by his more simple-minded followers, turned on them with scoffings at those who "showed their vanity by the clumsiness of their clothes." "A tattered hat, a red tie, and a tone of voice of religious repetition of Marxian phrases," he said, "may be as indicative of a man who has sold himself to appearances as the possession of a ceremonial dress to attend ceremonies which are an historical part of his duties." He is no fanatical Communist. "Certainly I am in favour of property," he said to his constituents only a fortnight ago; "a person cannot express his individuality unless he has enough property to make him independent."

Nor was it antagonism to all Liberals that gives the clue. The close and notorious intercourse between him and Mr. Lloyd George from 1910 to—shall I say?—the morning of that fatal third of August 1914 constitutes one of the unwritten chapters of contemporary history. Perhaps the secret of the hostility is to be found in the peculiar intensity of his dislike of Lord Oxford and Lord Grey. Balliol, too, is a trifle Olympian, and one Olympian does not love another.

But the final offence had to come. It is easy to forgive an injury, for there is a flattering sense of grandeur in the gesture. It is hard to forgive a benefaction, for a benefaction implies obligation. Mr. Asquith and the Liberals committed the grave indecorum of putting Mr. MacDonald in office. He pocketed the affront, but did not forgive it. His principal colleagues did not share the resentment. They were notoriously willing to work for an understanding. They were civil, even friendly, in private almost cordial. But Mr. MacDonald had another goal in view. He would use the weapon that had been put in his hand to destroy the giver. Never again would he suffer the ignominy of being put in office by a loathed rival. So through the summer the thundercloud of Killiecrankie hung over the Liberal benches, and when the hour struck the pillars were rent asunder and the temple collapsed. It was a resounding crash, and the air will be filled for a long time with its reverberations and its dust. Only the future will be able to estimate the repercussions of that prodigious throw of the Highland boy who became Premier.

Where the obscure working of his strong personal antipathies and of his political strategy are not engaged, his mind and outlook are enlightened and wise. He has boundless ambition and a mighty egotism; but ambition is not a crime in a man of great parts, and we do not think less of Chatham because he said, "I can save this country and I know that no one else can." His public spirit is high and his personal integrity above suspicion. He acted indiscreetly in the acceptance of the endowment of motor cars from a man to whom he subsequently gave a title, but it was the indiscretion of an honest man and it is a tribute to his character that no one seriously believed that the gift and the honour had any connection. If he is a "professional" politician, he is only a professional in the sense that every politician ought to be a professional. There is no more foolish gibe than that which assumes that politics is a polite relaxation for amateurs whose serious activities are elsewhere. His industry is a legend. No statesman of his time has laboured so hard to master his profession as he has done. He is the most travelled man who ever occupied No. 10, Downing Street, and he has travelled always with a purpose, notebook in hand. His administration at the Foreign Office was prudent, sagacious, farsighted, free from personal advertisement and impatience; and though the fall of Poincaré helped him much, he is entitled to claim a large share in bringing about the momentous change in European affairs which issued in the adoption of the Dawes report. His private life is plain, simple, refined, and the moving tribute he paid to the memory of his wife lifted for once the curtain of that "mysterious reserve."

He is the product of a great and sombre tradition, in which fierce personal animosities were interwoven with a gloomy religion. If the claymore is in one hand, the Shorter Catechism, or its modern substitute, is in the other; and if he does not smite you with the carnal weapon he is apt to damn you with the spiritual weapon, for he is a moralist who might have "wagged his pow in a pulpit," as well as something of a Scotch philosopher who would have been at home in a classroom. His gifts are conspicuous; a handsome presence, with that suggestion of hinterlands of thought to which you are not invited that keeps the mind wondering; a deep, powerful, and musical voice; a considerable rhetorical power, and that sort of genius which consists of the "capacity of taking infinite pains." But his mind is pedestrian. There are no wings to his thought. He lacks clarity and candour. His motives are obscure, his speech often equivocal. He is without the high and rare gift of dispassionateness, and personal feeling plays havoc with his judgment. But he has the quality of power and tenacity of purpose, is the most formidable figure the movement he so largely created has thrown up, and he has a future in spite of his recent past. If the final verdict goes against him, it will be because in great matters he permits the inferior passions to dominate the great argument.

XIV. Lord Birkenhead

IF THAT excellent person, Dr. Smiles, were among us to-day he would be in great perplexity about Lord Birkenhead. The golden moral that ran through Smiles's once famous book was that if you were honest, industrious, virtuous, modest, thrifty, sober, serious, the heavens would rain their blessings upon you and the earth would bring forth its increase. His heroes all marched "through terror to triumph" by the light of the Victorian stars, and success was measured out to them in exact proportion to their observance of the cardinal virtues. "Be good, dear child," he said in effect, "and you shall have the best of everything in this world and the next, but especially in this world." The seventeenth-century pilgrim was promised only a heavenly crown, but the nineteenth-century pilgrim was sure of an earthly crown as a payment on account. In this way, Smiles justified the ways of God to men and gave us a simple, satisfying solution of the riddle of this world.

It is not, however, a solution with which the story of Lord Birkenhead can be reconciled. There has been no more spectacular career in our time than his. He fulfilled all the external conditions of the Smiles "self-help" hero. He was born in poor circumstances, in an appropriate Nonconformist atmosphere; he got his foot on the ladder by his own unaided efforts; a scholarship at Wadham College; a brilliant University career; a swift success at the Bar; a dazzling maiden speech in Parliament; a seat in the Cabinet; the Lord Chancellorship and an earldom before he was

fifty. But while his achievements place him high in the
calender of Self-help hagiology, he would be the last to
claim that they have been won by the Puritan virtues. If
he has any of them, he frankly disowns them. He will not
even admit that he is industrious. Like the lordly Con-
greve, who wished Voltaire to know him not as an author
but as an English gentleman—"I should not have troubled
to see you if you had been only that," said Voltaire—he
wishes it to be understood that a man of his quality does
not owe his seat at the high table to so vulgar an attribute
as industry. He has as little respect for that virtue as he
has for modesty or thrift. "I profoundly regret many
hours which I have bestowed on mental labour," he says.
"I would not, if I could, recall one that I have spent on
games."

His aptitudes, indeed, fly flat in the face of the legend of
the industrious apprentice. He loves high living more than
high thinking, and moves in an atmosphere of magnificence
that scorns the thought of thrift. His society is the society
of the rich and the great, and his friends are the jolly fellows who mix their statesmanship with the gaieties of the
Empress ballroom. "I had arranged to spend the Christmas with my family at Blenheim" is the regal way in which
he opens his book on his visit to America, and that easy
familiarity with the splendours of life never fails him. The
House of Commons was his washpot, and over the House of
Lords he cast out his shoe. He shocked that august assembly by putting his foot on the Woolsack when he addressed
it, and on all occasions and in all circumstances he conveys
the impression that he is not subject to the niceties and decorums that apply to ordinary folk.

The magnitude of his pretensions has become a legend

enshrined in many a happy jest. When the eminent judge, attending the Liverpool Assizes, passed the vast premises of the Dock and Harbour Board, he gazed at them reflectively and observed, "Those, I suppose, are F. E.'s chambers," and when Lord Mersey was raised to the peerage, he is reported to have explained that he had chosen a title which would "leave the Atlantic for F. E. Smith." Only once did he indulge in a nodding acquaintance with the Smiles's axioms for success. It was when he became that loathed thing, a teetotaller, for the space of twelve months; but as he only did this in order to win a wager, the ignominy of the incident may be said to have been cancelled. In the gay world that he adorns, almost anything may be forgiven if it is the subject of a bet, and Lord Birkenhead has made ample atonement for the lapse by the gibes he has flung at "the solemn Puritans," at Prohibition in America, and at the advocates of temperance reform here.

In his tastes and his character alike, in fact, he belongs, not to the tradition of the nineteenth century, but to that of the eighteenth, and to find a parallel for him in the history of British politics we have to go back to that turbulent genius, Bolingbroke. Lord Birkenhead would prefer to be regarded as the successor of Disraeli. He has told us in those abundant contributions with which he used to brighten the Sunday Press—until, under compulsion of Parliament, Mr. Baldwin recently restored respect for the tradition that Cabinet Ministers must not be journalists too—how the glamour of Disraeli seized him. Up to that time he had only intended to be Lord Chancellor. His father had told him that "there was no reason in the world why he should not become Lord Chancellor," and he had been content with that modest ambition. But one day he read Froude's

"Life of Disraeli," and his ambition soared to higher realms. "I had never seriously considered the fascinating story of Disraeli's incredible emergence and genius before," he says. "At once I made up my mind that I must reproduce his career."

He has not done that. There was much more subtlety and depth in the sceptical philosophy of Disraeli than there is in the somewhat blatant and superficial pragmatism of Lord Birkenhead, and the romance that enveloped the one is entirely absent from the other. But in modelling himself on Disraeli, Lord Birkenhead followed the natural bent of his character and powers. He is the soldier of fortune who comes into the lists for the prizes of life, unburdened with any particular view of things; unhampered by tiresome principles or prejudices; ready to play the rôle of "Galloper" to Sir Edward Carson; equally ready to go over to the other side if circumstances change; swift with his sword but bearing no malice; fulminating against Mr. Baldwin and his "second-class brains" and enlisting under his banner while his fulminations are coming hot from the press.

There is no hypocrisy in all this. He is frankly an adventurer, and declares himself so, as, when speaking of Mr. J. H. Thomas, he says, "He is an adventurer precisely in the sense in which I am myself willing to be called an adventurer. And the great Disraeli did not disdain the name. Life is, in fact, an adventure, and he who (starting from nothing) fights hard, while conceiving ambitiously, must be an adventurer." His disagreements are never about policies, but only about place, and when he lashes the "Dolly Sisters" —Lord Selborne and Lord Salisbury—in the House of Lords, it is not because any grave issue is at stake, but because they are in office and he is out. His real personal antipathies

—in so far as so good-natured a man cultivates antipathies —are directed against men who stand for moral ideals which he neither shares nor understands. Ideals are to him irrelevant moonshine. The world is a stage where the play of material forces alone matters, and the wise man is he who manipulates those forces most skilfully and with the least regard for moral consequences. Even in America he did not trouble to conceal his scorn for the day-dreaming President Wilson and his maudlin sentimentalism about democracy and a world organised for peace.

What have these things to do with the realities of life? Life is an adventure, a jolly scrap, a rough-and-tumble affair, in which "he will take who has the power and he will keep who can." It has never been anything else, never can be anything else, and ought not to be anything else. He formally declared this gospel in his famous Rectorial address at the Glasgow University—an address that shocked even the martial spirit of the *Morning Post* by its coarse appeal to the savageries of human nature. "Self-interest," he said, "not only is, but must be and ought to be, the mainspring of human conduct." The League of Nations is a fantastic futility. The world continues and will ever continue "to offer glittering prizes to those who have stout hearts and sharp swords."

It would be unfair to dignify this swashbuckling swagger by calling it a creed, for Lord Birkenhead has no creed, not even the creed of force. If self-interest, in its most local application, dictates another creed he will adopt it without hesitation. Hence, his actions have the irresponsible waywardness of a wholly unreflecting mind. They are often better than his words, which he eats without visible discomfort. Take him on the subject of Ireland, and the Black-

and-Tan episode. When in the House of Lords the Arch-bishop of Canterbury protested against the doctrine of call-ing in Beelzebub to cast out Satan, the Lord Chancellor lightly dismissed the Sermon on the Mount as a cure for the mischiefs in Ireland and proceeded: "I do not believe there is one right reverend prelate who would be bold enough to offer the view that without the assertion of force—force in its most extreme and vigorous assertion—you can cure the mis-chief by which we are assailed in Ireland to-day . . . . We shall never deal with it except by these means."

Within four months the roar of the lion was succeeded by the cooing of a dove. He had renounced the whole doctrine of force as a cure for the mischiefs in Ireland, was deep in negotiations with the rebels, and was defending the conces-sion of Home Rule with the fervour of a new revelation. The policy of a life-time was shovelled overboard as so much lumber, and his dulcet accents were quivering to the gospel of peace and reconciliation. "Reconquer Ireland?" he said. "Well, suppose we did reconquer Ireland? How much nearer should we be to the achievement of a contented Ireland?" Yet, I have no doubt that Lord Birkenhead goes on thinking of Gladstone as a foolish old gentleman who did not know what the art of politics was, and bored every-body by pedantic nonsense which he called principles. And as his Rectorial address showed, the lesson of Ireland has taught him nothing.

His outstanding gift, of course, is his audacity, and, if this quality ever touches genius, he may be said to have genius. It was this gift, coupled with what used to be a singularly pleasing and youthful manner and appearance, which en-abled him to make the most effective début in Parliament that there has been in our time. He did not stumble at the threshold like his hero, Disraeli, but burst into the Chamber like a boisterous, confident schoolboy, equipped with the cool and calculating insolence of a *maître d'armes*. Read to-day, the speech leaves one wondering that it could have had such a sensational effect, for it is thin, undergraduate wit that has long since lost its effervescence; but it was the instinct with which it seized the occasion and the gay audacity with which it charged the victorious enemy and put heart into his cowed and humbled colleagues that made it famous.

Politically he has never made any substantial advance upon that astonishing irruption. In the legal sense, he has established a higher claim to respect. His judgments are the subject of general commendation in his profession, and his administration of the patronage of the Lord Chancellor showed that an active legal conscience may co-exist with an inactive political conscience. But in the field of statesmanship, he remains and will remain to the end a rather negligible free-lance, valuable for his gifts of speech and his still ready wit, but carrying little weight either with friend or foe. In politics, an enduring career can only be built up on a certain loyalty to ideas and a certain constancy of aim. The note of Lord Birkenhead's political life is the note of an easy flippancy. As the graces of youth vanish, his bankruptcy of the deeper wisdom of affairs and of the disinterested attachment to a considered philosophy of government becomes more apparent. Perhaps he had too early and too intoxicating a success. His brains, as Lady Oxford wittily remarked, went to his head. He can never fail of an audience or wholly lose his piquancy. But he is an extinct volcano, and his dream of "reproducing the career" of Disraeli will never be accomplished.

xv. Suzanne Lenglen

NO GALLERY of post-war portraits could pretend to completeness which did not include Suzanne Lenglen. She is not the most important woman in the world, for importance has little to do with notoriety, but she is easily the most celebrated woman in the world. She is known by her Christian name to more people than any woman in history has been. If it were not for the rivalry of Charlie Chaplin, she might indeed claim to be the most celebrated person in the world regardless of sex. And this she owes not merely to her supremacy in the beautiful game to which she has given a new lustre, though that supremacy alone would have been sufficient to command for her a high place among the famous women of the time. She owes it to the medium itself. Lawn tennis has conquered the world more universally than any other game. It is the most delightful and easily accessible of all recreations, and among the civilising influences of life I do not know what diversion would take precedence of it. Nothing has done more, I doubt whether anything has done so much, to add to the pleasure and health of so many people of all ages, and it is no small claim on our gratitude that Mlle. Lenglen has widened the appeal of the game and popularised its practice more than anyone past or present. To do anything which millions are engaged in doing incomparably better than it has ever been done before is alone a title to fame, and Suzanne possesses that title more unchallengeably perhaps than anybody in any sphere of human activity.

When she comes on to the scene, she dominates it as Bernhardt, of whom she is not a little reminiscent, dominated the stage. She carries with her the sense of potentialities that lift the argument to another plane. She is an embodied emotion. Her opponents walk the solid earth solidly; when they run, you are sensible of their specific gravity. But Suzanne skims the ground like a swallow, as though there were no such thing as gravitation. She is never at rest. Her whole body is in motion, her feet twinkle as lightly as if they carried a frame of air and fire, and were shod with wings. It is this extraordinary eloquence of her feet that first holds you and that strikes the note of contrast between her and her relatively slow-footed rivals. Most games that are fought with the hands are won by the feet. They set the pace, govern the action, control the strategy. The boxer who does not think from the feet upwards, as it were, is lost, and all the subtlety and precision of the strokes of a Hobbs or a Ranjitsinhji get their impulse from the swift, judicious play of feet. Suzanne's feet seem to talk and dance and sing. They are like feet that do not obey instructions from above, but are independent members with an intelligence of their own. This only means, of course, that the whole body is a unit of coherent, harmonious, instantaneous action, each member functioning with absolute truth of time and impulse, the hand completing the rhythm of the stroke that the flash of the feet has inaugurated.

It is this perfection of the relation of the parts that gives that sense of economy to the action. There is no waste of power, no idle effort, no superfluous display, no art for art's sake. Everything is severely businesslike. The mind is at full stretch, engaged with the move ahead, leaving the members to finish the immediate business in hand. They can be trusted to do their work while G.H.Q. above surveys the field, measures speed and distance, and prepares for the next stroke. For though I have said that it is the play of the feet that gives the first impulse to the visible action, it is by the quality of thought that Suzanne achieves her triumphs. When Nelson was asked to give the secret of his success, he said: "I always make it my business to be just a quarter of an hour ahead of the other fellow." Suzanne succeeds by the same token. She is mentally ahead of her opponent for the purposes of the action. Her sense of the game is a shade more acute that that opposed to her, and the well-disciplined feet have converted that foresight into action and have given her an advantage which the equally well-disciplined hand and eye convert into achievement.

The more accomplished her opponent the more readily is her supremacy admitted. The inferior player often pleads that the game was over before she got started, that she did not play up to her form, and did not get into her favourite stroke. There seemed to be something fortuitous, unintelligible, even unjust in the scheme of things. Give her another chance and her real powers would not thus be sterilised, thwarted, defeated by accident. But those who most nearly, however distantly, approach the level of Suzanne, are under no such illusion. They are equally sensible that they did not play their game, but they know that it was not the workings of accident that were to blame. "My pork pies don't turn out good by accident," says one of George Eliot's characters, and Suzanne does not reduce her opponents to futility by chance. She disarms her foe as the expert swordsman disarms his by superior craftsmanship. It is true that her opponent does not play her game, but she does not play it because Suzanne does not permit her to play it. She only does what Suzanne commands her to do. From her base line Suzanne controls the field, governs the action, dictates what the other shall do. Her initiative is never lost and she keeps her opponent breathlessly on the run while she herself is cool, collected, ready to leap to the volley and "Ping!" the point is won. Not that her victories are won mainly at the net. It has been estimated by one of her most competent antagonists that ninety-nine per cent. are won from the base line, from whence, with her power of taking the ball on the rise and controlling her stroke, she puts her opponent on the wrong foot, knows instinctively where the reply, if reply there be, must come and having established her command of the situation, scatters the enemy's front in an ever-increasing fever of motion while she, pirouetting lightly with the minimum of wasted effort, prepares the breach for the fatal stroke.

All this connotes a natural original genius for the game which no amount of practice could create; but it means also that it has been cultivated with extraordinary industry. Suzanne, like the poet, was no doubt "born;" but she was also "made." When Charles James Fox was asked how so bulky a man as he was could play so fine a game of tennis, he replied: "Well, you see, I am a very painstaking man." And Suzanne has been and is a very painstaking woman. She has been chained to the oar. She has toiled for tennis as the saint toils after virtue. That elasticity of frame, those astonishing gymnastics with which she electrifies the multitude, those Pavlowa attitudes in which the body is poised as light as a butterfly on the toes of one foot have only been achieved by infinite labour. The result is a lyric that seems born with a breath; but behind the lyric is the tireless drilling, exercise, discipline of a lifetime.

She was caught young. She was dedicated to the throne of the lawn-tennis world as definitely and deliberately as another is dedicated to the veil. It used to be said of the boys selected to win given scholarships by a famous headmaster of St. Paul's School that they either won the scholarships or perished in the attempt. Suzanne's training for the throne was rather like that.

Nature gave her the equipment, but her father gave her her discipline. His career has been to make her career, and her supremacy is his triumph. He has trained her from earliest childhood for the part he had allotted to her, and though she herself denies some of the legends of that rigorous apprenticeship, she admits that she owes everything to him. He invented her strokes, thought out her strategy, controlled every detail of her practice, chose her diet, selected her friends. It is said that if, when as a young girl forging her way to the front, she made a bad stroke, she turned intuitively to the taskmaster in the grandstand and exclaimed "Pardon!" to which there would come a minatory rattle of the stick to indicate that that sort of crime could not be tolerated.

"My father," she said on one occasion, "is very strict in the matter of training and makes not the slightest concession. Thus the various pleasures which sometimes mar the chances of other athletes do not exist for me." And it is recorded that when, on the occasion of her defeat of Miss McKane at Wimbledon, she asked him at the end of one of the games whether she could have a drink, he replied: "You are all right. You are playing a winning game." "I think I should like a drink," she said. "You go on playing," was the inflexible instruction, and she went on playing, drinkless, to the end. "Father is always right," she said afterwards.

"Sometimes I cry with vexation, but he always knows. Father is a wonderful man." The path to the throne is a thorny one, but Suzanne can at least say that she has seen

> The stubborn thistles bursting
> Into glossy purples that out-redden
> All voluptuous garden roses.

Probably the stern tutelage which has enabled her to possess those glossy purples of fame is not unconnected with that temperamental and histrionic side of Suzanne Lenglen which holds the public mind almost as much as her genius for the game. I have said that she is reminiscent of Bernhardt. That is so in the passionate absorption of herself in the drama of her life. She gives the impression of being trained down to a tenseness of emotion that leaves all her nerve ends bare. The sun shines and the court is filled with the singing of birds, and the Queen comes throwing happy glances and blowing gay kisses to the crowded tiers that salute her with "roses, roses all the way." There is a check —a rebuff. Some rude incident momentarily eclipses her glory. The sun darkens and the whole universe is hung with black. All is desolation and tears; vanity and vexation of spirit. Her life is a thrilling drama, centering in her emotions, and we are as interested in her personality as in her play. The details of her dress, her brilliant bandeaux, her jumpers, her ailments, her split shoe, her tears, her pearls, her curtsies, her reported engagements, her retirements from matches, her blistered hand, her heartbroken agonies, have all the quality of Bernhardt drama.

I do not know whether the stories of the scenes in which she has been involved are true, for when I have seen her the sun has been shining for her and her opponents have fitted their proper function of adorning her triumph like captives of a Roman conquerer. It may be true that when she disagreed with the decision of an English linesman she said "the English are pigs." She herself denied it, just as she denied that on another occasion she threw down her racquet and trampled on it in anger. "I was only trying to straighten it," she said. It is certainly true that on the occasion of her unhappy visit to America she burst into tears when Mrs. Mallory was leading, resigned from the game, and returned forthwith to Europe, where later she took an ample revenge on the American. She has become so much a part of the property of the descriptive reporter that I am tempted to make a substantial discount in her favour. She is expected to provide a sensation, just as Harry Lauder is expected to wear a large smile and a Tam o'Shanter.

But whatever the truth of these episodes, they represent the spirit of her highly wrought temperament as faithfully as the legends that gathered around the tempestuous Bernhardt represented that other woman of genius. It would be strange if with such a career of strain and achievement—the hard regimen of childhood and the world-din of acclaim in which she has lived since she was twenty—she never lost her head and her temper, never broke down under the excitement in which she lives from day to day and under the sense of the fate that dogs her. She is still only twenty-seven, and she has held her throne already for seven years —ever since that thrilling day in 1919 when at Wimbledon she snatched the world's championship from Mrs. Lambert Chambers. Such a reign is rare in any sport in which the demands of speed are so tyrannic that antiquity begins at thirty. The stimulus which her genius has given to the game has multiplied her potential challengers a thousand-

fold. All the world is mobilised against her sovereignty.
She is literally *contra mundum* in her defence of a throne
the possession of which is everything in life to her. From
California to Tokyo candidates are in training to dethrone
her. And they are inspired by the lessons she has taught
them.

For lawn tennis to-day, so far as women are concerned, is
what she has made it. She burst into the field with a new
technique. Until her appearance lawn tennis had been a
superior game of pat-ball for women. It was not conceived
that they could imitate the methods of men. Nature did not
permit it and decorum almost forbade it. They were content to play from the base line, receiving the ball and returning it, pit-pat, pit-pat, relying for success upon the mistakes of their opponents rather than upon the positive merits
of their own attack. They did not so much score as wait
till the other allowed them to score. Suzanne changed all
that. Trained in the methods of men, deliberately habituated by her father to measure her skill with men, she conquered an empire hitherto undreamed of by women. If she
executed her strategy from the base-line, it was not fear that
kept her there. When the occasion required, she boldly left
the base line, followed up her service, volleyed and smashed
with the greatest of the masters. In a season she banished
the old pit-pat game from higher realms of lawn tennis.
For seven years the world of women has been trying to
overtake that flying start of the young adventuress, and still
she leaves the pack—European, American, Asiatic—out-
paced, out-manœuvred, out-witted. She has improved by
her example the whole standard of women's play, and remains herself alone and unapproachable. But the "glossy
purples" will go. Helen Wills has already thrown the

shadow of coming eclipse across the luminary. The pressure of the pursuit will be intensified and the palm will be snatched from her hand. That is the cankerous thought that, as Caruso once said, eats at the heart of the wearer of the crown in any competitive art. Perhaps Suzanne will be wise and act on Nelson's maxim, "Go at your zenith." The world would regret to see so well-graced an actress leave the stage. We shall not look upon her like again.

xvi. M. Briand

M. BRIAND has made more eloquent speeches than anybody in Europe to-day; but it is not improbable that the moving little speech which he delivered in London after the signing of the Locarno Pact will be remembered when all the rest have been forgotten. It will be remembered because it rose to the height of the great argument and foreshadowed that in the act that had just been performed was the seed of the United States of Europe. That is the aspiration of all, except the barbarians who afflict most countries; but M. Briand will live in history as the first great European statesman who, on a momentous occasion, challenged the thought of the world by giving the ideal plain and unequivocal utterance. Locarno means what he said it means, or it means nothing. It is either the beginning of the consolidation of Europe into a single pacific organism, or it is an empty formality that the disillusioned future will deride.

If M. Briand can take the confident view of the occasion, if, as he said in his message to the *Daily News,* he can cherish the hope of living to see the vision of the United States of Europe realised, there is no reason why we should not share his optimism. For M. Briand is nothing if not a realist. *"Je suis un homme de réalisation,"* he once said of himself, and he spoke truly. He is a realist working through the medium of an enlightened opportunism. It is not uncommon to hear him compared with Mr. Lloyd George, and there is a large measure of truth in the comparison both in regard to his intellectual qualities and his methods. But there is a wide dissimilarity in the immediate personal impression they make.

M. Briand has none of the dapper alertness of Mr. Lloyd George. He rises slowly, almost sleepily, to greet you, and has the bearing of a weary man. His figure, with the round, sloping shoulders and the ungainly knees ("Ah, my knees!" is one of his favourite jests about himself), has a slouching carriage, and his appearance is not enhanced by a certain disregard of dress. His crumpled frock coat, his baggy trousers, and his ready-made tie are a familiar theme of the caricaturist, and he himself is not disinclined to make a joke of them. "My frock coat and my tie are almost as bad as my knees," he says—or used to say—with mock pathos. Nor would his face make him conspicuous in a crowd. The brow is narrow and the head, with its closely cut black hair now turning grey, is sufficiently ordinary. His complexion is sallow, and the wide, loose mouth, with the underlip that sags at the left corner as he talks, is more or less concealed by a thick moustache that hangs down almost to the chin on either side. The most noticeable features are the eyes. They are dark and commanding, with a suggestion of latent lightnings behind the steady considering gaze.

It is that gaze, so comprehensive and comprehending, which enables you to appreciate M. Clemenceau's *bon mot*. "Poincaré knows everything and understands nothing. Briand knows nothing and understands everything." You feel that, whether he knows everything or nothing, the steady gaze implies a capacious intelligence that envelops the subject with bold and flexible flight. He may be lazy and inert in movement, but in the hinterlands of the mind he is very busy indeed, and what he is busy about is not disclosed by the uncommunicative, unwavering glance. He has always had the faculty of solitariness, proper to a man whose only recreation is fishing, and though his reputation has been that of something of an idler, it only means that he has gone to books less than to life for his education.

As a youth and a young man he gave no promise of the powers which have made him the most constant force in French politics and have brought him to the Premiership more often than any statesman in history. The son of a small cultivator and liquor seller in Brittany, he won little distinction as a student, and, a trifle soiled by youthful frivolities, he drifted to the Paris boulevards, a not very heroic picture of a conqueror in shabby clothes. His interests were divided between law, journalism, and politics; but even now he seemed much more like a leisurely saunterer through life than an active and ambitious student. He talked more than he worked, and as he talked amazingly well he was a popular figure at the restaurants and cafés. He was in those days the *dernier cri* of extremism, the preacher of the general strike, of collectivism and direct action. He wrote leaders in the most advanced newspapers, and when Socialists came within reach of the law it was "our Aristide" who was always called in for their defence. And it was as a Socialist, the friend and colleague of the great Jaurès, that he was eventually sent to the Chamber of Deputies by the workmen of St. Etienne, who were proud of Aristide not only because he was a terrible fellow politically, but because he was so like one of themselves, so genial, unassuming, companionable. Also did he not go to see "my dear old mother" far away in the country, as his first duty on becoming a Cabinet Minister?

The disillusion that followed turned "our Aristide" into the "Judas" of the cause. It is not necessary to assume that "our Aristide" was an impostor. It has been said that the man who is not a Socialist before he is twenty-five has shown that he has no heart and that the man who is a Socialist after he is twenty-five has shown that he has no head. That is a crude gibe which is subject to qualification, but it represents a certain truth, and it does not follow that Aristide's youthful ideals were a sham because he treated them with such brusque disregard when he came into contact with the realities of government. We have seen in this country how warily the most convinced of Socialists have walked when the responsibility of administration has fallen to them. Even that pontiff and law-giver of collectivism, Mr. Sidney Webb, left office without one hint of the explosive philosophy that he preached. No one doubted his loyalty to his creed. Everyone recognised his wisdom and restraint in avoiding reckless experiments with the institutions of government. No man who is not a fool or a firebrand can act in office as he quite honestly believes he would act before he has had experience of office. Jaurès himself would not have survived the test. He might have avoided the methods of his old colleague, but he could hardly have acted with different purpose.

For the issue that converted "our Aristide" into "Judas" was whether government and the nation itself were to exist. The great railway strike of 1910 threatened France with paralysis. It brought into play the weapon of sabotage, and M. Briand saw in it and proclaimed it as a revolutionary plot to overthrow the State with the forces of violence. His reply was as ruthless and uncompromising as the challenge. He issued a mobilisation order which called all railway employees to the colours and rendered them subject to court martial. And when in the terrific storm that followed in the

Chamber he defended his action, he declared that if the Government had not found legal measures to enable them to remain masters of the railways, which were indispensable to the national defence and the national existence, they would have resorted to illegal measures to accomplish their ends.

Of course he went down before the storm in the end, as he has often gone down since, for that is the tradition of French politics, whether a man does well or ill. His eminence is his doom. If he rides boldly he is unhorsed as a despot, and if he rides feebly he is unhorsed because he does not ride boldly. M. Briand has spent twenty years in vaulting into the saddle and being thrust out on the other side. It would be truer, perhaps, to say that he is not thrust out, but anticipates the operation by alighting himself. For his sensitiveness to atmosphere is as remarkable as that *souplesse* with which he manipulates men and occasions alike. I am told that when, after the Cannes incident, he went to the Chamber to confront his enemies, he did not know whether he would resign or not.

He knew that his fall was nigh. All the reactionary frenzies had focussed themselves around the pedagogic obstinacy of M. Poincaré, and the madness of a Ruhr occupation had seized the nation. He was not brave enough to fight the wave of military insanity that was sweeping the country, and at the Washington Conference he had yielded to that wave in taking up an attitude on disarmament, and especially in regard to the reduction of submarines, which shocked America, and led to a memorable rebuke to France from Lord Balfour. But he had far too much intelligence to become the instrument of an incalculable disaster in the Ruhr. If he could have retained his control, that enormous tragedy would not have delayed Locarno for two years.

But for once his sense of the singular mentality of his countrymen failed him. He played a game of golf at Cannes with Mr. Lloyd George. He played a very bad game, for he held his club as if it were a fishing rod, but it was the most famous and the most disastrous game in history. If he had been guilty of a heinous moral delinquency that would have sent any English public man into permanent retirement, nothing would have happened to him. But a game of golf! A game, moreover, with the very man he was to outwit! Was there ever such levity? Was there ever such a betrayal? And he went to the Chamber fearing the worst. For once the enchantments of that golden and melodious voice that he uses as a master uses the violin, the swift rapier thrusts of his wit, the singular persuasiveness of his oratory, and the eloquent gestures of those delicate hands that are his principal claim to beauty, were in vain. His audience was cold with the horror of that scene on the links at Cannes, and interpreting the chill he did not wait for a vote, but vaulted out of the saddle as he closed his speech. And out of that tragi-comedy came Poincaré and the wretched episode of the Ruhr. Even the topless towers of Ilium fell for a more reputable cause.

But whether in office or out, M. Briand is always the most vivacious figure in the unstable world of French politics. The fact is not due merely to his unrivalled gifts of speech. It is due still more to his genius for affairs, his power of improvising upon the ever fluctuating theme of life, his tenacity, his dexterity, his mingling of slimness and persuasiveness. His mind is always accessible to ideas and infinitely fertile in expedient. He comes to the art of government not with theories, and still less with that vice of the French tradition, a reverence for the fetish of verbal logic.

"The logic of words is one thing; the logic of reality quite another," he says; and it is reality and not words that matters. The power of his utterance comes from its freshness and responsiveness to the temper and vision of the moment. He does not write a speech, and he uses few notes, but he prepares in the open air and saturates his mind with his theme, or gathers his friends about him and argues it out, setting up his own objections as if he were the opponent of his own proposal in order to find the weak places in his dialectical armour before he comes to battle. From this practice of talking the thing out dispassionately from all angles comes his gift of persuasion, his appeal to the intelligence rather than the emotions.

From all this it would seem that M. Briand is an unblushing pragmatist. He may respect the ideal, but he pursues the attainable. If the principle won't work, then so much the worse for the principle. I did not make human nature so intractable a material, he would say, and since I must work with it I must humour it even when it is wrong. If it won't have the best, then I must try the second best. It is not an heroic type, but M. Briand would not claim to be a hero. He claims to be a politician working with the materials that he can commend. He is not from Sinai, but from the boulevards. But if he has not the courage of Clemenceau, neither has he his barren cynicism. And if he has not the obstinacy of M. Poincaré, neither has he his pedantic provincialism. He sees the larger horizon of things and moves in spacious atmospheres. His spirit is humane and tolerant. *"La République est habitable pour tous,"* he says. He is a good Frenchman, but he is also a good European, and he is too sensible to nurse the infantile hatreds of war and too intelligent not to know that if Europe remains a bear garden the doom of France as well as of much else will not be averted. That is why his attitude in London represents him more truly than his attitude at Washington.

If his courage had been equal to his sanity and intelligence, he might have been the Moses of his people, leading them out of the wilderness of illusion in which they had wandered since the war. But he has not the tough fibre of those who "put it to the touch, to win or lose it all." He sees the best, but he will not sacrifice himself for it, and he trims his sails to the prevailing breeze of popular opinion with an easy confidence in his powers of persuasion and his own nimble genius for the manipulation of men and occasions. He is the prince of opportunists, and, like Mr. Lloyd George in England, has been the chief disintegrating force in French politics. It was he who conceived the notion of governing with shifting majorities, throwing a sop now to the left, now to the right, relying on this combination at one moment, on that combination at another and picking his way through the maze with the instinct of an infallible scent. The more crooked and devious the path the more he is at home in it, for it is through the perplexities and bewilderments of men that he seeks to govern them. He has as little respect for democracy as Mussolini has, but while Mussolini rides democracy with whip and spur he regards it as a petulant and irrational child that must be manœuvred unknowingly into reasonable courses. He is not of the stuff of dictators, and could not imitate the histrionics with which Mussolini dazzles his people. His genius is that of the diplomatist, and it is by the exercise of that genius that he has filled the highest office in French affairs more often than any one in the history of the Republic. He will never lead his people on an heroic adventure or risk his career for a faith. But though he is disillusioned, he is not cynical.   M. Poincaré and M. Clemenceau regard the League of Nations, not merely as a dream, but as a pernicious dream.   Briand may regard it as a dream, but he would at least like it to become true.   His significance is in the fact that he is the best European that has played a prominent part in French politics since the war began, and, making all allowance for the emotion of the occasion, his vision of a United States of Europe emerging from the reconciliations begun at Locarno is the most hopeful utterance that has issued from a responsible Frenchman in these days.

XVII. Henry Ford

IS HENRY FORD the greatest joke of his time or the greatest man of his time? Or is he, perchance, both? Let us equivocate and call him the most extraordinary man of his time, for he is that beyond all challenge. Whether we laugh at him or wonder at him, he is equally astonishing. He is like that child-man of Plato, who sees all the bewildering spectacle of life with the unsophisticated intensity of a first vision and with a mind that plays about the amazing revelation with the magnificent freedom of ignorance touched with genius. Hence the strange mingling of folly and wisdom with which he perplexes the mind. He belongs to no known category, conforms to no school of thought, acknowledges no sanctions except the empirical convictions which his own vision of the facts imposes on him. "History is all bunk," he said when he was once under examination in a libel action, and the comment represents his attitude to learning and the learned. He has carved himself with his own jack-knife and he has made such a surprising success of the job that he is tempted to think that the jack-knife is all that is necessary to solve the problems of life, and that making a new heaven and a new earth is as simple as building a new factory.

It is not that he is vain, or even self-important. The hurry of his spirit leaves him no time for moods of self-admiration or complacency. He does not exalt Henry Ford or think of him as an exceptional person. He wants to see all America and all the world filled with Henry Fords, their barns bursting with plenty, their roads black with their motor-cars, their lives saturated with the sunshine of universal benevolence. He combines, in a degree perhaps never before equalled, and certainly never excelled, the qualities of the man of action and the visionary. To think of him only as an astonishing manufacturer of machines is wholly to misunderstand him. He is a man who has had an apocalyptic vision, and though it was only a vision of a steam engine on the roadside it illuminated the whole of life for him.

He was a young farm boy of twelve when he saw that steam engine lumbering along a road in Michigan and learned from the companionable engine driver the mystery of its being and the range of its powers. No more momentous lesson was ever given on the roadside, for it inflamed a singularly receptive mind with a gospel which, however homely, is not unworthy. It was the gospel of taking the load off the back of labour and transferring it to steam and steel. In the beginning the gospel had a personal application. Young Ford did not like farm work, and he did like machines. All his toys had been tools, and now, with the vision of that steam engine, he was seized with the idea of emancipating the farm labourer by the aid of machinery.

It was to be many years before that idea materialised in the Ford tractor. His boyish experiments to apply power to machinery, stimulated anew by his first contact with the Otto gas engine, became diverted from the fields to the roads, from tractors to road cars, and in 1893 he emerged triumphantly from his apprenticeship when he drove the first gasoline buggy that he ever built through the streets of Detroit.

But the point is that his mechanical passion was then, as always, related to ideas. His realistic grasp of material facts had the momentum of a social purpose. He was less concerned to invent a piece of machinery than he was to invent a new and more efficient way of life. It is this mixture of the mechanical and the reforming motives that makes Mr. Ford so baffling, often so hilarious, and always so engaging a figure. He applies the philosophy he has learned in the tool shop to the whole complex issues of human society with a naïve directness that sometimes smacks of genius and sometimes of infantile credulity. His self-assurance is the self-assurance of a child, fortified by the completeness of his mastery over the concrete problems of his business.

That mastery has the signature of transcendent genius. What ingenuity of our time, for example, compares with that amazing device of the moving workshop? In its way it is as fine a claim to immortality as the discovery of Neptune. We can picture it coming to birth. I conceive Ford standing in his sheds, watching his workmen at their tasks, moving about here and there, now for this tool, now for that "part," the clock recording inexorably the wasted footsteps and the wasted labour. All this waste, he sees, goes into the price of the commodity, making it dearer while making the return to labour less profitable. How to save those wasted footsteps and that wasted time is the problem. Save ten steps a day only, he says, for each of 12,000 employees, and you will have saved fifty miles of wasted motion and misspent energy. You will have put that energy into production, lowering the price of the commodity while at the same time increasing the value of the worker. But how to do it? And we see him, as it were, with a leap of the mind conceive the idea of a moving workshop, so adjusted that the material comes to the hand of the worker as he needs it instead of the worker going to the material.

If that is not genius, I do not know how we are to define that quality. By such inspirations as this he has enabled 50,000 men to produce what, on the methods of twenty years ago, would have required the labour of 200,000 men, while performing the miracle of raising the wages of his men and reducing their hours of labour concurrently with cutting down the price of the commodity to a level that would have seemed incredible a dozen years ago.

And his ideas of the relation of his industry to the public have been no less bold, revolutionary and successful. Ford is said to be now the richest man in the world. His wealth is measured by hundreds of millions and threatens to become incalculable. But he has no pride in his riches and no use for them except to make still cheaper motor-cars, have still more highly paid labour, and bring more miracles of mechanics to birth. He belongs to the common people, and is not so much indifferent to as unconscious of social distinctions. His habits are the habits of the old Puritan strain from which he comes—no alcohol, no tobacco, no pleasant vices. You may see him, a lean, alert, noticeable figure, steal a little furtively into the hotel dining room and make his lunch off milk and crackers. And when he buys a railway, as he does sometimes, he has been known to stop the Sunday trains.

It is not an accident that a man so saturated with the democratic idea should have been the instrument of democratising the motor-car. He could not help democratising anything, for the idea of luxury is alien to his ascetic nature, and he does not cant when he talks of "service" as the only basis of business. And so, in the teeth of all advice and in the hour of darkest industrial depression, he increased his pro-

HENRY FORD

duction, cut his price, made cars more common and nearly as cheap as perambulators. If motor cars were good things, they were good things for everybody, and should be accessible to everybody. He did not care twopence about ridicule and still less about appearances. He would not cater for anybody but the million, or for anything but practical utility. He subordinated every consideration to efficiency and cheapness. "Any customer," he said, in his droll way, "can have a car painted any colour he likes, so long as it is black." And as for appearances—well, "A Ford will carry you anywhere—except into Society."

The effect of the revolution he accomplished is hard to overestimate. The motor-car which might have remained a luxury of the rich and a symbol of social inequalities, creating resentments and increasing class hostility, became instead, especially in America, a powerful influence for allaying social unrest by making power universally accessible and a new interest in life common to all.

It is when his ideas get outside the range of his business, that the visionary is apt to get out of hand. It was so in the case of the war, and the astonishing episode which engulfed him in the laughter of the world. He had a simple vision of the root of war and a simple remedy for stopping it. War was the instrument of the money power and against that power he would mobilise the peoples of the earth who were yearning for a deliverer. It is curious that the whole political thought of the richest man in the world centres in the evil of the money power. He sees the financier as a sort of bloated spider in the center of a foul web in which he enmeshes honest folk. He desecrates business by juggling with it as a money counter instead of ennobling it as an in-

strument of universal service, and he poisons the relations
of nations in order to plunder them.

From this conception comes his notorious anti-Semitism.
Financier and Jew are for him synonymous terms—it is certainly not true in America—and in his *Dearborn Independent* he has carried on a furious crusade against Jewry, which
he has now discontinued, because, with the American tradition of lynching, he has, I understand, come to fear that
pogroms against the Jews might follow, and before this
possibility his pacifist instincts recoil. But his hatred of the
money power remains. He has even designed a new currency—a currency based not on money but on units of
power—in the hope of disestablishing the financiers.

And there is no more dramatic episode in his career than
the story of his battle with Wall Street when, at one critical
period, early in 1921, it seemed that his vast structure had at
last fallen into its power. He was momentarily hard up for
money. He owed £12,000,000, with only £4,000,000 of
cash in hand. An emissary from Wall Street descended on
him with a plan for tiding him over his difficulties. Ford
listened until his visitor manifested an interest in the appointment of a new treasurer of the Ford Company. Then he
showed him the door and set out to defeat the spider that
was preparing to gobble him up. Before April he had converted his stock in hand into £5,000,000 cash, raised another
£6,000,000 by speeding up the delivery of goods, sold some
of his Liberty Bonds, collected from agents in foreign countries, amassed £6,000,000 more than he owed and kept Wall
Street at bay. Then he reduced the price of his cars, en-
larged his business, and at the time when almost every other
firm in the country was depressed and the motor business
seemed to be going into bankruptcy, he started triumphantly

on the most spectacular phase of his extraordinary career, which left him, not merely the greatest prince of industry in the world, but, as a mere by-product, the greatest banker in America.

It was the idea that the financiers were the real authors of the war that sent him out in his "Peace Ship," in December, 1915, to deliver Europe from the insane carnage that afflicted it. "The Boys out of the Trenches before Christmas" was the slogan he invented, but he had not the ghost of a notion how it was to be done beyond a dim vision of some miraculous waft of peace passing over the battlefields. Probably no such comedy was ever enacted outside the pages of "Don Quixote," and the world wrote off Henry Ford as the greatest jest of the century. He himself soon saw the folly of the adventure, realised that the people were to blame as much as the financiers, came home convinced that there were some diseases that could only be "cut out with a knife," and when America came into the war, flung himself into the production of tractors and ships with the feverish ardour of a crusader. On the day that America declared war this conversation took place between a member of the Government and Mr. Ford:

"Exactly how long will it take before your first delivery of cars, trucks, caissons and the like?"

"By three o'clock to-morrow afternoon my first delivery will be complete. The plant will receive the order in five minutes."

And by three o'clock the next afternoon Ford did make his first delivery, and at the close of the war he handed over his war profits, amounting to twenty-nine millions of dollars, to the United States Government.

There is the man. A simple, emotional visionary, a

dreamer of dreams, ignorant of politics, ignorant of history, ignorant of many things that any schoolboy knows, but with a public heart of boundless good will, with a practical philosophy of surprising wisdom, and with a genius for manipulating the ponderable things of life that has no parallel in our day. We are too near the portent to gauge its meaning and estimate its influence upon the life of mankind. But we cannot fail to see in Henry Ford one of those great natural forces that shape the destinies of the world, and there is such a soul of goodness in him that we can hardly doubt that his place will be high among the benefactors of men.

XVIII. Mr. John Wheatley

LORD DARLING remarked not long ago that his experience on the bench had led him to distrust appearances. He found that in the majority of cases he could not tell from the face and bearing of a prisoner whether he was innocent or guilty, a criminal or a respectable member of society. I think he overstated the deception of appearances. Generally speaking, our faces are not a bad index to our minds and our dispositions. The little boy knows instinctively the sort of person who will respond to the question, "Please, sir, can you tell me the right time?" in an amiable spirit, and in the ordinary exchanges of life we have all learned to rely on the certificate of the face. The tongue can lie, but the eye seldom lies. But we should all agree that people are not always to be taken at their face value.

For example take this bulky comfortable-looking person who passes us by in the lobby of the House of Commons on his way to the Chamber. He looks the soul of cheerfulness and contentment. His face is full and round, his eyes gleam brightly and blandly through his gold-rimmed spectacles, his hair is just enough dishevelled to show that he is not worried about appearances, his broad, massive frame bespeaks a healthy appetite and a good digestion, his shortish legs give just that agreeable note of stumpiness to the figure which is not uncommon in the companionable man, his clothes sit on him a trifle negligently and his pockets bulge with papers. No discerning small boy would hesitate to ask him for the right time, and no casual onlooker would

doubt that here was a man who had found the world a pleasant place, looked on it benignantly and even humorously,
had done very well out of it, and was quite satisfied with
things as they are. Why that, you would say, must be the
veritable Mr. Pickwick. Thus did he look, thus did he
beam upon the world, and with that comfortable, all-em-
bracing smile did he ensnare the heart of Mrs. Bardell.

And then, inquiring his name, you discover that this
placid, Pickwickian façade is the public aspect of the most
formidable revolutionary in the country. You feel that you
are deceived. If you must have revolutionaries you prefer
that they should look the part. "Yon Cassius hath a lean
and hungry look," and we expect all our Cassiuses to be
on the lean and hungry side too. They should haunt the
lobby like unquiet wraiths after the manner of Mr. Max-
ton, not like well-fed burgesses after the manner of Mr.
John Wheatley. But in spite of his physical disclaimers,
Mr. Wheatley is, as I have said, the most formidable revolutionary both in the House of Commons and in the country.

And this, not because his views are more extreme than,
let us say, Mr. Smillie's or Mr. Cook's. They are certainly
as extreme as they well can be. They are the sort of views
that make Mr. MacDonald or Mr. Thomas or Mr. Snowden
shudder, not merely by their extravagance, but by their folly.
They aim quite definitely at a social war, organised war, if
necessary bloody war, which, by the nature of this country,
will make the happenings in Russia and Italy trivial by comparison. I can imagine Mr. Sidney Webb turning pale at
the vision which Mr. Wheatley conjures up. Mr. Webb
and the Fabians are not revolutionaries. Their watchword
is "the inevitableness of gradualness," which I take it is
an evolutionary process as well as a verbal jewel. It is the

permeation of the mind of the country with the ideas of social reconstruction; and the attainment of those ideas not by a violent convulsion, but by organic changes and adjustments carried through by Parliamentary and constitutional means.

But Mr. Wheatley scoffs at "the inevitableness of gradualness." He wants revolution and he wants it now. He aims at a *coup d'état* as absolutely and unequivocally as Lenin aimed at it in Russia and Mussolini in Italy. Parliament to him is "a second- or third-rate debating society," that is only a nuisance which obstructs the path. It is not the instrument but the enemy of his policy. It may be five or ten years, he says, before labour is in power, and even then it will be helpless for his terrific ends, for in that wicked assembly there will still be people like Mr. Snowden and Mr. MacDonald and Mr. Webb, not to speak of Liberals and Tories and other shameless elements of the community, enemies of the "proletariat," unbelievers in the blessed gospel of Karl Marx. No, Parliament is a deceit; constitutionalism, a snare. If the proletariat is to be enthroned as in Russia, it must be done swiftly, immediately, violently. It must be done by direct action, by class war, by one crashing blow struck by ten million organised workers against the whole structure of a capitalistic society.

The method is simple and very candidly, even blatantly, declared. It contemplates the aggregation of all the trades unions into one gigantic body under a single control. The General Council of this vast organisation is to be endowed with practically absolute powers in administering the affairs of the unions. It will be a sort of Council of Ten which will initiate policy and exercise practically uncontrolled executive power. Its purpose will be not to bring peace into

the industrial world but a sword.   It will inaugurate the
class war, and its motives will be not the settlement of
disputes by negotiations, but the employment of disputes to
destroy the existing economic and political system of society.
Disagreements are not to be adjusted, but fomented, and
the dislocation of the machine is to be brought about by the
introduction of grit into its workings.   Prosperity in industry is not an end to be desired, but a peril to be averted.

This means bad trade and unemployment, which is unfortunate for the worker, but not so unfortunate as it
seems.   Unemployment, as Mr. Wheatley has said, is not a
bad thing in itself.   It breeds discontent, fans the fire of
revolution, and so brings the political end nearer.   Every
industry which is depressed and whose workers are conse-
quently unemployed is a new burden to the industries that
are prosperous.   Every subsidy paid to one trade, as in the
case of coal, has to be provided by taxation which falls on
other trades.   These trades in turn become depressed and
add to unemployment.   More subsidies.   And so the area
of depression widens—widens—widens, until the whole
trade of the country is involved, the prosperous industries
are all bled white, the sources of subsidies are dried up and
the whole capitalist system falls to the ground.

Then the new order will begin.   Then the paradisaical
conditions that prevail in Russia will prevail also in our
happy land, and the blessings of Communism will rain down
on us like manna.   There will be no need to worry about
Parliament, that "second- or third-rate debating society."   It
will be painlessly extinguished and government will pass to
the workers' Soviet—in other words, the General Council—
who will wield the sceptre.   The council will dig themselves into office as the organisers of the revolution have

[Photo Topical Press Agency

MR. JOHN WHEATLEY, M.P.

done in Russia, and the trades union delegates coming solemnly to their annual congress will have about as much power over affairs as the Russian Peasantry or the Russian artisans have over the little group of dictators who sit at Moscow. There will be no newspapers to complain. The only newspapers that will be allowed to be published will be, as in Russia, those which say what the dictators instruct them to say. We shall have full permission to drink in the wisdom that falls from Mr. Wheatley and Mr. Cook or whatever Robespierres may have got the dictatorship, but wicked people like Mr. Baldwin, Mr. Lloyd George and Mr. MacDonald (especially Mr. MacDonald, the leader of that feeble folk, the Menshiviks) will be suppressed—probably in exile.

This is not a caricature. It is a plain statement of the policy which is being preached daily in the country, and the seed of which trades unionism has been invited to plant officially and authoritatively. It shrank from that tremendous step at the Southport Conference of 1925, but when a little later the Government temporarily bought off the crisis in the coal trade by granting a subsidy to the industry, Mr. Wheatley's thanksgivings were ecstatic. He saw that Mr. Baldwin had himself opened the door to the sanctuary of capitalism. He had established the precedent of the State maintenance of industry. Coal was on the dole, and the path was miraculously cleared to the goal of communism through the universal bankruptcy of industry. He hailed Mr. A. J. Cook, the secretary of the miners, that "humble disciple of Lenin" as he described himself, as the architect of the social revolution that had now begun. "Capitalism," said Mr. Wheatley, "was winning in the commonest of canters" when the heroic Cook, derided by the intellectuals of the Labour

Party as a "blusterer," "a damned fool," stormed the position, swept through the country preaching revolution and a Red Friday to wipe out the memory of Mr. Thomas's Black Friday, brought the Government to its knees and prepared the position for the complete overthrow of our social order. Nine months (the period of the subsidy) remained in which to mobilise and equip, to organise trade unionism into one solid unit of striking power, to construct the battering ram that was to lay capitalism low and inaugurate in our midst the fairyland of Russia.

Much depended on the Army and Navy. And here as a member of the Privy Council and an extremely astute gentleman, Mr. Wheatley was discreet and veiled. "It looks like evens on a crash," he said. (How well he knows the blithe, hearty way of speaking to the proletariat.) "If working-class soldiers can be relied on to shoot down working-class strikers, capitalism will get a new lease of life by making Britain a land of coolies. Capitalism has no other policy. *If the working-class soldiers should fail,* then all is lost for capitalism." (My italics.) Meanwhile, mobilise! Mobilise!

"And should the workers arm?" inquired Mr. Ernest Bevin. It was a straight question, a serious question, put by one of the most responsible of trade unionist leaders. But our nimble Privy Councillor was not to be entrapped. His reply to this crucial question was a perfect example of his method. He scented danger. The cloud of vague suggestion descended upon him again. "We are told that it may lead to bloodshed. I sincerely hope it may not, but I frankly fear it may." The enemy will not hesitate to shoot, and "the workers, *true to their pacifist teachers*" (presumably people like Mr. Bevin), "may 'turn the other cheek,' and, having got a bullet in it, return to work, confident that they have done all that respectability demands. . . . This method (the machine gun) has often succeeded *with backward races.*" (My italics.) No man can foretell what sacrifices the workers in a crisis may make. The question is advance or retreat. "I want to go forward." This reply, with its skilful evasion of the direct question and its subtle hints and implications, deserves careful notice.

For it is not his extreme views that make Mr. Wheatley, as I have said, the most formidable revolutionary in the country. It is his quite unusual gifts. He is no shallow, soap-box orator of the Cook species. He has little in common with the sombre and in its way noble passion of Smillie. He has much more affinity to the Tammany boss. I do not by this mean to question his sincerity. I daresay he is sincere. I daresay he believes that if we can have a Russian revolution, the dethronement of Parliament, and the enthronement of a Workers' Soviet, the result will justify the bloodshed that he fears and invites. I should not doubt his sympathy with the class from which he sprang. A Catholic Irishman, born in Glasgow, he had an acute, personal apprenticeship to the social problem. "I was one of eleven persons," he told the House of Commons, "who lived, not merely for a month, but for years, in a single-roomed apartment in Lanarkshire." In these conditions, he tells us, he lived till he was twenty-four working from his twelfth to his twenty-second year in the coal mines, and emerging to a successful business as a publisher in Glasgow. With these memories as the background of his life, it would be unjust to doubt the sincerity of his feelings and convictions.

But a study of his utterances and his methods leaves even

less doubt that he is a remarkably gifted and audacious political engineer of the Tammany school. If he has rejected
constitutionalism for revolution—bloody revolution, he
"frankly fears"—it is not because he has failed in Parliament. On the contrary, I do not recall a first-class reputation being made in the House of Commons so swiftly as
he made his. He was fifty-one, I think, when he entered
Parliament, in 1922, and in two years he was on the Front
Treasury Bench, measuring swords on equal terms with
the best debaters of his time. He is not an orator, but a
debater, powerful in the statement of a case, agile in his intellectual manœuvres, quick in the cut-and-thrust of the
game. He knows how to keep a cool mind in a heated atmosphere, and he is never taken off his guard. He can
sustain an argument, however shady, and juggle impudently with a grotesque fallacy, as in his notorious assertion
that the advance in the Bank rate of 1 per cent. was equiva-
lent to 50 per cent. increase of the building costs of a house,
and added, in the interests of the financier, a burden of £3
a year to the small householder. It was, as so clear-headed
a man must have known, a silly travesty of the fact, a piece
of sheer debating legerdemain, but it served his purpose,
and so far from withdrawing he insisted that the real increase was 100 per cent.—"but I like to understate the
facts. It is merely an example of my well-known modera-
tion."

His good humour is invulnerable and his effrontery sublime, as when he went to Dundee and made a bitter attack
on Mr. E. D. Simon, to whom he owed his measure to
protect poor tenants from eviction, after he had failed with
his own. In a party inordinately deficient in humour, he
alone has claim to wit, as when he observed, "If the world

were run by moral gestures, and if all trade and class disputes could be referred to Heaven for settlement, Mr. Baldwin would be a great statesman, second only to Gipsy Smith."

In the large sense the history of the Labour Government is seen to have been a duel between Mr. MacDonald and Mr. Wheatley for the soul of the Labour Party. Mr. Wheatley won. He was subtle where Mr. MacDonald was only obscure. He had a policy while Mr. MacDonald only had an animus. He was unequivocal where Mr. MacDonald was always hedging. Mr. MacDonald's constitutionalism was subordinated to his hatred of the Liberals, and he surrendered to the man whose aims he loathed rather than be civil to the party which had put him in power, and whose fundamental policy he approved. Under Mr. MacDonald's protecting umbrella, Mr. Wheatley dug the grave of the Parliamentary Labour Party, and carved a new channel of Sovietism into which the current of Labour could flow. He derided Parliamentarism, preached revolution, the class war and the proletarian dictatorship, repudiated the official program of Labour and scoffed at its Free-Trade sympathies as frankly as the *Morning Post*. He converted the Communist element in the Labour Party from a negligible fraction into the fighting wing of the organisation, and behind the triumph of the egregious Mr. Cook is the strategy of this bold and adventurous Tammany boss who sees in the subsidy idea the weapon, not of economic stabilisation, but of the economic overthrow of the existing system of society.

"Now to the recruiting offices," he cries. Now for the final assault on society. Now for the dis-establishment of Parliament and the establishment of the proletarian dictatorship.   He fears there may be bloodshed.   He hopes not, but it is about "evens" that there will.   But no one can say that he has urged the workers to arm.   Nor that he has not.   He has simply hinted that they belong to the backward races if they don't.   Yes, a revolutionist, but a revolutionist who knows how to leave the risks to others.

xix. "Father Hindenburg"

IF LINCOLN had died at fifty he would have died unknown. He died at fifty-six, one of the world's immortals. If Benckendorff von Hindenburg had died at sixty-eight Europe would never have heard of his existence. He would have been remembered among the gossips of Hanover City as an enormously bulky old boy with a formidable bearing, a dauntless chin, a mighty moustache, and a head as bristly as a scrubbing brush; an army pensioner with a bee in his bonnet that had made him something of a jest among his military colleagues, spending the evening of his days at the Linden café, where he played chess and drank beer with the gravity of a hippopotamus. He lives to-day as the first man in Germany and the most singular legend of the war, an epic figure standing stubborn and vast above the wreck of a mighty empire. He has seen the twilight of the gods he loved fade into night and survives to greet the dawn of a new and incalculable day as the representative of ideas that his whole life repudiated and of hopes that he accepts valorously but without faith. The Kaiser he worshipped is a negligible exile in a foreign land and he stands in his place; a lonely, valiant old man keeping guard over the Fatherland.

When Germany elected him President of the Republic there were rejoicings in the Nationalist camp. Germany in electing him had declared against the Republic and for the revival of monarchism and the creed of war. With Hindenburg, the idol of the army and the symbol of an embattled Germany, as the figurehead of the State, the old régime would be restored and the pursuit of revenge would be the motive of German policy. The calculation was wrong in two particulars. It misapprehended the mind of the German people in electing Hindenburg. It elected him, not because it wanted the monarchy and the war lords' gospel back, but because in the vast tragedy through which it had passed he had played the part of a hero and an honest man. His hands were clean, his record unstained. He was not elected for his opinions, but for his character.

And the calculation was still more wrong in its estimate of Hindenburg. It was assumed that so stubborn a loyalist could not be loyal to the Republic, and that so hardened a militarist could not be the instrument of peace. This estimate, the estimate of Ludendorff and all the Die-hards, was wrong, not because Hindenburg is an obscure character, but because he is a simple character. He is so simple a character that clever men, like Ludendorff, do not understand him. Intellectually he is probably one of the most limited men among the great figures of Europe. He is not so much indifferent to modern thought as unaware of it, and in opinions he is as archaic as one of Frederick William's Pomeranian guards. His whole life was spent to the rhythm of the goose-step and the drill book was his only gospel. He came into the world at Posen when Napoleon was still a living memory, among a hard-bitten tribal family which had seen Prussia trampled under foot and had shared in the resurrection that culminated in the Battle of the Nations. He imbibed militarism with his mother's milk, saw life in the simple terms of a perpetual battlefield, and beyond that absorbing vision his thought and interest never strayed.

But if his intelligence was that of a drill sergeant, his morality was intense and fervid. It was embodied in his sense of duty. That is the idea that runs through his actions and his autobiography like a refrain. No one who was present at the great meeting at Hanover, when he was candidate for the Presidency, will forget the thrilling effect with which, suddenly breaking away from his elaborate written document, he struck his great fist on the table before him, and thundered, "I am a man who is accustomed to do his duty." And if he has any political philosophy to offer it is the philosophy of duty and discipline. "I fail to see that any citizen has rights on whom equal duties are not imposed," he says. In so far as he had any political ideas, they were the ideas of Bismarck. "A powerful self-contained State was the world in which I preferred my thoughts to move," he says. "Discipline and hard work within the Fatherland seemed to me better than cosmopolitan imaginings."

His Trinity was God, the Kaiser, and the Fatherland, and when the conception of his duty compelled him to choose between the Kaiser who had fled and the Fatherland which had renounced him, he took his stand by the Fatherland, even though it had assumed a form of government he loathed. He held himself aloof from all the futile intrigues and conspiracies of which Ludendorff was the centre, and, being elected President, instead of becoming the tool of the Monarchists and Nationalists, he acted within the strict limits of his duty. The Republic had become the Fatherland, and he obeyed it as the will òf the Fatherland. It might be painful, but discipline was discipline. And it is because they do not understand this simple code of duty that the Nationalists are aghast at what they regard as his betrayal of the cause, and Ludendorff openly denounces him as a traitor for signing the Treaty of Locarno, and not less for his message to the Chairman of the Ambassadors' dinner at the London Press Club, in which he expressed his "profound desire that a new spirit of mutual esteem and desire for understanding among the nations may arise from the deliberations at Locarno."

It is probable that no one could have piloted Germany through this difficult channel except this stalwart friend of the old order. For through all the vicissitudes that have filled the years since August, 1914, the legend of Hindenburg has remained undimmed. Victory could not add lustre to it, and defeat could not detract from it. It even survived the grotesque idolatry of the famous wooden statue and its iron nails. And though criticism has played havoc with his claims to military genius, the legend still remains for Germany the one glorious and indestructible memory of the war. It began, of course, with that astonishing episode in the first weeks of the war, when, called from his chess and his beer at the Hanover café, Hindenburg suddenly became the most resounding name in the world; but its true significance is to be sought later in far other circumstances.

Whether he or Ludendorff was the real author of the strategy which resulted in the most thrilling and dramatic victory of the war need not be considered here. But it cannot be denied that it was Hindenburg's obsession that made the victory possible. That obsession had caused him to be something of a joke in the army, and he was known alternatively as the "old madman" and the "man of the lakes." He had a bee in his bonnet, and after a not very illustrious career he had retired on his pension to Hanover, and "General Mud," as he was sometimes called, had apparently disappeared from the stage. His various nicknames were all derived from his obstinate fanaticism about the Masurian lakes, and their defensive importance to East Prussia. There were two military theories about the lakes. One, that of Hindenburg, was that the Russians must be received there and driven into the marshes. The other was that the Russians must not be allowed to reach the lakes. The dominant view was hostile to Hindenburg, and he came to be regarded as an honest, but stubborn crank.

When it was proposed to drain the region, he fought for his marshes as a tiger for its young, and finally overwhelmed the Reichstag, to which he was delegated to state the case, by the energy of his advocacy. The region had been his favourite theatre of study, and in the manœuvres there he unfailingly engineered his foe into the marshes. "We're going to have a bath to-day," was the saying of the soldiers when "Old Hindenburg" was against them. Even when he was pensioned, he still spent his holidays among the Lakes experimenting and nosing about. He borrowed from Königsberg a gun on its normal gun-carriage and had it dragged from morning to night out of one pool into another. He measured how deeply a cannon of a certain size sank in the mire, he ascertained how many horses were required to drag a cannon over the fairly solid ground that formed passages through the swamps, and discovered the swamps out of which not even twenty horses could drag a cannon.

Then came the war and the Russian advance into East Prussia. Berlin was in panic, and, at Ludendorff's suggestion it is said, the Kaiser sent for the old pensioner at Hanover. He had no weakness for him, for Hindenburg was not a courtier and had had the misfortune to incur his disfavour. The Kaiser and he had commanded rival armies at manœuvres, and Hindenburg of course had been beaten. At the close of the day the Kaiser asked the vanquished general what his views of the campaign were: "It was very pretty," said Hindenburg, "because it was all pretence, but if we had really been fighting I should have taken your men in the flank and all those I did not kill I should have driven into the Baltic." The Kaiser, it is said, never forgave the remark, and Hindenburg was under no illusion as to why, when the war came, he was left eating his heart out in Hanover, with his chess men, his beer, and his dogs. With the sudden panic call and the overwhelming sequel, the Hindenburg legend sprang to life. The country was swept by a frenzy of idolatry. Towns and villages were renamed after him; the Hindenburgstrasse became as common as the Friedrichstrasse; the Universities showered their dignities upon him; Hindenburg marches were composed by the score; gifts, decorations, telegrams descended on him in a torrent. He took everything cheerfully except the remedies for gall-stones. "Those gall-stones," he said, "are the plague of my life. Not a day passes without my getting sovereign remedies for them sent to me, whereas I never suffered from them in my life."

Never again, in the four years that followed, was there any faint repetition of that dazzling episode of Tannenberg; but the legend of Hindenburg survived all disappointments. Generals rose and fell, but Hindenburg was invulnerable to failure, and above criticism, and when he had reached the position of Commander-in-Chief no question of his supersession ever arose. The belief in his military genius became an empty creed; but the belief in his character and his star had passed beyond the realm of reason.

And it is significant that the legend became brighter as the darkness fell over the nation and all the other lights were extinguished. It was in the last phase of the war, when the bitterness of defeat and humiliation had come, and the army was in collapse and the nation dared not think of the morrow, that Hindenburg's name counted for most. It was then that "Old Hindenburg" became translated into "Father Hindenburg." All the gods were discredited and in flight from the Kaiser downwards, and only this stout old soldier, with his iron sense of duty and his indomitable spirit, shepherding home the routed and dispirited troops and trying bravely to sustain the heart of the nation, was left to remind men of what Germany had been and might be again.

In that dark hour he was the single stay and bulwark of the shattered nation. Reactionary though he was, even the "Reds" who hoped to see the extension of the Bolshevism of Russia to the Rhine shared in the common feeling for his loyalty to the Fatherland. "Our Hindenburg is expected to visit us this afternoon," ran one proclamation issued by a Soldiers' Council. "Comrades must see that the greatest of living Germans is enthusiastically welcomed." And it was as the greatest of living Germans that this old Monarchist was made head of the Republic. It was not a tribute to his opinions or his intellect. His opinions are mediæval and his intellect, outside war, negligible. "Since my boyhood I have never read a book which did not treat of soldiering in one aspect or another," he says. But he was trusted as a pillar of fidelity in a faithless and reeling world. He had shown himself worthy of the trust. May he live long to lead his broken country to those victories of peace which are no less renowned than those of war.

xx. John Maynard Keynes

IN THE dark sky of December, 1919, Mr. Keynes flared up like a rocket. He published a book. It was a book on what is supposed to be the dullest of all subjects. It had a title—"The Economic Consequences of the Peace"—that seemed like a sentence of death on its prospects. The argument of the book was so unpopular that its author, had he been recognised in Trafalgar Square, would probably have been ducked in the fountain pools as a pro-German. It was stated with such uncompromising audacity that it seemed to be an invitation to public ostracism, if not a public horse-whipping. The book was damned by the critics and sent a shudder through the "Coupon" Parliament. And it went like a prairie fire. It was read as "Uncle Tom's Cabin" was read in the days of our grandfathers. It crossed the Atlantic and set America aflame. It was translated into every Continental tongue, and was discussed from China to Peru. Incidentally, the young David who had gone out alone against the embattled Philistinism of the time was famous. His reputation was as wide as the world.

He would have become famous in any case, for no bushel, however impervious, could permanently hide the light of such an incandescent spirit as John Maynard Keynes. There are few men to whom Johnson's remark about Burke would apply. It has been my fortune to see much of most of the men who have played the great parts on the stage of the world in the last twenty-five years, and the not infrequent impression left is that of wonder how such ordinary men get such greatness thrust upon them. But there are rare cases in which the question does not arise. Mr. Keynes is one of them. If you met him sheltering from a shower of rain you would have no doubt that you had met a remarkable man. It would not be his appearance that would impress you. It is pleasant and interesting without being distinguished. Slight of build, sallow of complexion, with dark eyebrows, a thin face and a longish nose—at Eton, I am told, he was known as "Snout"—his most noticeable features are the vivacious eyes that gleam with intelligence and suggest a mind that is always cool but always at the gallop. His habit of speech is as swift as his glance. He talks like a man who has to race to keep up with his thoughts, and whose utterance stumbles a little in the vain struggle to go the pace.

It is the talk of a man who thinks in many quantities, whose glance ranges over wide horizons, and whose eye has alighted on a new fact before his tongue has disposed of the last. But it is not gabble, because behind the eager speech is a mind moving cool and composed through the labyrinth of explanation and proof, the goal clear in view, the course sharply defined as a razor edge. He seems to be bringing up unseen and unsuspected resources from all the circumference of things to support his argument and to envelop you in ruin.

> Thousands at his bidding speed,
> And post o'er land and ocean, without rest.

It is talk as unlike that of the dry-as-dust economist as the seed is unlike the flower. It is lit by many lights. Art, science, literature, knowledge of men and of affairs all come in at easy call to adorn and illustrate the theme. There is no pedantry, and his learning is carried so lightly that it does not impede the adventurous hurry of the spirit. His certainty would be intolerable if it were not so gaily garbed, so sprightly, and so boyish. He rides you down with such debonair grace that you have not the heart to feel angry. He has no respect for persons, and I am told that people go to the Senate at Cambridge for the delight of hearing him say things that make the dignitaries of that seat of learning shudder. But they respect him, if he does not respect them —not for his opinions, but for his gifts, and particularly that rare gift among scholarly men of being a brilliant man of affairs.

For he has not only written a book on the "Theory of Probability," which, according to some commentators, only three men are capable of understanding, but he has worked a miracle in the financial basis of his college which has placed it in a position it had never before enjoyed. His versatility, indeed, is bewildering. He flits from the lecture room at Cambridge to the public platform, and from the platform to the City, which he has taken, as it were, in his stride, becoming the chairman of one great company and the director of another; he looks in at the *Nation,* of which he is chairman; edits the *Economic Journal* in odd moments; writes innumerable articles; makes innumerable speeches; mangles Mr. Churchill in one brochure, and gives the French press an apoplectic seizure with another; carries on a campaign against the gold standard, which he regards as effete as the golden calf; discusses the currency of India with as much animation as the philosophy of contraceptives; and in the intervals is discovered as one of the arch-priests of the Bloomsbury school of intellectuals, discussing art and æsthetics with the Lytton Stracheys and Clive Bells who form the dilettante fringe of this amazing whirl of activities. He

writes of the virtues of the London Group with as much
enthusiasm as he writes on the vices of deflation, and his
walls at Bloomsbury are hung with the challenges of the
modern anarchs of art. He has no ear for music and no
taste for early rising, and he plays patience to cool the
ardours of his mind.

It was quite in the spirit of this whirlwind career that it
should be rounded off with a romance that set the tongues
and pens of two continents as busy as "The Economic Consequences of the Peace" had made them. And though the
marriage of the most brilliant young man in England to the
most famous dancer in the world was celebrated at a drab
register office, and though, to the application for his photo-
graph, Mr. Keynes wired, "There isn't one in existence,
thank God" that, too, is in the spirit of the man. For even
in his romance and his art, he is an uncompromising realist.
He is as absolute as mathematics, and his emotions never
escape the dominion of the intellect. The fact is remarkable, because his origins might suggest a certain congenital
sentiment. On both sides he is of Puritan stock, his grandfather on the maternal side being that Dr. John Brown who
long preached in Bunyan's church at Bedford, and who was
one of the great historians of Nonconformity, while his
father, also a professor at Cambridge, was the son of a
famous Nonconformist, whose memory is still fragrant in
Salisbury, not only for the roses that he grew but for the fine
spirit he brought into the religious and public life of the
place. There is little trace of this tradition in the severe
rationalism of Mr. Keynes. And he suffers, as the severe
rationalist usually suffers in the popular esteem, from a certain lack of atmosphere.

It is this fact, I think, that rules him out of a great part on the political stage. He has many of the gifts for such a part, a swift, apprehensive mind, a bold, imaginative, wide-ranging thought, an unusual power of unravelling difficult problems and making obscure things plain, and a genius for action. But his sympathies are cold. Facts are the stern realities and fancies are for the foolish. Things are what they are, and their consequences will be what they will be—why therefore pretend? His cool, expert mind, moving unfalteringly among the wilderness of perceived facts, is contemptuous of the emotionalism that seizes the mass mind and plays havoc with the judgment of things. He makes no concessions to the mob and will deal in no anodynes for the weaker brethren. He has no superstitions and no faith.

> He is clear of the pines and the oak scrub:
> He is out on the rocks and the snow.

If you will take your stand with him on these bleak highlands—good. If not, he has no medicine for the mind diseased. His fervours are not moral fervours: they are intellectual fervours. It is the folly of things, not the wickedness of things, that revolts him. If the Peace Treaty had been practically right, I do not think he would have complained because it was spiritually wrong. It was the offence against the reason and reality of things that was, to him, the sin against the Holy Ghost. He saw the statesmen of Europe dealing in lies. He saw them whetting the appetites of their wretched peoples with Barmecide feasts of unthinkable millions. He saw them laying a rotten foundation of falsehood over the abyss of the war through which Europe must inevitably crash with utter ruin.

And with the courage, not of a moral crusader, but of a mathematical divine whose faith rested on the impregnable

rock that two and two make four and that it is a sin to pretend they make five, he threw up his post at the Peace Conference, shook the dust of this infatuated society off his feet,
and set out to tell the world the truth about the Treaty.
What he wrote looks obvious enough to-day, but it needed
courage to talk sense in the midst of the screaming frenzy
of those days, and Mr. Keynes took the risks of a very gallant adventure. Even in taking them, the young David
showed that worldly wisdom that so strangely consorts with
his scholarly and artistic gifts. He published at his own risk
and reaped all the profits of one of the greatest publishing
successes on record.

That success was due not merely to the matter but to the
manner of the book, for in his abundant armoury is one of
the keenest blades in contemporary literature. He has a pen
that cuts like a whip-lash and a wit that stings like a scorpion.
I think that his treatment of President Wilson was cruelly
unjust; but the brilliancy of his picture of the "blind and
deaf Don Quixote" being rounded up, manacled and
strapped down by the supple minds about him is a spirited
bit of literature as well as of history. Take this thumbnail:

What chance could such a man have against Mr. Lloyd George's un-
erring, almost medium-like, sensibility of everyone immediately around
him? To see the British Prime Minister with six or seven senses not
available to ordinary men, judging motives, character and subconscious
impulse, perceiving what each man was thinking and even what each
man was going to say next, was to realise that the poor President would
be playing blind man's buff in that party!

Is it quite so sure that fifty years hence the poor, bamboozled
Don Quixote will look such a fool to the eye of the historian
as he looked to that raging young onlooker who saw him
being bound and trussed at Paris? Don Quixote wanted one

thing, the League of Nations, and though the price he paid for it was high—among other things it was his life—it is reasonable to hope that time will say that he did the greatest service to this distracted Europe of any man in history. If he had not been deserted by his own country, it is not unreasonable to think that the fruits of that service would have been more visible to-day than they are.

But it is not by the wisdom of his judgment on this or that issue that judgment on Mr. Keynes himself will be passed. Homer nods sometimes, and Mr. Keynes may occasionally be suspected of napping. It would hardly be decent for any man to be quite so omniscient as he seems. If he were, he would be in danger of being hanged at the lamp-post or ostracised like a modern Aristides. His merit is in the rare combination of a wealth of diverse and solid attainments with an unrivalled power of clarifying the public thought on obscure and erudite issues. If he had a little patience and a little of that detestable but necessary thing called tact, he might be the Moses to lead Liberalism out of the wilderness.

For to his question, submitted to the Liberal Summer School, "Am I a Liberal?" the answer is in the affirmative. We may dismiss his quaint notion that Birth Control should be a cardinal Liberal doctrine, not because Birth Control is illiberal, but because it does not belong to the party issue. But his outlook is essentially Liberal. For Labour's theories he has intellectual contempt, and for Labour's sentimentalism and animus, the scorn of the dogmatic rationalist. "Throughout the Labour Party," he says, "there is secret sympathy with the policy of catastrophe. . . . It is necessary for the successful Labour leader to be, or appear to be at least, a little savage. It is not enough that he should love his fellow men; he must hate them too."

But Parliament is not the sphere where Mr. Keynes would be happy. He is too aloof and unsympathetic with the common mind, too lonely and independent an adventurer in the fields of thought and speculation ever to sit in harness on the Treasury bench. His function is perhaps greater. It is to be a lamp hung aloft the parties to scatter the darkness and the lies that dwell in the darkness.

XXI. Chicherin

WHEN on the night of January 3, 1918, the gates of Brixton Gaol were opened and Georghi Vasilievich Chicherin passed out to recovered freedom, it did not seem to the un-aided vision that anything momentous had happened. It is true that the case of M. Chicherin had been much discussed in Parliament, and that his continued internment had been the subject of severe criticism by the late Lord Sheffield as well as by the Labour representatives and by such disinterested observers as Dr. Hagberg Wright. It is true also that Trotsky had intimated to the British Government that he would not permit Sir George Buchanan, the British Ambassador, to leave Russia until Chicherin was released from his London prison. It was even stated, though this was not the case, that the new Bolshevik masters of Russia had nominated Chicherin as Ambassador at St. James's.

But all this implied no special significance in the slight figure that emerged in the darkness of the winter's night from Brixton Gaol. In the feverish circumstances of those days, when the terrific shape of Lenin had risen from the welter of the Russian revolution, and when the menace of Bolshevism competed with the menace of the war itself to terrorise and inflame the public mind with unknown perils, any incident served to focus the passions of the time. The battle raged round Chicherin, not because he was important, but because he typified the Terror. There was nothing in his story which distinguished him from scores of refugees who had for a generation found freedom in this country from the tyranny of the Tsardom.

Like Prince Kropotkin, he came of a "noble" family, which had filled great positions in the intellectual and public life of Russia. He was a nephew of the great Russian jurist, Boris Chicherin, who was Mayor of Moscow at the time of the coronation of Alexander III., and who was summarily dismissed from that office because he had dared to suggest to the new Emperor that the first duty of a ruler was to inaugurate reforms. He, himself, had begun his career in the Russian Foreign Office, just as Kropotkin had begun his in the Russian army; but becoming imbued with Tolstoyan sentiments, he had thrown up his appointment, renounced the large estates that he inherited and associated himself with the Socialist movement. This meant voluntary or compulsory exile, and after the abortive revolution of 1905 he, like Lenin, Trotsky, and many another rebel, evaded Siberia by taking refuge elsewhere. He became an exile in many lands, and to this fact is due, not merely his exceptional linguistic powers—he speaks and writes French, German and English with equal facility and correctness—but that extraordinarily intimate knowledge of the affairs and personalities of other countries with which he is equipped.

We hear of him in Berlin in 1907—then a man of about thirty—as a member of the Central Committee of the Berlin Social Democratic Bureau, playing a leading rôle as a Socialistic propagandist amongst the numerous and needy Russian emigrants in Germany. He did not escape the attentions of the Prussian police, and in 1908 he was arrested at Charlottenburg, fined for bearing a false name, and banished from Germany. Thence to Paris, where, still living a refugee among refugees, he remained until the outbreak of war, when he came to London to work and wait, not for the downfall of Germany, but for the downfall of the Russian despotism. Here he developed that close intercourse with the Labour and Socialist movements in this country which have served him in such good stead since, and when the fall of the Tsardom came and Russia once more had a welcome for the political refugees of the past and a flaming sword for the new refugees of the old aristocracy, he in his office at Finsbury Square provided the clearing house for the stream of repatriated Russians.

He might have had office in the brief Kerensky interlude between the fall of the Octobrists and the triumph of the Bolsheviks, but he preferred to stay in London and shepherd his flock home, and he paid the penalty when the goblin shadow of Lenin fell across the map of Europe and panic spread from Warsaw to London. Russia was no longer an ally, but an enemy, and Chicherin, on the ground of "enemy associations," was whipped off to Brixton Gaol, from whence we have seen him emerge into freedom.

Nor, apart from the commonplaceness of his record, would the warder at Brixton Gaol, as he watched his late prisoner off the premises, have been disposed to regard his departure as historic. There is nothing formidable or commanding in the presence or bearing of Chicherin. Slight of stature, with sloping shoulders, an oval face, dark, absent-looking eyes, reddish moustache, long nose and sparse Van-dyke beard, his appearance is ordinary. He would pass unremarked in a crowd, and his indifference to dress—heavy overcoat, woollen scarf, and bulging pockets—adds to the general lack of distinction that marks him. His manner is polite and graceful, with a touch of timorous apology, his voice and speech those of a well-bred European, his habits solitary and ascetic. He has no gifts for public consumption, his oratory being lame and halting, and his manner nervous rather than forcible.

And yet in the eight years that have passed since Chicherin walked through the gates of Brixton Gaol he has been the most constant figure of eminence in the drama of world politics. Lenin has gone, Trotsky has fallen, and in every great State Minister has succeeded Minister with almost the frequency of the seasons. But Chicherin remains what he became on the morrow of his release from Brixton Gaol, the intellectual spearhead of Russian Communism in its struggle with a hostile world. Wherever the battle has been critical, at Lausanne, at Genoa, in Paris, he has been in the thick of the fight, using the most accomplished cunning of the old diplomacy in the service of his new gospel, now appealing, now truculent; answering the contempt of a Curzon with the scorn of a Chicherin—"the Chicherins are of more ancient lineage than the Curzons," he said, when smarting under Curzon's hauteur—penning more State documents with his own hand than any Foreign Minister on record; passing judgments on foreign statesmen as acute and often as vituperative as those of an irresponsible journalist; manœuvring now with Germany, now with Poland, now with Turkey, now with China; setting his cap at America in one phase; flinging his challenge at her in another; and all the time watching the central pillar of the capitalistic world, the British Empire, for symptoms of that collapse without which the world conquest of his idea cannot be consummated.

For he lives for his idea with the single-minded devotion of the fanatic. Wifeless, childless, for most of his life homeless, he has surrendered himself to the task of creating a new heaven below with the fervour and intensity with which Loyola sought to turn men's thoughts to the heaven above. It is a very simple faith. Private property—"*viola l'ennemi*." There is the crux of earthly battle, there the vision of the heavenly reward. Two irreconcilable conceptions are at death-grips for world empire—"one holding property to be the means for individual enjoyment, the other holding it to be something to be employed for the commonweal." Between these conceptions no compromise. It may be necessary to appear to compromise. The hosts of the capitalistic Midian that prowl and prowl around the Communist ark have, by virtue of their shameful gospel of private property, precisely those sources of power that Russia needs. It is a tragic irony that a Communist State should need money, still more that it should have to seek it from its capitalistic enemy.

But there it is, and the problem with which Chicherin has wrestled for seven years has been how to reconcile the pursuit of the political destruction of the enemy with the enticement from that enemy's pocket of those large reserves of capital which he has so infamously secreted. That, I think, is not an unfair statement of the issue. Chicherin would not perhaps admit it, for in his mood of suppliant he proclaims the readiness of the Communist lamb to lie down beside the Capitalist lion—in other words, he seems to admit the co-existence of the rival systems. But in his more challenging moods and in his statements of policy it is clear that he holds the view that the lion and the lamb cannot permanently survive in mutual amity.

He has excellent reason for thinking so, and excellent reason (given his point of view) for regarding this country as the enemy-in-chief. For when he left Brixton Gaol for the New Jerusalem of Communism, did he not find all the

GEORGHI VASILIEVICH CHICHERIN

capitalist States, with the clarion call of Mr. Churchill to
whoop them on, and the money of this country to arm them,
promoting one reckless adventure after another to destroy
the Russian revolution? It is necessary to remember this
disgraceful phase of the story if we are to understand Chicherin's present attitude. He can very well ask, "Who began
it?" And we cannot very well answer that we are blameless."

But in granting this I do not suggest that another policy
on the Allies' part would have changed Chicherin's course.
It would have changed events in spite of him; but it would
not have changed the fanaticism of the fanatic. I do not
think anything would change that, and those who think that
he is willing to be brought within the ambit of normal continental relationships ignore the undeviating drift of his
policy. He is frankly hostile to the League of Nations and
all that it connotes. He sees in it the consolidation of
Europe on those capitalistic lines which it is his mission in
life to obliterate.

I do not condemn him for this. If any man in the public
life of Europe in these great years has given proof of his
disinterested passion for the common good, as he conceives
the common good, it is Chicherin. He is of the stuff of
martyrs and of heroes. But his aim is clear as noonday. He
regards Locarno as the heaviest defeat he has sustained, not
because he does not want peace in Europe, but because he
wants the overthrow of the European social system and
because the absorption of Germany in the League means
a Europe mobilised against his ideals. He turns to Turkey
and the East, and coquets with the idea of an Asiatic bloc
founded on the yellow and dusky millions who are to be
redeemed by the gospel of Bolshevism.

But the tide of that gospel is ebbing. It has left Europe

from the Vistula westwards and it is visibly ebbing in Russia itself, where compromise after compromise with private property has had to be conceded and where we have seen the Central Executive of the Soviet itself shattered on that cardinal issue, and Kamaneff and Zinovieff fighting a losing battle against the majority. Chicherin himself went back to Moscow after Locarno with the sense that the battle had been lost to him and his cause on the fields of Europe. Germany had made her choice. She had chosen to throw in her lot with Europe. The Allies spent six years in trying to drive her into the arms of Communist Russia. If they had succeeded, Chicherin would have succeeded. But they failed and Chicherin has failed. Even the squalid fiasco at Geneva, which went perilously near to obliterating the work of Locarno, failed to turn the current of Europe in his favour. It failed because, shamefully though Germany had been handled in the miserable tale of intrigue, she did not allow her resentment to deflect her into the new channel that Chicherin had so laboriously excavated for her. In the struggle of the Communist ideal for the possession of Europe it is the constancy of Germany which has been the breakwater that has kept out the revolutionary tide. It is that breakwater on which the purposes of Chicherin have broken in vain. But whatever his fate, he has made an heroic fight, and the prisoner of Brixton Gaol remains as the only Foreign Minister in Europe who has survived the torrent of events through all the post-war years.

He survives also as the most significant product of the greatest social upheaval in history—not a man with normal appetites and cravings, but an embodied idea, living his hermit-like life in his office with closed windows, rarely going out, working ceaselessly through the night, shuffling about in ill-matched clothes like a night watchman, interviewing this man at midnight and that one at two in the morning, unconscious of time and unaware of the habits of the normal world, a symbol of the Nemesis that overtakes tyranny and is itself a tyranny. Well would it have been for Russia and for the world if Alexander III had harkened to Uncle Boris instead of dismissing him from his office.

XXII. Lady Astor

"IT WAS a good thing," said Lady Astor, not long ago, "that the first woman to get into Parliament was an ordinary woman, because it made it easier for other ordinary women to succeed her." If Lady Astor were given to that self-depreciation which is the most unpleasing form of self-praise we might assume that she knew that she was talking nonsense. But as among her qualities none is more conspicuous than her shattering veracity, both about herself and about other people, it is necessary to say that a less "ordinary woman" does not exist than the member for the Sutton Division of Plymouth. If I say I shudder to think what the world would be like if all ordinary women were like Lady Astor, I do not wish to convey disrespect. I mean that if such torrential personalities were the rule instead of the exception, life on this planet would be too thrilling an affair to contemplate with composure.

There have, of course, been in the past and there are to-day more intellectually remarkable women than Lady Astor. Her qualities are not of the head, but of the heart and of the spirit. She is an embodied emotion, bursting into the sobrieties and decorums of the world with the same impulsive gaiety with which, as one of the Langhorne sisters, she careered in youth over the Virginian pastures. This does not mean that she is a modern woman of the aggressively emancipated type. The modern woman is apt to be self-consciously defiant in the enjoyment of her new freedom. The chains of the past have fallen away, but the memory of them is still fresh, and she flings herself about a little tempestuously as if to remind herself that they no longer encumber her.

But the engaging audacities of Lady Astor have nothing of this conscious triumph over the male. She would be what she is to-day if there had been no woman's revolution. Hence, with all her passion for the freedom of women she is no sex fanatic, does not declare her equality with men by imitating their habits, and does not confound political and social freedom with moral unrestraint. Indeed, in morals she is old-fashioned rather than new, with a good many of the Puritanical inhibitions which used to be associated with the New Englander of the Mayflower tradition rather than with the aristocratic Virginian culture to which she belongs. Not only does she neither smoke nor drink, but she loathes those habits and wages ceaseless war against the trade in and out of Parliament. She was the first woman to enter the House of Commons, but I fancy she will be the last woman in England to bob her hair.

And if she is free from the feverish unrest of sex, she is equally indifferent to the frailties of fashion. When she was first elected for Plymouth, she appealed to the reporters to regard her as " a regular working member of Parliament and not as a curiosity," and she appeared in the House in a garment of sober black, a practice from which she has never departed. If there is anything in the ways of men that she desires women to imitate it is their freedom from the vagaries of fashion. "They do not change the length of their trousers every two years," she says, "as women change the length of their skirts."

It is not her opinions, therefore, that make her so unprecedented a figure in English public life, but the gallop of the spirit with which she enters the lists, her terrific pugnacity, and her gay indifference to the formal "respectabilities" of behaviour. "The House of Commons," said Bolingbroke, "loves the man who shows it sport." And wherever Lady Astor's "view halloo" is heard there is the assurance of sport.

Her fearlessness, both of speech and action, would be terrifying if it were not touched with such gaiety and good nature, and if it did not proceed from so slight and sylph-like a foe. When it was reported in certain newspapers that she had "mauled" Sir Frederick Banbury and hung on to his coat tails when he talked out her Bill for prohibiting the sale of wine and spirits to persons under the age of eighteen, she denied the aspersion. "I went to Sir Frederick," she explained, "and said jokingly, 'I have tried kindness; I have tried rudeness; now I shall try force—I shall hold on to your coat tails and you shall not rise.'" He replied, "You are not strong enough," and rose to talk until the clock told him the Bill was dead. Lady Astor rose beside him (it was now daybreak, and she had been in the House from eleven to four on "a hard-boiled egg and a glass of water") and strove to save her offspring.

"I wonder," said Sir Frederick, pursuing his thesis of the virtues of drink, "I wonder if the honourable lady member for the Sutton Division has ever taken any hard, violent exercise."

"I never felt more like taking violent exercise than at this moment," said the voice beside him. But she did not "maul" him, and when he had won she only fired at him a parting shot—"Oh, you old villain," she said, "I will get you next time." And she did, for in the end she got her Bill passed.

LADY ASTOR, M.P.

Her courage is equal to any emergency. When, returning from a night meeting at Plymouth, she found a ruffian in her entrance hall, who threatened to kill her, she overawed him by the sheer impetus of her mind, and he fled into the stables, whither she pursued him. Again he ran from this astonishing fury, plunged into a public-house and out at the back, with Lady Astor still on his heels. And when, having run him to earth, the police arrived she refused to prosecute. "I only wanted his name in the public interest," she said. She is as dauntless in the face of a hostile audience as in the presence of a burglar. When, while speaking in Glasgow, the Communists tried to howl her down, she started singing "Keep the Home Fires Burning" with such enjoyment of the fun that she silenced the uproar and won a hearing.

But she can be a formidable enemy if the occasion requires. That conscienceless bravo, Horatio Bottomley, made one of the mistakes of his life when he set out to destroy Lady Astor by issuing an infamous poster entitled "Lady Astor's Divorce," and raking up the unhappy story of her first marriage. There was nothing to conceal about that incident, nothing but what was honourable, however painful, to herself, and she went to Plymouth and told her constituents the facts in a speech that revealed the deeper and finer qualities of her nature. But she did not forget the cowardly blow, and I have something more than a suspicion that in the final exposure of Bottomley her hand was operative if not visible. "The brewers paid Horatio Bottomley to try to take my moral character away," she said, at the election at Plymouth, in 1922. "Well, I've still got my character, but Bottomley is in gaol." And one day, when a person of a certain reputation interrupted her offensively, she paused in front of him, and in even tones that were heard, and intended to be heard by those about, said, "Take care. Bottomley slandered me and I have put him away. I know enough of you to put you where he is, and I warn you that I shall not hesitate to do so." Yes, a formidable woman, even though she did not hold Sir Frederick Banbury down by the coat tails.

A day in her life, any day, is more full of motion and excitement than a day at a fair. She seems to have the secret of perpetual motion, and inexhaustible animation. She rises early and retires late, and whirrs like a spinning wheel the whole time. She reads the papers, arranges the details of her domestic life, plans lunch and dinner, writes and dictates innumerable letters, telephones to no inconsiderable fraction of the population of London about this, that and the other; takes the vice-chair at her luncheon table, which she keeps in a ripple of merriment with her sallies; is spirited away to the House of Commons to ask her questions, and meet constituents, co-workers in the temperance cause, and deputations interested in questions affecting women and children; cracks her jokes, makes a speech, perhaps interrupts the pomposity of a bore; vanishes, it may be to an afternoon meeting, it may be to see her son ride in a steeplechase; is back at the House in time for committees, still untired; whips off to St. James's Square to become the centre of a dinner party at which Tories, Liberals, and Labour men, Churchmen and Dissenters, aristocrats and democrats, business magnates and trade-union secretaries with whom they are at war are all cheek-by-jowl, and all warmed by the glow of her incandescent presence. A ring at the telephone, and she is away to the House for a division; then back to her guests with more fun, more laughter, more stories of the day's doings, more genial pricks for the solemn and dull, more appeals to the stony and obdurate. Perhaps when the last of her guests has gone, she flashes to some other planet to enliven other realms with her surplus gaiety. It is difficult to conceive that, like the rest of us, she goes to bed.

Falstaff said that he was "Jack" to his brothers and sisters, "John" to his neighbours, and "Sir John" to all the world. But Lady Astor is less eclectic. She is "Nancy" to two continents. She is "Nancy" by a sort of royal patent, as Kings are "Edward" or "George," or as Archbishops are "Ebor" and "Cantuar." The fact indicates the free range of her sympathies. There are no fences in the boundless prairie of her adventure—neither in politics nor in society. It may be said without disrespect that she is "hail-fellow-well-met" to all the world. She is nominally in the Tory fold, but she leaps the political hurdles as lightly as she will skip over a five-barred gate in the country, and her party has long ceased to hope to discipline so independent a mind. She is as ready to back Mr. Baldwin or Mr. MacDonald as she was to pull the coat tails of Sir Frederick Banbury, and she has declared that she would go to Timbuctoo for the joy of fighting a brewer.

For amid all her enthusiasms for the under dog, it is the cause of temperance that most serves to keep her at white heat. It was in that cause that her maiden speech—the first utterance of a woman in the British Parliament—was delivered, and her open hostility to the dependence of her party upon the drink trade once led to her being howled down at a Unionist Conference. Not that she believes in compulsory Prohibition. "I have just enough of the devil in me," she once said, "that the moment anyone prohibits anything, that is the very thing I want to do." But she is the sleepless enemy of the trade, and her duels with Mr. Macquisten in the House are historic. When he complained that the habitués of public-houses were not represented in the Liquor Control Board, she leapt up with the demand that the victims of the habitués of public-houses, "generally their wives," should be represented on the Board. Her gift of retaliation is, indeed, inexhaustible. When the member for Dunfermline said she should confine herself to milk and babies and leave the Navy alone, she retorted that if he would drink more milk and *less lemonade* he would be more polite to the only woman in the House.

It was an unjust implication in regard to an eminently reputable member of the House; but Lady Astor shares the censoriousness of Johnson who, in his teetotal interludes, was apt to think that anyone who drank was *ipso facto* drunk. "I will not talk to you, Sir," he once remarked to the courtly Reynolds: "you are too far gone." Lady Astor has a dash of that suspicion which occasionally involves her in attacks, such as that on Mr. Hayday, which would be unpardonable in a man and are not easily pardonable in a woman. Her tongue knows no respect either for persons or occasions and it falls with impartial severity upon friend and foe. It was one of her own leaders of whom she said that he had "a face like a Meat Trust," and it was another to whom, meeting him in the lobby after she had been opposing him in the House, she remarked, "I have been defending you against the Labour members. They say you are not fit to feed with pigs. I say that you are."

She sees everything from the angle of the woman and the child. "A woman is always thinking of the world she wants for her children," she says. Hence her enthusiasm for the League of Nations, and the courage with which on a famous visit to America—a visit on which, said the *Daily Telegraph*, she made forty speeches and not a single *faux pas*—she rebuked her own people for standing aloof. "That's where we dropped the treacle jug," she said breezily to the Virginians. "You need not call it the League of Nations," she said elsewhere. "Give it a new name every week, but give it a chance." If her sincerity and high spirits were tempered with judgment and discretion, she might crown her galloping career by being the first Ambassadress to America.

xxiii. Mr. W. R. Morris

IT IS a saying, I think, of the Zend-Avesta, that the man who makes two blades of grass grow where one grew before has done more to win salvation than he who utters ten thousand prayers. From this it is evident that the great controversy between salvation by faith and salvation by works is not confined to the Christian religion. If, accepting this doctrine, we assume that the multiplication of motor cars is as beneficent an achievement as the multiplication of blades of grass, Mr. William R. Morris has advanced as far along the road to salvation as any Englishman of his time. He has incidentally done a conspicuous service to British industry.

It is probably true that if there had been no Mr. Morris the blades of grass would have multiplied all the same; but it is certainly also true that the culture would not have been of a home-grown type. The genius of Henry Ford, soaring up in far away Detroit, had seemed to transcend competition. He had taken the world for his parish. His missionaries were out in all lands, and the sound of his gospel was heard on every highway from China to Peru. He had taken this country in his stride and scattered motor-cars among us as plentifully as the wind scatters leaves in autumn. I remember driving along the Bristol road from Birmingham some five years ago, when the chauffeur, commenting on the vehicles we met, said he estimated that 95 per cent. of the cars normally on that road were Ford cars. If they were not flagrantly Fords, they were Fords in disguise.

Today on that road, as on any other road in the country, the overwhelming majority of cars that would be met would bear the signature of W. R. Morris. He has, as a witty friend of mine observed, given us "a Ford with an Oxford education."

His achievement does not of course detract from the title of Henry Ford to be the supreme adventurer into the vast kingdom that petrol opened up for exploitation. It may not be true, as is sometimes said, that if there had been no Ford there would have been no Morris, but it is true that to Ford belongs the conception of the vast potentialities of the baby he had done so much to bring into the world, and that it was his bold pioneer work that blazed the path for others. If there had been no Ford, the astonishing development of the industry would certainly have been delayed, but it is by no means certain that if there had been no Ford the impetus would not have come from Morris. For though, as will be apparent, there is little likeness between the two men in one respect, they are extraordinarily alike in those matters which are relevant, that is, the practical application of imaginative ideas to strictly business ends and the force of will that overcomes difficulties.

In a word, the priority of Detroit over Oxford may only be due to the fact that Henry Ford chanced to come into the world before William Morris. In the year (1893) in which Henry Ford drove his first gasoline-propelled motor-car through the streets of Detroit, to the amused curiosity of a world which did not realise what a revolutionary portent had appeared in their midst, young Morris, then a lad of seventeen, entered the lists. In the matter of time, therefore, Ford had arrived before Morris had started. Morris was twenty years behind, and he had to travel precisely the same road as his forerunner. There was no golden road to the Samarkand he reached. In an established industry where all the routes are marked and all the possibilities explored, there may be golden roads, but in a new and uncharted field like that of the motor industry, such an adventure as that of the Fords and the Morrises is only possible to a man who has worked every inch of the way and fought every difficulty with his own hands.

This is the key to Mr. Morris. He does not stand out as the creator of the most remarkable "one man show" in contemporary British industry by virtue of luck or financial skill or any occult power. He would be the last to deny that he had had luck—or that he had had the wit to take it by the hand—and he will readily admit that he owes much to the facilities which the bank accorded him. But the "glittering prize" he has won is the reward, not of the astute financier, but of the working man, the mechanic, the engineer who has saturated himself with the knowledge of his subject and has built his vast structure upon the foundation of that knowledge. It is because he is a great mechanic that Mr. Morris is a prince of industry—a great mechanic with a genius for concentration. "Young man," said the first Rothschild to young Buxton, "stick to your brewing and you can make yourself the first of brewers. But squander yourself in banking, in business, in this, that, and the other and your name will soon be in the *Gazette*." No one can doubt the tyrannic absorption of Mr. Morris in his one theme. He is the spirit of the motor-car made flesh. The bewildering lightnings, gaieties, idealisms, irrelevancies that coruscate around the personality of Mr. Ford are wholly absent from this one-idead man.

He carries his burden lightly because he has no other impedimenta, and because all his driving energy is applied to a single purpose. His physique is powerful, though spare, but it gives the impression of being overengined, of a dynamo that is running ceaselessly and always at high voltage. He has no gift for relaxing the strain, and he will tell you that when he was once induced to take a holiday on the Riviera he found it an intolerable affliction. He has no personal tastes to gratify and no uses for money except that of fertilising the astonishing business of which he is the sole creator and, until recently, the sole owner. He has the natural pride of the creator in his own creation, and claims that it is the product of one thing only, his power of work. If you suggest to him that it was the fortuitous direction of that power of work into a certain channel that had something to do with the result—that if, for example, events had thrown him into the building of ships in these days instead of the building of motor-cars, his success would have been somewhat less sensational—he will gaily admit the thrust.

But while making that thrust you suspect that even in shipbuilding this driving energy would have found some way through the murk and stagnation of things. For you cannot doubt that he is of the stuff that will not be denied. Scott said of Hogg, the Ettrick Shepherd, that he was "born under a six-penny planet." He was a defeatist. He was born to failure and, having the spirit of failure in him, everything he touched took the blight. I do not know what planet presided over the birth of W. R. Morris, at Worcester, in 1877, but it must have been the most auriferous planet in the firmament, for it endowed him with just those qualities that make for material success, and denied him all those qualities that divert success.

He struck out adventurously from the start. With no

education except that which he had got in the village school at Cowley, the suburb of Oxford where his great factories cover the fields in which he played and where now a new motor-car is born every few minutes, and with not so much as a £5 note at the back of him, he took the decision to work for himself, on the principle that W. R. Morris would pay him a higher salary than anybody else. "So I started to work for W. R." And what so natural for a boy to work at as jolly things like bicycles? He repaired them, he built them, he rode them in races. Men who were up at New College twenty odd years ago will remember the bicycle place in Holywell and the bright, active young fellow who owned it, and from whom they occasionally hired a not very thrilling motor-car that he also owned.

One of those men has reason to remember it, for he became interested in the ambitions of the bright, active young fellow, lent him some money and helped him on the road to victory. Morris had conquered all the mysteries of petrol power, matriculated, as it were, with the Morris motor-bicycle, and being now well under way worked night and day for his "degree." He would make a motor-car of his own—a motor-car enriched with all the experience he had got from the repair of myriads of motors. He had analysed them, dissected them, compared them, observed the weaknesses here and the virtues there, and out of the wealth of knowledge with which he had charged himself he evolved during a gestation of ten years a machine which should approximate to the Ford in price and eclipse it in appearance and solid merits. He had leapt to the idea which Ford had conceived and the exploitation of which had become Ford's monopoly in the world—the idea that the future of the motor-car was not with the rich few but with the multitude of moderate-circumstanced people—and fourteen years ago, with the purchase of land at Cowley, he embarked on his great adventure. In his first complete season he turned out some 500 cars, but with success in sight, though not yet achieved, there came the killing frost of the war, and the Morris car, like so much else, went into cold storage, its inventor and his works being commandeered for the manufacture of mine sinkers for the North Sea.

For all practical purposes, the great Morris structure is a growth of the last six years, and the creation of one bold decision. It was taken, curiously enough, at the same moment and in the same circumstances as that crisis in Ford's struggle with Wall Street with which I have dealt elsewhere. In the first year after the war he had an output of 1,500 cars. Then the cloud of depression descended. The bubble of inflated business burst, industry collapsed, most of all, industry, like that of motor-car manufacture, which was of the nature of luxury. Some firms were broken, most ran in for shelter until the storm passed. Morris was urged to run in to shelter, too, to cut down his production, to reduce his liabilities, to play for safety. Instead, with the instinct of great generalship, he seized the moment when everybody was fleeing to advance with all his banners flying and trumpets sounding. He increased his output and announced the sensational "cut" of £100 in his model. It was magnificent and it was war. The trade was hilariously incredulous. The thing was insane. It could not be done. The public marvelled and Morris became a household name. Across the Atlantic the Goliath of the cheap car became aware that a David had entered the lists to challenge his reign in one part of his world empire.

And in the result it proved the most triumphant calculation in modern business. Morris had risked every penny he had, and probably more, on the throw; but he will tell you that the choice was not whether he should keep it or risk it, but whether he should lose it in running to shelter or risk it for a prize of inconceivable magnitude. Had he had shareholders to consider and directors to consult, he would have been driven to shelter. It was his freedom of personal initiative that won him a kingdom. The fact is worth noting in relation to the conduct of business. There is no need to dwell on the fruits of that dazzling coup. The world knows all about the vast growth of the Morris enterprise, the companies at Oxford, at Birmingham, at Coventry, in France; the increasing torrent of cars that flows hour by hour out of the gates at Cowley; the turnover exceeding £20,000,000 a year; the output that has risen from 500 a week to 1,000 a week and 1,500 a week, and that will soon be 2,000 a week. Mr. Morris thinks—unlike Mr. Ford, who says, "Tariff isn't a graft: it's a nuisance"—that it is duties that have made him great. He is too modest. The abolition of the McKenna duties not only did not check him. He increased his output, lowered his price, and increased his staff after the abolition. But Mr. Morris is not of interest as a political thinker. He is only of interest as a brilliant business man who has won a famous victory for British trade, and whose career is a sufficient proof that even in this country the ranker of industry can still find the marshal's baton in his knapsack.

xxiv. Jack Hobbs

LET us sing the praise of Hobbs. It is a work of supererogation, as the poet says, to paint the lily and gild refined gold and add a hue to the violet, and it may savour of a like "wasteful and ridiculous excess" to exalt John Berry Hobbs and attempt to add a lustre to his fame. But no picture of the life of our time, set down in the terms of personalities who command the public attention, would be complete without him; and though the kingdom he rules is only the kingdom of play, the man who can claim to have given as much innocent pleasure as any man living to as many people from the Oval to Capetown and from Capetown to Brisbane has as good a title as any to a place in the gallery of celebrities. In making a list of household names in the English-speaking world we could no more exclude his than that of Bernard Shaw, or Charles Chaplin, or Lloyd George. He is a link of the Commonwealth and in far-away Melbourne the city workers pour out in tides to see him more eagerly than they would pour out to see a prince of the blood or the victor in a war.

He is the representative man of the most English thing we have done in the world of recreation. Give an Englishman a bat and a ball, said Emerson, and his cup of happiness is full. He said it, I fancy, with a note of scorn that we should be so easily amused, and though since Emerson's day, America has become as infatuated with the delight of hitting balls both large and small as we are, it is, I think, true that nothing better illustrates the difference between the

English spirit and the American spirit than the fact that the sun of English cricket has never risen on the dark continent across the Atlantic.

It explains much that we find alien in the American culture, for cricket is not merely a personal affair of hitting a ball more skillfully than someone else hits it. Cricket is a frame of mind, it is an attitude to life, it is a discipline, a comradeship, a thing of serene and joyous memories. It embodies our philosophy of conduct. When we have said, "That is not cricket," we have passed a judgment from which there is no appeal. I will not go so far as to say that no people can be truly civilised that does not love cricket; but I do say that the humanising spirit of the game is one of our most precious possessions, and that if I were to be born into the world again one of the conditions I should wish to impose would be that I should be born in a land where I could recapture one of the purest and most enduring joys that sweeten the adventure of life.

And if I could make a further condition it would be that I should be a contemporary, if not of "W. G."—of course I should prefer that—then of Hobbs. He is so easily the first cricketer of his generation that it is unnecessary to look for his rival. There are strokes in Frank Woolley's repertory—that crashing shock with which he plays a ball from the pitch to the off boundary for example—that are more thrilling than anything that Hobbs has to offer; but in the completeness, variety and exquisite finish of his equipment, Hobbs is matchless, the perfect artist among the great craftsmen of the game. He belongs by a sort of inherited authority of nature to the royal line, and in any team of the world's best he would have his place without challenge beside W. G. Grace, Ranjitsinhji, and (less assuredly) Victor

Trumper. He is of their class, and there is no other of that class. He differs from them, but he is not inferior to them. He has not the overwhelming personality that counted for so much in the case of Grace; nor has he that panther stillness and swiftness, that touch of magic, which made Ranjit-sinhji's cricket seem so much more subtle, so much more delicate, so much more inspired, than any other cricket that lives in the memory. But his mastery of the art is as great as that of either.

If I were to attempt to define the peculiar quality of his play, I should say that it lay in the perfect balance of both physical and temperamental elements. A great cricketer, like a great poet, indeed, like a supreme artist in any order, is born, not made. Genius has been described as an infinite capacity for taking pains, and it is true that without that capacity the highest natural gifts are lodged with us useless. But the original gift, the quality of temperament, the power of co-ordinating thought and action, must be there for the industrious apprentice to polish and refine. Hobbs was born and bred in the cricket atmosphere—his father groundsman at Jesus College, Cambridge; his childhood spent in the ardent practice of the game on Parker's Piece at Cambridge; his horizon bounded by the cricket field—but that might be said of thousands who are no more like Hobbs at the wicket than a dray horse is like a Derby winner. It is the perfect adjustment of all the faculties of mind and body for the task that alone explains him.

See him come out from the pavilion at the Oval and take his place at the crease. Note the neat, trim, slight figure, the ease of movement, the loose, free action of the limbs, the alert economy of motion, no idle expenditure of effort either for display or for restlessness, no hint of egotism or self-consciousness, no suggestion of panic; but every gesture to the point and under the control of a mind at once eager, vigilant and self-possessed. He is neither too tall nor too short for the powerful weapon that he carries. In the hands of Grace, with his huge black-bearded head, his mighty shoulders, and his bare blacksmith arms, the bat looked like a top. In the hands of Bobby Abel it looked like an encumbrance. You wondered how so small a man could flourish so large a weapon, and half the delight which that famous batsman aroused was in the sense of the triumph of art over matter. In the hands of Ranjitsinhji the bat was a magician's wand. It seemed to whisper its secret to the ball and sent it flying on its errand with a touch, a flick, a glide that was almost impalpable as a breath of wind.

Hobbs and his bat are of a piece. The bat is so controlled, so responsive, that it seems only an extension of himself. It is not an instrument, but a limb, a part of the anatomy, answering his thought as hand and eye answer it. The bearing of the man at this early stage is so undemonstrative and untheatrical as to allay alarm—if you did not know his past. He is so pleasant and modest in appearance, the sort of good boy of the family—he has sung in a Church choir since he was a boy, and when his father died he set out with his bat to help his mother to bring up his eleven brothers and sisters—that it is hard to think any harm of him. He does not look pugnacious; he does not look cunning; he looks just nice and friendly and ordinary.

You would feel quite happy about getting his wicket, but for that neatness and economy of action of which I have spoken, and that disquieting self-possession. He is feeling his way, taking his soundings, testing the bowlers, the ground, the field, all the circumference of things. No

hurry, he says; all the day before us. He taps the ball and
steals a run just to break the ice and show how cool and self-
assured he is. No judge of a run like him since "Monkey"
Hornby—"Oh my Hornby and my Barlow long ago"—
used to delight the Old Trafford crowd. But even in this
short sprint, not hurried, everything accurately and coolly
calculated.

And now, the foundation well laid, he begins to build.
He has taken the measure of the bowlers, he has got the
disposition of the field, and "That for you" he says as the
ball comes bounding along the carpet—always along the
carpet—between point and cover, or slip and deep slip. The
opposing captain shifts his field, this man a little forward,
that a little back to fill the gap that has been revealed. Well,
well, there is another gap here, captain, and away goes the
ball with a glance or a high stroke to leg or a push past mid-
on. And as the field moves, the strokes vary. The bowler
changes his attack as the fisherman changes his bait; but with
every change comes the unfailing reply, for here is a man
who has the solution to every problem, and can produce
every stroke for the occasion.

It is not the bookish, formal solution that made the cricket
of that other great Cambridge batsman, Tom Hayward, so
invulnerable and so uninspiring. Every stroke is fresh and
entertaining. He has not the genius for improvisation that
was the glory of J. T. Tyldesley, who played every ball as
if it were a new revelation to which he had to give a new and
joyous welcome. He was the great empiric of the game, and
next to MacLaren the finest flower of Lancashire cricket.
But if he is less spontaneous than Tyldesley, Hobbs is no
less various, and his all-round accomplishment, his aware-
ness of things, his imperturbable command of himself and

his resources, place him in a higher class than Tyldesley. No great batsman missed his century so narrowly and so frequently as Tyldesley, and no one ever missed it so rarely when it was within his grasp as Hobbs. It is this union of brilliant executive power with a coolness and deliberation of mind that are never wanting that supplies the key to his mystery. That deliberation is remarkable in nothing more than in his genius for placing the ball, in which no one except Grace has equalled him. It was said by one of the professionals who bowled against Grace, "I puts it where I likes, and he puts it where *he* likes," and any bowler of this generation might make the same comment on Hobbs.

And he plays the game. He does not dole out runs as if he were a miser hoarding them. He spends his riches freely, and as if he enjoyed spending them. In a time when cricket is threatened with sleeping sickness, and the pursuit of places in county tables and positions in averages has superseded the old hearty delight in the game itself, it is not the least of his claims upon our gratitude that he has kept the spirit of the sport glowing in his play. He hits as though he loves hitting, and his art is not in making easy bowling appear difficult, but in making difficult bowling appear easy. He fields, as he bats, with zest—and there has been no better cover point since Vernon Royle. For him the game is the thing. It is an adventure, not a safe five per cent. investment.

Upon that adventure the struggle for points and averages falls like a blight and a curse, turning it to a dull, mechanic, soulless business, and obliterating the rapture and gallantry of the game—Yorkshire playing for safety the first day, and Lancashire playing for safety the second day, and the third day being a weariness to the flesh. I do not suggest that there was no stonewalling in other days. Scotton, Barlow, and Hall have never been equalled in that funereal rôle. Scotton was once in for sixty-five minutes without scoring a run, and Barlow once batted for two and a half hours for five runs. But, apart from the case of those monumental dullards, it is true that the temperature of the play has fallen, that one run per man in three minutes on a good wicket is becoming far too common, that the habit of treating batting as a science of defence instead of an art of attack, and of putting a respect for decimals before a healthy appetite for boundaries, is trying our patience and making us yearn for a Jessop to come like a whirlwind into the stagnant atmosphere.

Hobbs is not a Jessop, but the supreme exponent of the whole range of the batsman's art. But he gives us runs, he gives us sport, he gives us the finest vintage of the noblest of all games. And though I loathe measurement by the footrule of records, I share the interest with which the world of cricket watches him passing the mighty achievement of "W. G." and planting his flag on a yet higher pinnacle of "centuries."

xxv. Earl Haig

THERE is no more shadowy and elusive figure in the events of our time than that of the man who, in the military sense, played the leading British rôle in those events. From the background of the Napoleonic wars the personality of Wellington stands out sharp and clear, an abrupt, masterful man who made up for his brevity of speech by the strength of his language and whose hard decisiveness of thought and action live in the appropriate sobriquet of the "Iron Duke." And so, out of the welter of other wars, there always emerged one figure that seemed to dominate events, to personify the action and to hold the attention—Clive, Wolfe, Marlborough, Cromwell. But in the records of the greatest war in which this country has ever been engaged there is no presence that has seized the public mind or seems likely to make an impression on the mind of history. The fact is the more remarkable because it has seldom happened that one man has filled the leading part so uninterruptedly in a war as Earl Haig did. With the exception of the first year of the war, when he held the second position in the field, he was Commander-in-Chief throughout. He saw the mighty struggle through from the first day to the last, and he emerged from it with as unequivocal a triumph as ever fell to any British commander. Nevertheless he is "caviare to the general"—little more than a great name, vague, almost impersonal, a sort of ghostly presence which suggests no clear outline and no brave colours to the mind.

Was he a great general? Was he even a good general?

The question is still open and controverted, and I do not hope to solve a problem which has puzzled far more experienced minds. Part of the perplexity is no doubt due to the change in the methods and magnitude of war. The day of the Cæsars and Hannibals and Napoleons has gone for ever. The swift movement of small, professional armies, with its possibilities of surprise and decisive overthrow, has given place to the slow, grinding war of attrition in which the motive is not so much the capture of positions as the exhaustion of the life of nations, and in this new kind of warfare there is no place for the romantic hero who by a sudden inspiration turns the tide of battle and settles the fate of empires. The science of war is governed by the material of war, and a century of scientific discoveries has made the scientist, the chemist, and the engineer, rather than the soldier the real potentates of war. The man who can invent the most deadly gas is in future more important in war than any Hannibal or Napoleon.

But apart from this vast change that has come over the character of war, there is a more personal explanation of the fact to which I refer. It is in the character and temperament of Lord Haig himself. When, just before the battle of Loos, I was being motored to his headquarters not far from Festubert, the general who accompanied me grew eloquent on the subject of his chief. "You will find him," he said, in finishing his eulogy, "not only a great soldier but a great gentleman." Whatever doubts might linger on the first point there could be none on the second. Nothing could be more remote from the conventional idea of the great commander in the midst of war than the calm atmosphere which the personality of Douglas Haig exhaled. He looked—and still looks—young for his years, a fact due to the smooth, untroubled character of the face.

The first impression is certainly not one of force, still less of egotism. The forward thrust of the heavy chin is more than countered by the mild candour and kindliness of the blue-grey eyes. His manner had no hint in it of the rough life of camps, but was attuned to the note of the family lawyer or the family physician. It was quiet, temperately assured, entirely unaggressive. I do not know whether he has ever been known to lose his temper; but it is impossible to associate any ungovernable passion, anger, fear, resentment, jealousy, with that disciplined bearing. It was a manner which seemed to persuade rather than to command, to express itself by suggestion rather than emphasis, and which diffused a certain air of sweet reasonableness and open-mindedness about him. I felt that it would be difficult to make a breach in that armour of panoplied courtesy, which at once put you at your ease, won your confidence and loosened your tongue. He talked in quiet tones, simply, sincerely, without exaggeration or dogmatism, and he was a good listener. He laughed little, but smiled revealingly. It was a smile that could be a rebuke without a word being uttered and without a wound to the feelings. It was as though he at once corrected you and forgave you. Garrulousness, cocksureness, bumptiousness, assertiveness withered in that urbane atmosphere.

He did not impress me then, or afterwards, as a great man; but he impressed me as a wise man, the sort of man who might make mistakes, but not foolish mistakes, who was the victim neither of impulse nor vanity, who would face the facts with plain, undistracted scrutiny, and having come to a decision could be relied on, in the words of another famous soldier, "to fight it out on that line if it takes all summer."

It follows from this that, whatever the military merits of Haig, he was not the type of man to project his personality across the footlights. He had no dramatic gift, no sense of the theatre, no political instinct. I do not say this to his discredit. I say it to his honour. In a somewhat patronising sketch of Lord Haig, Lord Birkenhead has formulated the view that there can be no great soldier who is not also a great statesman and that, inferentially, the great statesman is *ipso facto* a great soldier. It is a comfortable doctrine for the eminent statesman, but it is not supported by a survey of the history of the war, and there is in the public mind as well-grounded a distrust of the political soldier as there is in the Army of the amateur strategist. No breath of suspicion of political manœuvring ever touched Sir Douglas Haig, and his entire disregard of the arts of advertisement has to be borne in mind in attempting an estimate of his merits and services. Had he cultivated parties or the Press during the years in which his own fate as well as the fate of Europe was in the balance, he would not have done his work better, but he would have fortified his own position, he would have been less vulnerable to intrigue, and he would have made himself more actual and intelligible to the public mind.

But both during the war and since, often in circumstances the injustice of which few men would have been able to resist, he has preserved a steady aloofness from the field of controversy and has left his reputation to take care of itself. As the air clears and the larger issues of the struggle become defined, that reputation does not suffer. Lord Birkenhead speaks of the "whole Paschendaale offensive, futile in its results and bloody in its consequences," as "a tragic illustration of obstinate error," and of the prolongation of the Battle of the Somme, "entirely indefensible in its inception," as "one of the greatest follies of the war." Lord Birkenhead is here of course speaking from a brief, but a more cruel and grotesque travesty of the truth could hardly be conceived. Its aim is clear. It is to justify that political control of strategy which marked the later phases of the war.

It is not true that the Battle of the Somme was "entirely indefensible in its inception." It is not true that it was "one of the greatest follies of the war." The Battle of the Somme was notoriously the answer to the Battle of Verdun. It was the heroic attempt and the successful attempt to save the French by diverting the German offensive on the Meuse to a defensive on the Somme. It was so successful that—as we now know from Ludendorff's book—the Germans at the end of 1916 knew that in a military sense their fate was sealed. If the sequel to that campaign on the Somme had been carried out as Ludendorff feared it would be carried out, and as Joffre and Haig intended it to be carried out, it is more than arguable that a military decision would have followed in 1917.

But the political *coup* in London, in November, 1916, changed the whole strategy. Joffre's plans were scrapped; the politicians took command; the sacrifices on the Somme were converted into fruitless sacrifices; there followed a brand-new strategy, and the lamentable fiasco associated with the name of Nivelle, which nearly brought France to the ground. And it was because of this reversal of policy and this tragedy of errors that the tragedy of Paschendaale was enacted. It was a desperate attempt, delayed till the autumn and defeated by the weather, to recover the ground that had been lost, not by Haig, but by those politicians who had scrapped the soldiers' strategy and substituted their own.

And the more the crisis of 1918 is studied the more the historian will support Haig and condemn his political masters. The catastrophe to the Fifth Army was the work of politicians who, in the pursuit of a decision in the East, had fatally weakened the Western front, and the establishment of unity of control at the eleventh hour, which alone saved a fatal breach in the Allied line, was due to Haig as much as to Milner. Nor must it be forgotten that it was Haig who ended the war in 1918. At the beginning of September, both the authorities at Versailles and our own Government were convinced that victory was not possible before 1919 and the arrival of more Americans. Haig insisted that he had the measure of the enemy and could break through the Hindenburg line. He was allowed to make the attempt on condition that he took the entire responsibility on himself— "heads I win, tails you lose." He knew that he had been long marked for slaughter, and that failure would be the end of his career: but he took the risk, and the collapse of the Germans and the abrupt end of the war sustain his title to bold and imaginative generalship.

It would be absurd to suggest that history will rank him with the masters of war, or will attribute to him the quality of genius. He did not inspire men by the fervour of his spirit or solve great problems by the light of inspiration. His gifts are not intellectual, but moral. He is a slow-thinking, prudent Scotsman, a trifle conservative in his habit of mind—witness his obstinate belief in the cavalry arm— not very ready to accept new ideas or to reject old ones; but painstaking, wise, imperturbable, firm in the dark hour and modest in the hour of victory; free from the vices of envy, jealousy, and ambition that so often play havoc with greater men than he is; never subordinating the cause to baser considerations, patient under misrepresentation and injustice, and strong enough to resist the temptation to retaliate.

I find that the list of his virtues is of a negative kind; but the total is positive. If it does not bear the signature of genius it betokens a character that stands the wear and tear of time and the vicissitudes of fortune better than ill-regulated genius. He was the only commander of any army who lived through all the mighty ordeal unshaken, and he emerged with a victory as complete as any in history. I doubt whether genius of the most resplendent sort would have done as much. It could not have done more.

xxvi. M. Caillaux

WHATEVER may be said to his discredit, M. Caillaux
is a very brave man. He has that rare and invaluable gift
in a public man of daring to tell the public the truth and of
offering it unpalatable medicine. There is no country in
which that quality is more rare than France, and it is this
fact more than any other which is at the root of the failure
of the peace and of the present condition of Europe. France
has lived for seven years on a fiction as transparent as that
of Madame Humbert's safe. In the safe were colossal
riches. Only find the key to it—and was not the Ruhr the
key?—and everybody would be prosperous. Why pay taxes
when any day the safe might be opened and its contents
poured in a golden stream into French pockets? Let us go
on borrowing; let us go on not paying our debts, let us go
on pretending, and suddenly all will be miraculously well.
It was not so much the fault of the people as the fault of
the statesmen. They knew the hoax, but they had not the
courage to expose it. To preserve the hoax had become
their career.

"When are you French statesmen going to tell your people
the truth?" asked a famous Englishwoman of one of the
post-war Premiers of France who was sitting by her side at
lunch.

"*Jamais*," said the statesman with a cynical shrug.

M. Caillaux turned that "never" into "now." He told
the French people what was the nature of their disease and
he prescribed the medicine they had to take. It was very

unpleasant medicine—all the more unpleasant because it had been so long delayed. It was so unpleasant that the people still refused to take it, and M. Caillaux, having been thrown up by one convulsion, was thrown down by another. But the credit of being the first statesman to tell his country-men the truth is undeniably his, and though he fell when he suggested that France should pay her debts, his fall was not inglorious, and it was not out of keeping with his varie-gated career.

His life has been as rich in melodrama as a film play. His exits and entrances have been many and tumultuous, and thunder and lightning are his unfailing accompaniment. If he is not being hissed as he comes on to the stage, he is being hooted as he goes off, and even when he is behind the wings there is a rumble of speculation as to what he is doing out of sight. He has been Prime Minister and he has narrowly escaped being shot as a "traitor." He has sat in the Cabinet with Clemenceau, and he has been banished as a public criminal by his formidable chief. He has been a hero in the trenches at the moment that he was fleeing for his life from the mob in the street, and there can hardly have been a day in his life for years when he did not think that the fate of Jaurès or of Calmette might be his before nightfall. There is not an infamy, public or private, of which he has not been accused, or at least held capable of committing, and an atmos-phere of scandal, real or invented, hangs about him like a garment. If his enemies are to be believed there was never such a scoundrel. If he is to be believed there was never a more disinterested patriot.

I do not accept either view, though there is something in both. There was probably an element of truth in the venom-ous vendetta with which Gaston Calmette pursued him in the *Figaro*. Many of the allegations were grotesque. Calmette told, for example, how, when Prime Minister, M. Caillaux had promised to restore the great Prieu estate, which was in the hands of the French Government, to the heirs who claimed it on the understanding that 80 per cent. of the value was paid into the party funds. This shocking story, which has a family resemblance to things that have happened in countries nearer home, and similar tales fell to pieces in derision, but they were followed punctually by others. "*A demain*" was the favourite ending of the Calmette articles. "To-morrow" there would be something still more startling about this political brigand. Calmette was moving to some grand climax.

What was it? What did Madame Caillaux think it was when she set out for the *Figaro* with her loaded Browning on that March day of 1914? Did she think it was the Fabre document which was found in the dead Calmette's pocket? Put quite bluntly, the suggestion of that document was that M. Caillaux had been involved in the Rochette scandal and that it was his influence in 1911 that delayed the proceedings and enabled the adventurer to escape to Mexico. Rochette was a young man in a hurry to get rich with other people's money, and he built up such a fabric of doubtful companies—financing one with the money of another, and so on—that the Government in 1908, decided to deal with him. Rochette was convicted; appealed; lost his appeal; again appealed. It was in connection with this second appeal in 1911, when M. Caillaux was in office, that the delay that enabled Rochette to escape was engineered; and the Fabre document pointed directly to Caillaux as the medium.

The story of that document takes us into the underworld of French politics. M. Briand, who had been a Radical colleague of Caillaux in the past, became possessed of it when he joined M. Poincaré's Cabinet in 1912. He did not publish it; but when he went out of office he passed it on to M. Barthou, who, on his fall from the Premiership, took the precaution of keeping it. Then its existence began to be whispered abroad, and Calmette became the instrument for firing it off at the critical moment and blowing Caillaux to bits with it. "To-morrow." But to-morrow Calmette was dead, slain by Madame Caillaux.

It is an ugly story, and where the truth lies is hard to tell. M. Monis, who was Prime Minister when the Rochette appeal was on, denied the truth of Fabre's allegation. So did the President of the Court. But why did Madame Caillaux fear the publication of a lie, if lie it was? On the other hand, the history of the document was as suspicious as that of the Dreyfus "bordereau." Whether true or false, it was to be used as a political weapon for making an end of a man who was hated and feared by his opponents more than any man in French public life.

And that fact brings us out of the sewers of French politics on to the plane of ideas. For whether M. Caillaux is the scoundrel that his foes picture or an honest man, it is not his moral character that makes him the best hated man of his generation. If moral probity were a *sine qua non* in French politics, the mortality among French statesmen would be high. Without putting an excessive valuation upon M. Caillaux's moral standards, I am disposed to think they are not below the average of his class. You would take him for a very astute man of business, but you would not take him for a rogue. There is something of the dilettante in this dapper little man, with his polished bald crown, his bright, alert eyes, his neat, well-groomed figure, and his spirited talk and bearing. Nor, accepting the philosophy of the "Northern Farmer"—

'Tisn' them as 'as munny that breeäks into 'ouses and steeäls,
Them as 'as cooäts to their baäcks and taäkes their regular meals—

has M. Caillaux had any temptation to join the criminal classes. He comes of a prosperous stock, had an excellent introduction to life, began his career as a teacher of political economy, speaks English—thanks to an English governess —better than any French politician except Franklin-Bouillon, and if he had not entered politics could have made any fortune he pleased in finance.

In saying this I am not suggesting that he is any better than he ought to be. He may be worse than he ought to be. He may even be as wicked as the Barrès and the Daudets would have us believe. My point is that if he had been as virtuous as the Archangel Gabriel he would not have escaped calumny. For the real crime of M. Caillaux is not his moral behaviour, but his political opinions. And, if putting aside all the scandalmongering and suspicions, we judge him by his loyalty to those opinions, the judgment will place him, not below the standard of French statesmanship, but above it. What he believes he stands to. What he is fighting for to-day, he fought for thirty years ago. And the things he has fought for are not the things that make a man popular. If he had been a mere adventurer he would have adopted another cause, or he would have deserted his own cause when the opportunity offered.

For the two things for which he stands before everything else in the mind of France are taxation by the English method and peace with the historic enemy. "To tax and be popular," said Burke, "is as hard as to love and be wise."

And nowhere is taxation less loved than in France. As a former Chancellor of the Exchequer observed to me during the war, "the French will give their blood for their country, but they will not give their treasure: they will only lend it." Against that national characteristic, M. Caillaux has waged war ever since, as a man of thirty-six or so, he entered the Cabinet of that great statesman, Waldeck-Rousseau, in 1899. He loathed the pettifogging expedients of indirect taxation and Protection, and the tricks and subterfuges by which successive statesmen had made the French budget a Chinese puzzle that no one could decipher and no one was intended to decipher. He saw his country getting deeper and deeper in the mire of illimitable borrowings, and he nailed his colours to the mast of the Income Tax and fought under that ensign in and out of office with the courage and tenacity that never fail him.

That was his first offence. His second was no less heinous. He was a pacifist. He opposed the Three Years' Service law, he was openly and candidly for an accommodation with Germany, and it was his brief tenure of the Premiership, in 1911, that prevented the Agadir episode anticipating the catastrophe that came three years later. He was accused of making terms with Germany, in 1911, behind the back of his Foreign Minister, and the accusation may be true. And it is certainly true that in 1917 he was in favour of a peace by negotiation, and took risks in that respect that might have cost him his life, and did lead to his expulsion from Paris and his isolation as a political and social leper.

But the infamy of these proceedings is much less indisputable in the light of what the knock-out blow policy has cost the world. It is said that he was treacherous to France in wanting to establish livable relations with Germany, but at the end of seven years of the "peace with a vengeance" the establishment of those relations is seen to be the key to European restoration and the only true guarantee of French security. It was said that his pro-German attitude implied hostility to this country, but I have seen no evidence put forward to support that view, and there is no sensible Englishman to-day who would not rejoice if the age-long feud between Gaul and Teuton could be reconciled, and no intelligent person who would deny that such a reconciliation, in lifting the shadow of war from Europe, would lift the shadow of depression from us also.

On the two capital issues—finance and peace—with which his career is associated, therefore, the verdict of time is with him, and it is not improbable that the future will see in the outcast of 1917-1925 the wisest, as it will certainly see the most courageous, mind in French politics. He may be all that his enemies paint him. I do not know, but I suspect that his enemies hate him not for his sins but for his virtues. And the greatest of those virtues is that he has had the courage to tell France the unpalatable truth, and to risk yet another fall in standing for it. And if that is not patriotism, I do not know what test to apply.

xxvii. Charles Chaplin

IT IS probable that when the time in which we live is seen in perspective, it will not be the Great War which will be regarded as the most significant thing that happened in it. Even the greatest wars are only episodes. Cæsar shook the world; but it was not Cæsar who shaped the world. The thing that dictated the history of two thousand years was something that happened in an obscure province of the Roman Empire, something that seemed so negligible at the time that it was not until a century or two had passed that solemn historians began to give it a casual and contemptuous reference. The last of the great religious wars devastated Europe for thirty years, but that tremendous event passed like a cloud, leaving nothing but a memory behind, while the thought of a solitary scholar on the Vistula changed the conception of the universe and the history of mankind.

And it may be that in the mind of the future the two most momentous happenings in the period which we regard as the period of the Great War were the invention of wireless and the invention of the film. These two things have this in common, that they make the whole world one. They obliterate space and bring all mankind from China to Peru within the orbit of the same intimacies of speech and action. The astonishing vogue of Charlie Chaplin is the symbol of this new miracle of universal communion, the ultimate results of which are incalculable. He is not a joke; he is a portent. He is the forerunner of enormous potentialities that will still be shaping the future of civilisation when the war is as vague a legend as the Thirty Years' War. He is important less for what he is than for what he fore-shadows. He is the first man who has realised for us the magnitude of the agency that has projected his personality over the globe.

It is not merely that Chaplin is the most celebrated man in the world, using "celebrity" to imply one who is personally familiar and personally interesting to others: he is the most celebrated man the world has ever known. If you go into the Strand any afternoon or evening you will see the pavement lined with queues of people waiting to see his latest film. Those crowds are typical of what may be seen all the world over, regardless of race or speech, on the plains of Nebraska and on the steppes of Russia, in Tokio and Capetown, in Berlin and in the islands of the Pacific. Everywhere, all round the earth, people—white, black, or yellow—are standing in queues to see Charlie Chaplin. It has been calculated that his daily audience is twelve millions, and it would not surprise me to learn that more than half of the inhabitants of the world's surface are as familiar with his grotesque figure and his quaint antics as I am. He was born in London, but that has nothing to do with the quality of his appeal to those queues in the Strand. He is as intelligible to the Chinese coolie or the Russian peasant as he is to the city clerk, the Lancashire weaver, or the university don. He is as universal as laughter and as common as tears.

It would be idle and foolish to depreciate such a phenom-enon. No doubt Chaplin is the creation of his medium. If there had been no film he would probably have lived and died relatively unknown. It may be so, but I am not sure, for so individual a genius would conceivably have found some expression for itself. But in the dimensions of his success he is of course the creation of his medium. No film, no Charlie. But that being conceded, the fact remains that among all the exploiters of the film, he is not merely first; he is a hierarchy apart. He is so much the King of the film, that he has no rival and no visible successor. He has done what no other experimenter has yet done. He has created an atmosphere. He has projected on to the flat surface of the film a three-dimensional personality that lives and moves and has its being as vividly and intensely as if it moved on the stage or in the street. He is as real and intimate as Harry Lauder. If you pricked him he would bleed and if you tickled him he would laugh.

This extraordinary illusion of reality is due to his intuitive sense of the medium and the delicacy with which he adapts himself to its requirements. His effects are broad, but they are achieved by an infinity of touches, so subtle, so appropriate, so deeply considered and yet so apparently negligent, that they convey the sense of sudden improvisation that belongs to life. He holds the attention by the fecundity of his invention and so creates in the mind of the audience the impression of movement, space, atmosphere. He understands that the language of the film is not that of words, but of gesture. That, of course, is a commonplace which every film artist knows. But his contemporaries conceive of gesture as the accompaniment of the spoken word. They cannot escape from the hypnotism of speech and their action is the action of the stage. Chaplin realised that another medium required another technique. He has created an independent philosophy of gesture which supersedes speech. His body is talking all the time in an idiom of his

CHARLIE CHAPLIN

own, swift, sensitive, eloquent, and as intelligible to the Egyptian fellaheen as to the eyes of Mayfair.

But this technical genius, while it is largely the secret of the illusion of realism, does not explain the unrivalled place which Chaplin holds in the film world. It enables him to make his personality live, but it is the appeal of that personality that counts and it is his creative faculty that is the source of his power. If he is comparable with anybody, it is with Dickens. It is certainly of that great man that he reminds us, both in his art and his outlook. Their origins were not dissimilar. Like Dickens, Chaplin was born in poor circumstances, and lived his most impressionable years in London in surroundings not unlike those which Dickens has immortalised in "David Copperfield." He was an actor at ten—he is still only thirty-six—and such formal education as he had was acquired here, there, and everywhere, at Kennington, at Manchester, and elsewhere, in the intervals of a wandering career.

But he had that sensitiveness to impressions of life that for the artist—as in the case of Wells or Dickens—is so much more important than anything that the schools have to offer. He took those impressions with the same mixture of the comic spirit and the sentimentalism of pity that Dickens had, and it is that early saturation in the humanities of London that colours his feeling and outlook. In the articles which he wrote describing his triumphal visit to London in 1921, it is not the public enthusiasm and the meetings with the celebrities that occupy him so much as his wanderings in the haunts of his boyhood in Kennington, and the human documents that he rediscovers. Here is a passage quite in the spirit of Dickens:

Who is that old derelict there against the cart? Another landmark. I look at him closely. He is the same—only more so. Well do I remember him—the old tomato man. I was about twelve when I first saw him, and he was still here in the same old spot plying the same old trade, while I——

I can picture him as he first appeared to me standing beside his cart heaped with tomatoes. His greasy clothes shiny in their unkemptness, the rather glassy single eye that stared from one side of his face, staring at nothing in particular, but giving you the feeling that it was seeing all.

I remember how I used to stand around and wait for him to shout his wares. His method never varied. There was a sudden twitching convulsion, and he leaned to one side, trying to straighten out the other as he did so, and then, taking into his one good lung all the air it would stand, he would let forth a clattering, gurgling, asthmatic, high-pitched wheeze, a series of sounds that defied interpretation. Somewhere in the explosion there could be detected "ripe tomatoes." Any other part of his message was lost.

And he was still there. Through summer suns and winter snows he had stood and was standing. Only a bit more decrepit, a bit older, dyspeptic, his clothes greasier, his shoulders rounder, his one eye rather filmy and not so all-seeing as it once was. And I waited, but he did not shout his wares any more.

And he is vulgar, as Dickens was, loving the "juicy" vernacular of things and the warm contact with the raw life of the mean streets. But it is a vulgarity touched with a childish innocence that makes even the mean streets full of poetry and wonder. He comes into the great, big, bullying world like a visitor out of fairy land, a small, shuffling figure, grotesque yet wistful, a man yet a child, a simpleton who outwits the cunning, moving through an atmosphere of the wildest farce, yet touching everything with just that suggestion of emotion and seriousness that keeps the balance true. He is in the world but not of it, and the sense of his aloofness and loneliness is emphasised by the queer auto-

matic actions that suggest a spritelike intelligence inform-
ing a mechanical doll. He is always a little sad, and his
large, wondering eyes and faunlike face bespeak a helplessness that asks for mercy from a rough world. He preserves
an elaborate gravity in the most preposterous situations, and
only the ghost of a smile reveals that there is feeling behind
the motions.

It is the contrast between that static innocence and the
demoniacal swiftness and efficiency of the motions that perplexes and delights the mind. Indeed, his art is the art of
contradiction. His clothes are banal and hideous, and would
be unthinkable on anybody if he had not bewitched them.
They are only the accidental reminiscence of his first adventures in the film world and would long have been discarded
if his audience would allow him to discard them. But hideous though they are, they add that quality of bizarre contradiction to the essential delicacy and refinement of the
little chivalrous gentleman inside them. To see the elaborate courtesy with which he lifts his Derby hat to some
outwitted intruder, or the solemnity with which he hitches
up his trousers in some dreadful emergency is to be left
wondering that dignity of manner can redeem vulgarity of
episode and issue in such delighted and innocent mirth.

The key to his drama is as old as drama itself. His
theme is the triumph of the humble and meek over the embattled tyrannies of the world. His innocence is matched
against the overbearing vanity of power, and he is most
successful when he fights the hulking villain who represents
the fatness and iniquities of life. In "The Gold Rush" he
has deserted this motif and made friends with the fat man.
That and the "happy ending," which is not worthy of him,
are the root weaknesses of a film which in other respects

shows his genius and invention at their highest. There should never be a conventional happy ending to a "Charlie" film. He should always be seen shuffling along a lonely road, fading away into the darkness, a grotesque and solitary knight errant, a little melancholy like the immortal Don, having slain the dragon and borne aloft the flag of innocence and virtue in a naughty world, but having achieved nothing for himself, and destined to reappear once more upon the horizon for fresh heroisms, still gloriously absurd, still magnificently triumphant, still bringing gales of laughter with him, but still a little sorrowful, a figure in which the comedy of life is touched with a hint of the abiding pathos of life.

It is no small claim to the gratitude of the world to have brought more innocent merriment into the whole company of mankind than any other man who lives or has lived, and that claim is Charlie Chaplin's. He would not pretend that he has exploited the highest possibilities of the silent drama. In certain respects, in a sombre power of suggestion and beauty of setting, the German film producers are moving that drama on to a plane undreamed of at Hollywood. But Chaplin's contribution to the development of this enormous potentiality is still the greatest personal achievement associated with it, and in the realm of comedy as applied to the film, he is alone. I doubt whether he will explore farther. I doubt whether he ought to explore farther. I think I would have him static, like Father Christmas or Mr. Pickwick, never growing older, never being different but just gathering the world around him and telling it a merry tale with a sad face.

xxviii. Miss Maude Royden

THE pulpit is the last stronghold of sex exclusiveness. It is still inviolate from the touch of feminism, still the preserve of man as the only channel of spiritual communication. The last few years have been loud with the crash of the falling barriers of sex predominance. "The Monstrous Regiment of Women," to use John Knox's phrase, has broken through the sacred enclosure of masculine privilege, and in the secular world the sex discrimination has entirely vanished. In the political, the social, and the professional spheres alike woman has established her right to a place in the sun beyond challenge. There is no career, no recreation, no freedom that man enjoys which woman does not enjoy in equal measure according to her capacity. She has not only won the vote, but she sits in Parliament, and has even made her appearance on the Government bench.

No such revolution in social relationships has ever taken place in human society in so brief a space of time. The whole structure has been shifted from the basis of sex to the basis of citizenship, and the marvel is that so vast a transition has produced so little visible dislocation in the machine of life. Those who feared that the emancipation of women would be the end of all things, and those who believed that it would instantly usher in an earthly paradise have been alike disillusioned. We are hardly more sensible that anything has happened than we are when spring merges into summer, or summer into autumn. The world seems to wag much as it did before, and though we cannot doubt that the ultimate consequences of the revolution will be great and far-reaching, the superficial results are almost negligible. Our alarms have subsided and our hopes have moderated, and if the Duchess of Atholl succeeded Mr. Baldwin as Conservative Prime Minister the only discussion that would be aroused by the change would relate to her intellectual fitness for the office. The fact that she was a woman would not arise. So far have we travelled, almost unconsciously, from the traditions of the past.

But in the spiritual sphere the woman still lies under the ancient stigma of inferiority. "All equal are within the Church's gate," said good George Herbert; but it is probable that when he said it the logical corollary of the utterance— the admission of women to the priesthood—was so unthink- able to him that it did not occur to him. And the thought of the Church on this subject has not advanced appreciably since the seventeenth century. In a few communities, like that of the Society of Friends, the spiritual as well as the temporal equality of the sexes has long been recognised, but alike in the Church of England and the Church of Rome woman is banned.

She has no access to the mysteries. She is inexorably ex- cluded from the priestly function. She may be as saintly as Theresa, as heroic as Joan of Arc, as intellectually powerful as Elizabeth, but not through her can flow the stream of grace. She may be Queen of England, or Prime Minister of England, but she cannot be Bishop of London or Pope of Rome, or even a parish priest or a country curate. The faith that was delivered to the saints in that Upper Room at Jerusalem was delivered into the hands of men only, and in the hands of men only it must remain. The tidal wave that has swept away the secular inequalities of the sexes breaks against the spiritual rock in vain. The world may do justice to woman, but the Church will not. She may worship from the pew, but she must not ascend the pulpit. She may receive the sacraments, but she must not administer them.

And against this exclusion Miss Maude Royden has issued the most formal and sustained challenge that has yet been made. The challenge is implicit even more than explicit. It is expressed in her life and character more than in her actions and words. If it can be said of any that they are born to the priestly function, that they have received the commission to minister to the spiritual needs of men from a source more authentic than any ecclesiastical ordinance, it may be said of Miss Royden. Putting aside the question of sex as an irrelevance, it would not be denied by anyone who has followed her career that she is singularly equipped with the gifts of the preacher and teacher.

When at the invitation of Dr. Fort Newton she went as assistant minister at the City Temple, in 1917, Lord Beaverbrook's newspaper dubbed her a crank, but there are few people to whom that derisive term could be less truly applied. There is an admirable balance and equipoise in her activities and bearing. Intellect and feeling are in harmonious relation. She is neither a blue stocking nor a fanatic. Her feeling is strong, and she is not afraid to give it free expression; but it is under the control of an excellent intelligence and an educated outlook. She comes of a stock that represents the best element in English life. The name of Royden is a name that rings true in Liverpudlian ears. It is the name of a family which has always been prominent in public-spirited causes, and has always stood for the best standards of commercial integrity. Her father, Sir Thomas

Royden, was chairman of the Cunard Line, a position which her brother occupies to-day. She herself, after her educational career at Cheltenham and Oxford, engaged in social work in the slums of Liverpool, and subsequently in parish work in a country district. Then for a period she was an Oxford Extension lecturer in English literature, and later editor of the *Common Cause*.

But she was born for the pulpit and the spiritual life, and she was not the kind of person to be denied her vocation by the obstinate traditions of the past. *"Elle a la voix de cathédrale"* was said of her when, the first woman to occupy Calvin's pulpit, she preached at Geneva. It is resonant and musical, and is the vehicle of a mind that is fresh and vigorous, and of an emotion that is sincere and never extravagant. Johnson's famous gibe does not apply. "A woman preaching," he said, "is like a dog walking on its hind legs: it is not done well, but the wonder is that it is done at all." Johnson was an honest man and if his spirit ever wanders on Sundays in the neighborhood of Eccleston Square, it will have to admit that it is "done well." But of course the gibe never had any truth. The faculty of public speech is as common among women as among men, and in the impoverished state of the pulpit to-day the rejection of the resources which women would bring to its service is lamentable.

Miss Royden is only the most conspicuous example of these resources. She was born in the Anglican communion, and wished to fulfil her vocation within that communion, but the flaming sword of sex inequality has barred her from the pulpit steps. "Women have prophesied, evangelised, converted," she says, "from Priscilla to St. Catherine of Siena, and from St. Catherine to Mrs. 'General' Booth. It avails not. The Church still says 'Let the women keep silence.' Or: 'If they must be talking, let them talk to one another, and in any case don't call it preaching and don't let it be in a church.' But the spirit of God, like the wind, blows where it lists, and even the English Church Union can not prevent the inspiration descending upon a woman."

Against this antiquated denial that women can be the vessels of spiritual service, Miss Royden has warred valiantly, incessantly, but not violently. She has never tied herself to the railings at Fulham Palace or in Dean's Yard, as the political rebels used to lash themselves to the door knocker at 10, Downing Street; but she has nevertheless been a thorn in the side of the Bishop of London. He, good, honest, embarrassed man, does not know what to make of this problem, and in dealing with it has presented a somewhat forlorn figure of amiable futility.

The struggle began in 1918 over the invitation by the rector of St. Botolph's, Bishopsgate, to Miss Royden to preach at the Good Friday service in his church. This, after some hesitation, the Bishop "prohibited," whereupon the rector, Mr. Hudson Shaw, arranged for a service in the parish school. This procedure was repeated in subsequent years. But a new phase of the trouble presented itself later. Shut out of the ministry in her own Church, Miss Royden had become assistant minister at the City Temple, where her pulpit eloquence and her social labours were so successful that when her colleague, Dr. Fort Newton, returned to America, her succession to the pastorate was seriously discussed. Instead, she joined Dr. Percy Dearmer in the establishment of a spiritual and social Fellowship movement at the Kensington Town Hall on Anglican lines. The enterprise was extraordinarily successful, but the need of a church became apparent, and Dr. Dearmer applied for permission to use St. Philip's Church, a chapel-of-ease in Buckingham Palace Road, which had long been closed. At first the Bishop seemed to be disposed to agree; but subsequently panic seized him and the permission was refused.

With the failure of this attempt to carry on her work within the Anglican Church, Miss Royden and Dr. Dearmer secured the lease of the Congregational Church in Eccleston Square, where, since the retirement of her colleague, Miss Royden has carried on the work alone. If it is as the protagonist of women in the claim to equality "within the Church's gate"—equality not merely in the pew, but in the pulpit—that Miss Royden acquires significance, she is not without importance as a personal influence apart from that fact. It is not on the ground of sex that she exercises that influence. She fights for the liberty of women not as women, but as citizens. "Who is the greatest and wisest woman in England?" asked Dr. Fort Newton of Jane Addams on his appointment to the City Temple. "Maude Royden," she replied; "for she wants women to be recognised as human beings and not as a sex." And on the strength of that recommendation by the most famous woman in America Miss Royden was invited to the City Temple.

I should hesitate to say that she is either the wisest or the greatest woman in England, even though the present generation of Englishwomen is not rich in personalities or conspicuous gifts. But she holds the most individual position among the public women of the time. She has devoted herself to religious and social, rather than political work, but her activities touch secular affairs and moral issues. She represents as effectually as anyone the conscience and the moral sense of the community, and her piety is charged with a modern spirit and a freedom from cant that are always refreshing and sometimes a little startling.

"I have learned more of religion from scientists than I have from theologians," she says, and she insists on the frank facing of facts and the honest following of truth wherever it may lead. "I have preached in churches after a service in which the hymns sung had tunes so sentimental and words so dishonest that I have felt when I started to preach that the congregation was debauched. An artist will not worship a god of ugliness, nor a scientist a god who lives on lies. Unfortunately, this is too often the god who is proclaimed from Christian pulpits." She would rather "pick oakum than play whist," but, like another less reputable character, she insists that "there is no reason because we wish to be virtuous that we should give up cakes and ale." She denies at the rejection of the Virgin birth touches the question of t : divinity of Christ, and in regard to the smaller conventions of the Churches she is apt to be a little contemptuous.

Thus, having removed her biretta before preaching on account of the heat, she explained the fact, adding: "But I would seriously ask you: Do you think God really cares whether we are with or without a hat in church?" She has views on all questions from women's dress—"never more admirable than to-day"—to the legitimate child of what she calls the "illegitimate parents," and the starved instincts of the superfluous women who find a baffled release in the adulation lavished on a lap-dog or the parson worship of emotional "religion." Her views on marriage, divorce, and sex are unconventional, and she holds the opinion that human beings can rise from moral lapses much more easily than from "subtler spiritual sins which have so much more respectable an air."

Perhaps, after all, the Bishop of London may be forgiven for not wishing to have so outspoken a spirit on his hands. Has he not Dean Inge already to keep him awake at night with apprehension?

xxix. Mr. L. C. M. S. Amery

IF I were asked to name the most influential member of
the Government, I should not select the Prime Minister.
Mr. Baldwin drifts amiably about from all points of the
compass according to any breath of wind that blows upon
him or any turn of the tide that overtakes him. Nor should
I choose Mr. Churchill, in spite of his restless energy and
his intrepidity in debate, for Mr. Churchill is an adventurer
without any philosophy of life or affairs except the philosophy of action. I should name the most dour, the most
drab, the least popularly attractive figure in the Cabinet.
To the public, Mr. Leopold Charles Maurice Stennett
Amery is a name and nothing more. In private relations he
is a man of attractive parts and manners, but in public life
no man has reached the front rank with so few of the arts
of popular appeal or with so little success in impressing his
personality on the public mind.

Pugnacity and personal courage are often a way to the
general heart. The plain man loves a first-class fighting
man. It was his quality of pugnacity that largely endeared
Joseph Chamberlain to the populace. It admired him much
as it admired a champion boxer who could always be relied
on to "down" his man and give the company good sport.
But even Mr. Amery's pugnacity and physical courage have
not succeeded in making him a popular character. His taste
for the noble art is notorious, and he has brought the practice of it into the political arena and even on to the floor of
the House. At one of his meetings, when someone called

him a "liar," he promptly leapt from the platform and knocked him down. And when Mr. Buchanan, the Labour M.P. for the Gorbals divisions of Glasgow, resenting Mr. Amery's reference to his "sob-stuff," called him "a swine and a guttersnipe," he approached him as the members were separating: "Did you say that?" he asked. "Yes," replied the other. "Well, then, take that," said Mr. Amery, striking him a blow on the face, and but for the intervention of members there would have been "ploody noses" that day on the floor of the House. But, somehow, not even this episode succeeded in making Mr. Amery either famous or infamous. It left the public curiously indifferent and antipathetic to him.

And the reason is not obscure. His public form, contrary to his private manner, is hard, arid, vitriolic. No humorous legend attaches itself to his name, and no kindliness of spirit or gaiety of expression graces his acts or utterance. When he came into the House for South Birmingham, in 1911, after a series of electoral defeats at Wolverhampton and Bow and Bromely, he became immediately conspicuous, not only by his extreme Die-hardism, but by the insolence of his controversial methods and the intensity of his personal animus towards opponents. Thus, on one occasion, he described Mr. Asquith as "a worn-out old party hack" and on another, Mr. Lloyd George as "the Welsh cheapjack." These civilities may pass on a country platform, but they were new to Parliament, and, as the "guttersnipe" incident later showed, Mr. Amery can resent them as vigorously as anybody when he is the object of them.

And just as he did not hesitate to fling stones at his enemies, neither did he fear to break the unwritten rules of public life. He would drag the name of the King into public controversy, as in a speech at Dewsbury in the midst of the Ulster rebellion in 1914, in which, warning the King against being made a party to the coercion of Ulster, he said:

If that happens Ministers would be disgraced and I hope they would also be punished. I daresay the people in their anger will string some of them up to the lamp posts, but nothing will take away the remorse of his Majesty if he has to put his hand to an instrument of blood guiltiness.

Acerbity of this extravagant sort needs some quality of wit and good nature or of imaginative flair to make it palatable even to the partisan, and as that quality is absent from Mr. Amery's equipment, his failure to reach the public mind is explained. If he disappeared from public life to-morrow he would leave no sense of vacancy behind him even in his own ranks.

Nevertheless, I do not think it can be denied that he is the most influential member of the Government. It was he, more than any other single person, who engineered Mr. Baldwin's plunge into Protection, in 1923. It was he who, when he was First Lord of the Admiralty, initiated the Singapore naval-base scheme. It was his pertinacious industry and quality of will that revived the scheme after the MacDonald Ministry had fallen and Mr. Baldwin had returned to power with Mr. Amery himself now in office as Minister for the Colonies. It was he who was chiefly responsible in the Cabinet for defeating Mr. Churchill over the construction of new ships for the Navy, and it is he to-day who had his masterful way in the controversy over Mesopotamia. Wherever action is afoot, wherever Diehardism is lifting up its head, wherever the spirit of force, untaught by the war, is in the ascendant in the affairs of the Government, it is Mr. Amery who is the driving force.

And while the reason for his personal unpopularity is plain, the reason for his influence is no less intelligible. Stuart Mill said that one man with a conviction is more powerful than ninety-nine who have only interests. Now, whatever Mr. Amery's deficiencies, no one will deny the intensity of his conviction and the obstinate, almost inspired, tenacity with which he pursues it. He has, what few men in public life have, and what no one in the present Government has in anything like the same measure, a constant philosophy of affairs and an undeviating aim. There is about him the fixity of the fanatic and the force of the fanatic. His appearance bears the signature of this intensity. The square, pugnacious face, the stiff, challenging carriage of the head, the taut little body and the exiguous but astonishingly active legs give the impression of a man of enormous physical vitality and of inflexible purpose. You would say he was a good man to go tiger-hunting with. You would never need to worry about what he was doing or whether he was playing the game. You would know he was after the tiger all the time, and not too concerned about his own skin.

The form his fanaticism takes is that of Imperialism. It is customary to compare him with Milner, and it is true that he may be said to be a pocket edition of the Milner of the Boer War period. But he is a Milner without the large, humane interludes of the original, without his glimpses into more spacious atmospheres and that deep sympathy with the social problem that underlay his cold exterior. It is of the Milner of the "Damn-the-consequences" that he alone reminds us. Like Milner, he is a product of Balliol, where he graduated after a career at Harrow, where he was a contemporary of Mr. Churchill.

Like Milner, too, he has alien blood in his veins. It is

THE RT. HON. L. C. M. S. AMERY, P.C., M.P.

a little singular that the two most fanatical Imperialists of our time should have had this in common. It is the more singular in Mr. Amery's case because his passionate Nationalism has none of the liberal sentiment and tolerance of other peoples which Milner possessed. He is a Chinese Wall of national exclusiveness. Yet on the maternal side he is a product of those larger sanities of British rule of which he is the bitterest foe. His mother, married to Charles F. Amery, an officer in the Indian Forest service—Mr. Amery himself was born in India in 1873—was a sister of Dr. Gottlieb Wilhelm Leitner, a Hungarian. Dr. Leitner was a very remarkable man. Born in Budapest, the son of a Jewish doctor in Constantinople he became distinguished as an Oriental scholar and a linguist. He spoke twenty-five languages, and while still little more than a boy was appointed an interpreter to the British forces in the Crimea. He afterwards became Principal of the Government College at Lahore. For in those days this misguided country even used foreign brains in its Indian service. If it had not done so there would have been no Mr. Amery at the Colonial Office, for it was in the Punjab that the sister of the Hungarian Principal of Lahore College and Mr. Amery's father met. And it is to his Hungarian ancestor that we must attribute his remarkable gift of tongues.

With this somewhat cosmopolitan origin, it is strange to find in Mr. Amery the most intense expression of nationalism in public life—a Die-hard after the heart of and pattern of the *Morning Post*. It is as though he would wipe out the element of the alien in his origin by being more English and more patriotic than any mere Englishman can possibly hope to be. He envisages a world in which the British Empire, armed to the teeth, self-contained, neither buying nor selling with mere foreigners, looms menacing and tremendous over the world. The war and its lessons have passed him by like a rumour on the wind. Prussianism, destroyed in its birthplace at infinite cost, lives triumphantly in his fiery and aggressive spirit. He thinks only in terms of force and scorns the soft-headed and soft-hearted slobberers who prattle of peace, disarmament, and the substitution of the reign of law for the reign of gunpowder in a world where gunpowder is King. His philosophy is indistinguishable from that which seemed so incredible in the days of the war when it came to us in the name of Treitschke and Bernhardi. Was it possible that there could be men who thought like this?

Mr. Amery thinks like this. Being an honest man, he acts like this. No lip service from him to that nonsense about the League of Nations. No sham pleas for disarmament. "I do not believe that actual disarmament is anything but a figment of the imagination," he said at Oxford, in 1923, when he was First Lord of the Admiralty. "I do not believe that we can go far towards a reduction of armaments by a mere mechanical scheme." That was, and is his attitude toward the "mechanical scheme" of the Washington Conference, towards the League, towards all the chicken-hearted sentimentalists who want peace in a world constructed as a stage for eternal war. What do we want with Leagues? Is not the British Empire League enough—"no artificial" League, but the real thing, founded on reeking tube and iron shard?

And he acts accordingly. He drives through his mischievous Singapore folly. He fights his own Government when gleams of sanity visit them. When the Geddes inquiry proposed reductions of expenditure in the Navy he came boldly out with a document aimed at destroying what was in fact the policy of his Government. He has revived Singapore: he has overridden Mr. Churchill's crusade for naval economy: he would commit us to the permanent occupation of Mesopotamia, not because he cares twopence for the mandates of the League, but because the passion to paint a bit more of the world red is irresistible to his infantile conception of what constitutes a greatness of a nation. The League will go like the shadow it is and like the figment that it stands for, and leave us masters of a bit more desert. The story of Ireland, the story of Egypt, the story of South Africa are lost upon him just as the story of the war is lost upon him. The more the crude Die-hardism which enslaves him is exposed the more obstinately he clings to it, for he learns nothing and forgets nothing. He broke the Baldwin Government of 1923 by his infatuated belief in the nostrum of Protection: "Protection is the only policy which can give us a cheap loaf, cheap boots, or cheap anything else," he said then—and it would be no reckless indulgence in prophesy to predict that he will break Mr. Baldwin again on the same derelict issue.

For he has the force as well as the wrong-headedness of the zealot. "Damn the consequences" and forge straight ahead is his maxim, and he has learned that by the impetus and driving power of conviction it is possible to ram any gospel down the throats of colleagues who have none. A formidable man. Able, industrious, brave, sincere, with the philosophy of a barbarian, the vision of a heathen world and the sombre frenzy of a dervish of the desert.

xxx. "Jim" Thomas

MR. J. H. THOMAS probably knows more people by their familiar names, Tom, Dick and Harry, than any man of his time. If you, being, let us say, a person in high politics, asked him whether he had seen "Arthur" lately, he would not say "I beg your pardon." He would quite understand that you were referring to Lord Balfour. If he had anything to relate in connection with his esteemed leader it would be related in the terms of "Mac" and "Jim." This colleague is "Philip" and that one "Josh," a certain eminent Elder Statesman is "the Old Man," and a distinguished lady politician "Nancy." Nor is this companionable spirit confined to the upper classes or the celebrities among whom he moves in public life. There is hardly a railway man in the land who would not call him "Jim," and whom he would not call Jack or Reub or Tom, as the case might be.

In short, Mr. Thomas is very much at ease in the world. Some of us are never at ease in it. We are doubtful about ourselves or doubtful about other people. We are either too haughty or we are too humble, or we are both. We share the disquietude of the poet:

> In this house with starry dome,
>   Floored with gem-like lakes and seas,
> Shall I never be at home,
>   Never wholly at my ease?

There has never been a moment in his life when Mr. Thomas was not entirely at home and very comfortable indeed. He comes into the inn of the world with the breezy assurance of an old habitué, who has known the landlord since he was a boy, and is as hail-fellow-well-met in the best parlour as he is in the taproom. He beams his broadest smile all round, cracks his joke with the easy liberality of a man who has plenty of them to scatter abroad, thumps this one on the back, and digs that one in the ribs. He will be as confidential with a duke as with a dustman, and will give either of them the civility of a wink in the most agreeable manner. He does not pick and choose. He spends himself royally, and will be as cordial and nice to a prince of the blood as he will to Tom the engine driver or Dan the signalman.

He has made the discovery that a cheery way will carry you anywhere and that human nature in the best parlour is much the same as in the taproom. The railway men love "Jim" because he is obviously one of themselves and the social world delights in him because he is so refreshingly unembarrassed. He neither fears the great nor frowns at them, but just makes them feel at home. He gives them the comfortable impression that they are as good as he is, and that it has never occurred to him that they are any better.

Mrs. Sidney Webb has suggested that there is artifice in this, and that his "deliberately persistent dropping of his 'h's,' like the red rouge on a star actress's lips, is an artistic touch" that gives an unmistakable note of audacious and uncompromising personality. I am sure Mrs. Webb means well, and I do not suggest that Mr. Thomas is not an artist— still less that he is not artful. No one who can put so much significance into a wink can be quite innocent of artfulness. And indeed he is artful. I can imagine him, like Joey Bagstock, confessing to himself that "Jimmy T. is sly, sir, devilish sly."

But it is a mistake to suppose that the liberties he takes with the parts of speech are a calculated cleverness. They are not a defiance of law, but a natural expression of himself. If he wants an "h" in or out for emphasis he puts it in or out, as the humour seizes him. He is not ashamed that he is not scholarly, but neither is he proud of the fact. He is content to be himself, plain Jim Thomas, and you must take him or leave him at that. There is nothing to be excused or explained. If you have started your career as an errand boy at nine, and graduated as a cleaner of engines and spent the prime of your life as a fireman and engine driver, there is no need to apologise for a lapsed aspirate or a singular verb with a plural noun.

Mr. Thomas's education has been acquired not from books but from first-hand contact with vast masses of men, and he has emerged from the experience one of the most skilful and agile figures on the public stage. He is the most representative and powerful trade unionist of his time, and his generalship of the great organisation with which he has been associated has by common consent been a triumph of good sense and sagacity. No trade union official, perhaps, ever did so much for his men as he has done. The position of the railwaymen before the war was a notorious scandal. One hundred thousand of them were below the £1 a week line, and the service was seething with discontent. All this has been changed, and to-day the railwaymen, instead of being the underdog in the industrial world, are in a more enviable position than almost any other section of the working-class community, with a decent wage, reasonable hours, and a secure employment.

It is these practical results of his leadership that give him so strong a hold on his fellows. They do not mind his hobnobbing with dukes on such easy terms if he "delivers the goods" to them. Indeed they rather like it. They like to hear of him patting Prime Ministers on the back and putting his arm affectionately through that of the American President, and telling Majesty itself a few plain truths about things. They like it because in spite of it all he remains so indubitably their man. And they like it none the less because he is also their master.

That is the most remarkable thing about the relationship. For the trouble in the labour world is the distrust of the leaders and the insecurity of their position. They are always under criticism from the firebrands who want their office and are ready to bid relentlessly for it. If they are honest, they fall; and if they are dishonest and timid, they yield and are stampeded into courses which they know to be mistaken. It is Mr. Thomas's rare distinction that he has kept the confidence and loyalty of his men without sacrificing his judgment in order to do so. He has the courage to throw his career into the balance—"to win or lose it all."

There was a remarkable instance of this intrepidity, in 1918, when, in defiance of the official decision, an unauthorised strike of grave dimensions broke out among the railway men in South Wales. Mr. Thomas went down and battled with the insurgents on the spot, and when, after four days' desperate conflict, he had triumphed he delivered his master stroke. He resigned his leadership of the union. If authority was to be disregarded, then let someone else be responsible for the anarchy that would follow. If the spirit of discipline was to be restored, the men themselves must restore it.

It was an adroit piece of strategy. It was indeed more than strategy. It was a stroke of statesmanship, for it compelled the men to face the conditions on which organised labour could alone exist. And the result justified the wisdom of the challenge, for from every quarter an avalanche of resolutions of confidence in Mr. Thomas poured in from the branches of the union, and he resumed the office he had vacated with the new authority that so decisive a verdict for constitutionalism in the labour movement had given him.

That is typical of the man. He is capable of bold decisions and masterful strokes. He has, among other resemblances, much of the nimbleness of his fellow-countryman, Mr. Lloyd George. He can be deaf when he does not want to hear, and smother a point he does not want to see. Thus, at the Trade Union Congress at Portsmouth, a delegate rises with: "A point of order, Mr. Chairman." The Chairman listens, and when the point has been stated remarks briskly: "That's your point of order? Right. Now let's get on." And before the interrupter can recover from the breezy irrelevance of the chair, the discussion has passed him by.

It is this agility that has made him one of the most successful Parliamentarians that the Labour movement has produced. There are better speakers among his colleagues. He has fluency, but no sense of form, and his emphasis is overemphatic. The week-end tonics he has for years administered to his railway men have communicated a certain sensationalism to his speech which is apt to sound forced and flamboyant in Parliament. But no one plays the Parliamentary game with nimbler foot than he does, and few men are so adroit in getting out of an awkward entanglement in debate. He knows the use of red-herrings as well as anyone, and, when on the Treasury bench, was as ready to save the face of a colleague as his own by setting the hounds off on a new scent. It does not surprise me to be told that he is among the first-class bridge players of the day, for he has that combination of quick wits and calculating judgment which I imagine are the essentials of success in that art. In all this and much else he is a Welshman. Mr. Lloyd George knows all his methods and his arts. When at some conference he was engaged in exploiting those arts his fellow-countryman observed: "That's all very well, Thomas, but you must remember that I'm a Welshman too."

It has been said by a witty member of the Labour Party that the British working man is about as revolutionary as the Christmas pudding. In this respect, Mr. Thomas is as representative of his class as anyone. I do not suppose that he has ever read Karl Marx, and though he pays homage to the jargon of the street corner, and makes the necessary allusions to the "proletariat," he has the Christmas-pudding view of things. It is the conviction that he is only a sheep in wolf's clothing that makes him so insufferable a torment to the more austere comrades. They do not believe that he really wants a revolution, and I think they are right. They hint darkly—after the manner of that hot-gospeller, Mr. A. J. Cook—at his riches, openly denounce his painful familiarity with loyalty and aristocracy, scoff at his Privy Councilorship, and reproach him with the infamy of having his sons educated at the University. When they draw a portrait of him, it is like this (from "The Worker"):

The crawling, slimy, tearful hypocrite, crooning like a dove and acting like a noxious reptile, garbed like a lamb, but with the hidden fangs of a cruel wolf, friend and councillor of Labour so that he might deliver it to the shambles more easily—this is the Labour leader type that has made British Labour a by-word and a reproach throughout the world. Does Mr. J. H. Thomas approximate to the above?

The answer, from the Clydeside point of view, is un-doubtedly in the affirmative. He does not want a bloody revolution, and he has no belief in the cure of human ills by a surgical operation. He has found the world a very toler-able place, and he has no complaint against a social and political system that has enabled the Newport errand boy to ride with the King in the train that he used to drive and to become a Minister of the Crown and a potential Premier. He is not a doctrinaire, but an empiric and an opportunist, not forgetful of himself, but genuinely loyal to his class, doing his best to improve their condition and, so far as he has a political philosophy, working for an accommodation between the opposing interests of society. He would rather have a peace by negotiation than by the knock-out blow, and he is happier in stopping a strike than in fomenting one. His bark is very loud, but he bites only under compulsion, and he incurred the undying enmity of the "fight-to-a-finish" advocates by smashing the Triple Alliance rather than hold the nation at ransom. He has no passion for dying in the last ditch or battling for forlorn causes, and though he will sing the "Red Flag" as heartily as anyone, he was a warm corner in his affections for the Union Jack. How long he and Mr. Wheatley will feed out of the same trough under the humorous fiction of the solidarity of Labour is not the least engaging problem of politics.

xxxi. Bernard Shaw

I AM sorry for Mr. Shaw. Joan at least had to wait some centuries before she was canonised, but Mr. Shaw is in peril of being canonised while he still walks the earth. He is already as respectable as a Minor Canon, Deans have been known to invite him to their garden parties and Archbishops are not unfavourably disposed towards him. The critics, worn out with years of vain effort to suppress so pestilent a fellow, have swung round to the view that he must, after all, be a man of genius. They no longer laugh when they mention him in connection with Shakespeare. They are beginning to be apprehensive lest the future should discover that they were dunces who did not know a great man when they saw him and who were incapable of understanding what he was talking about and what he was driving at. He is a best seller in the book world, and the public flock to his plays and come out with a shine in their eyes and discuss his meanings. He has already become a classic, and there is a dim but unmistakable gleam of an aura about his brow. If I do not mistake the symptoms, he is on the way to the calendar of saints. He has passed the threshold of his seventieth year, and though the fiery red beard has turned white, he still "treads the ling like a buck in spring, and looks like a lance in rest." He may quite well become one of his own Ancients and live to see himself in stained glass windows as the St. Bernard of a new dispensation.

And this would be the most insufferable revenge that the world he has flouted and scourged and mocked for a generation could inflict on him. For he knows that when a prophet is accepted and deified, his message is lost. The prophet is only useful so long as he is stoned as a public annoyance, calling us to repentance, disturbing our comfortable routines, breaking our respectable idols, shattering our sacred conventions. If Mr. Shaw were a vain man, of course, he would enjoy being popular, respected, and admired. But he is not a vain man, although he has said more vain things about himself than any man of his time. "I am a natural-born mountebank," he says, and he has played the trumpeter to himself with the brazenness of a showman at a fair. "With the single exception of Homer," he once wrote, "there is no eminent writer, not even Sir Walter Scott, whom I can despise so utterly as I despise Shakespeare when I measure my mind against his. The intensity of my impatience with him occasionally reaches such a pitch that it would positively be a relief to me to dig him up and throw stones at him."

That extravagant nonsense—and in the vast output of the man it can be frequently matched—sounds like vanity turned to delirium; but I repeat that Mr. Shaw, in spite of his public pose and his showman's tricks, is not merely not vain, but is one of the least self-regarding and self-absorbed of men. He is, quite frankly, an imposter who has, for the purposes of advertising his wares—that is, his ideas—carved a caricature of himself, decked with cap and bells, to keep the public gaping and talking, reserving for his friends the discovery that behind the absurd grotesque there is a man of rare sweetness of manner and infinite good nature, who does not care twopence for his own career, but will go to endless pains to help you in yours, and who is more free from the smaller vices of jealousy and envy than any contemporary of similar eminence, save one. His generosity is as unflagging as his wit, and I have known him refuse handsome offers that he could have fulfilled with consummate ease, because he was busy re-writing a play for a friend, or performing some equally disinterested office.

The atmosphere he exhales is curiously impersonal and cleansing, and his gay, vivacious talk is as free from the artifice of the conscious wit as it is from the vulgarities of the gossip. It pours out fresh from the mint, bright and scintillating, idea chasing idea, without a note of malice or a touch of personal feeling. He is an impossible man to quarrel with, as Mr. Henry Arthur Jones found, for though he may riddle your fancies with his irony and his mockery, he disengages you from your follies and goes on loving you as a fellow-mortal. He does not, therefore, want the deification with which he is threatened to soothe his vanity, and I am sure that he fears it as an enemy to his influence. He does not want to become an established reputation—a prophet who is accepted, worshipped and ignored. He wants to be a battle-cry, a bone of contention, a theme for eternal wrangles at street corners. For only in that way can his preaching remain vital.

That he is a preacher first, and only the prince of modern dramatists and a score of other things by the way, goes without saying. Whatever medium he adopts, he converts it into a pulpit, and however fantastic his utterance may be, it is always a sermon. It is only a shallow convention that the preacher must be dull and decorous. "The great," says Emerson, "will not condescend to take anything seriously; all must be gay as the song of a canary, were it the building of cities or the eradication of old and foolish churches." And though Shaw is as gay as a canary he is as obsessed as

Bunyan by the plight of the City of Destruction and as passionate a missionary of salvation as Loyola.

The popular idea that he is a mere iconoclast, an agent of destructive purposes, is at last seen to be mistaken. It should have been apparent long ago, for his religion of life has been implicit in all his multitudinous activities. It is not an orthodox religion, although it approximates to it much more nearly than it is customary to suppose. It is the religion of the Living Spirit in man triumphing over the dead letter of prescription. It is the religion of the optimist who believes that the best is yet to be, and that growth, Creative Evolution, is the law of our being. But to nourish that growth the vital flame must not be quenched by custom and convention. It must be eternally renewed, and the lamp must be unceasingly cleansed of all the accretions of time.

He would not have the dead Joan canonised, but the fierce spirit of Joan working in the living hearts of men. If he throws stones at Shakespeare, it is not because he is so foolish as not to appreciate the greatness of Shakespeare, but because he believes Bardolatry is as deadening as any other idol worship, and because the creative power that kindles us to life must express itself in new forms and new terms. "Sponge out the past," he says—not because the past has nothing to teach, but because we must rewrite its faded script ourselves. Let us press forward to the new vision and the new adventure, and escape from the tyranny of the past to wider horizons and free untrammelled thought. Every generation should have its own fresh, fearless expression. "All this academic art is far worse than the trade in sham antique," he says. The cake of custom rests like a blight on the living spirit of men. The cruelties of society are cruelties practised by kind people who have ceased to feel and whose understanding is sterilised by tradition.

And filled with this fury he launched his shafts of satire and mockery at the structure of society, turning the theatre that had become the temple of a stale, unprofitable drama of "situations" on the sex theme, into a forum where ideas wrestled and tumbled each other in an atmosphere of boisterous fun, and where effete marriage laws, and empty creeds, and outworn political systems, and sweating in the factories, and the cruelties of vivisection, and the ways of doctors, and the meaning of prostitution, and a score of other aspects of the social and spiritual malaise that was the inheritance from an unchallenged and obsolete tradition were brought under the scalpel of his criticism.

In this prodigal outpouring of his comments on society, he has incidentally changed the whole function of the drama, dismissed the sentimentalisms and romantic falsities on which it rested, and made it the vivacious vehicle of the urgencies and realities of life. But the reform of the theatre and the rekindling of the flame of ideas in the drama were only the by-products of his larger purpose. His theme was not art but life. It is not surprising that so challenging and uncompromising an attack on all the accepted sanctities of custom filled the timid and the comfortable with alarm and disquiet. Nothing is so sacred as a rut, and no one more annoying than he who jolts us out of it.

And Shaw took no pains to make his medicine pleasant. He laughed at us, gibed at us, insulted us. He brought "Britannicus" on the stage as a gorgeous guy to pillory our hypocrisies and sentimentalisms. And we retaliated by seeing in him only a desperate anarch, filled with the hatred of our holy things, smashing our images, and defiling our sanctuaries. The fastidious asceticism of his life was too notorious to make him suspect on the grosser plane of things, but his mockery of our moralities left him, nevertheless, the most undeniable lieutenant of the Prince of Darkness.

And then, with "Androcles and the Lion," with its brilliant preface on the Christianity of Christ and the Christianity of the churches, the sky began to clear about the activities of this extraordinary man. And with "St. Joan," the sun of Shaw shone full and clear. We began to see that his aim was not destructive but restorative, and that he sought only to ridicule us out of our bad habits and our obsolete moralities in order that the flame of life might be trimmed afresh to burn more purely and brightly. His religion became clear in its appeal to the individual conscience. He has shed something of his faith in democracy and, as Mr. J. S. Collis shows in his illuminating study, "Shaw," he touches Toryism on the one hand and Bolshevism on the other in his views of government. Democracy, he says, must decide the thing to be done; but democracy doing the thing is like leaving the passengers to run the train.

But if confidence in the collective wisdom is weakening, the faith in the individual conscience is undimmed. His Puritanism is nearer to the "inner light" of George Fox than it is to the harsh determinism of John Calvin. The divinity that shapes our ends works within us as well as without, and conscience can make cowards or heroes of us all. When Blanco Posnet is asked what he means by a noble action, he replies that if you do the wrong thing you have "a rotten feel," and if you do the right thing you "lose the rotten feel." It is not the Fox vernacular; but it contains the core of Fox's teaching, and of Shaw's, too.

In spite of his many virtues you are conscious that there

is some deficiency in him that leaves him a little unhuman, rather like one of those "Robots" in the play, an astonishingly perfect and accomplished machine, but bloodless, tearless, laughterless. He is not one of us as greater men have been of us, as Shakespeare was of us. He is outside the cosy family of men, a bleak, companionless spirit who pities us, scoffs at us, derides us, but does not understand us, because something is missing. He has given us a clue to the mystery. He does not play games. He not only does not play them, he is puzzled at the folly of people who do play them. Still more at the folly of the people who go to see them played. He was born into a playless world. He sits aghast at the silliness of all sport. It is meaningless to him. "I cannot endure the boredom of sport," he says. Least of all, apparently, can he endure the boredom of cricket. He went one day to witness the "Baseball madness," and though he was left wondering at the end which was the bigger fool, the man who plays it or the man who goes to see it played, and though he frankly confessed that he did not know what it was about, he wrote an article to prove that it was a better game than cricket, which "in slowness and stupidity is without parallel or rival."

But with all his extravagances and limitations, he is the brightest spirit in the world to-day, and there is no one whose passing would so eclipse the gaiety of nations or so impoverish the spiritual exchequer of mankind. He once told me that Tolstoi complained to him, apropos of "Blanco Posnet," that he seemed to be treating life as if it were a joke, and that he replied that if it was a joke, he wanted to make it a good joke. He has worked gloriously in that enterprise, and we are all his debtors. He has whipped us for our sins, but he has made us merry in spite of our stripes, and we cannot help loving him because, in his translunar way, he loves us. Hence the halo that begins to gather about his brows. It will be a great nuisance to him, but he will have to wear it. And there are compensations. Just as in his red-beard days he was an excellent Mephistopheles, so in his white-beard eld he will be a most presentable saint. For why should a saint not have a twinkle in his eye and a jest upon his lips?

xxxII. Sybil Thorndike

I SUGGESTED that we should go to the Empire. My visitor, a decorous and no longer youthful lady from the provinces, made a gesture of surprise, touched with just a suspicion of having heard something scandalous. "The Empire!" she said. . . . "In Leicester Square!" she said. "Yes, the Empire in Leicester Square," I said, ruthlessly. "But ——" "Yes, I know. You are thinking of the 'nineties and Mrs. Ormiston Chant. But the former things have passed away. To-night we will go to the Empire to see Sybil Thorndike in 'Henry VIII.'" The surprise remained, but the horror was transfigured. If I had suggested going to St. Paul's to hear the Archbishop of Canterbury, I could not have made a proposal more *comme il faut*, as the ladies of Troy Town would say. For it is not the least of Sybil Thorndike's claims on our respectful attention that her name has become a standard around which the earliest of Victorians may safely foregather, and when, like St. Joan, she advanced her banners into the midst of the naughtiness of Leicester Square, she brought with her all her ever-widening circle of admirers trooping to her call with the bright-eyed enthusiasm of crusaders.

The interest she arouses is unlike that awakened by any other contemporary personality of the stage. There may be room to question her supremacy of the stage, merely as an artist. When, on the occasion of the Manchester University conferring on her the degree of Doctor of Laws, Dr. Alexander, in his eulogy of her at the Free Trade Hall, com-

261

pared her with Duse, she shook her head deprecatingly. If politeness forbids us to shake our heads with her, we may at least hold them in suspense. She is certainly a very considerable actress, with a remarkable range of gifts; but it is too soon to allot her a place among the stars of the first magnitude. We have not yet seen the full orbit of her powers, for she is still young, and she is still learning with astonishing industry and intelligence, and there is about all she does the promise of unexplored possibilities.

But there is a sense in which Sybil Thorndike is more important than she would be even if her rank among the stars of the first magnitude were already assured. She exhales an influence that transcends the stage, that relates the stage to life and the things of the mind and the spirit that is quite new and individual. There is nothing more narrowing than the professional training. It is exclusive and excluding. It exalts its own fetish and sees all outside the communion as the Jew of old saw the Gentile rabble. The more skillful the professional man is in his calling the more limited the range of his general sympathies is apt to be. There was wisdom as well as experience in Bethsheba Everdene, in "Far from the Madding Crowd," when, wanting a sensible opinion on a plain matter of conduct, she went, not to her lawyer or her doctor, but to Farmer Oak, who had no professional limitations to conform to.

This absorption of the profession in itself is nowhere more marked and more limiting than in the case of the stage. The professional actor is subdued to what he works in. He becomes saturated with the atmosphere of the theatre. He lives in a world of artifice and shadows, on a plane which is not life, but a phantom projection of life. He reverses the truth of things. His artifice is the reality, and the world of action outside is seen through the veil of his artifice. The more successful he is the more remote he is from the actual current of things. Irving was as much an actor off the stage as on and Sarah Bernhardt smacked the face of her manager just as histrionically as she died her thousand deaths on the stage. Beerbohm Tree was an amazingly astute man of the world; but, then, he was not an actor. It is true that Garrick lived on terms of equality with the most brilliant company of his time; but even he, if we are to believe Goldsmith, did not escape the penalty, and was most an actor when he was off the stage.

Now, Sybil Thorndike is free from this tyrannous subjection to the medium she works in. She is an actress with a personality that escapes the histrionic atmosphere. Her intelligence is not exclusively of the stage. Her life does not begin with the footlights and end with the painted scenery. Her art is not a self-contained and excluding interest, sufficient to itself, intolerant of any competing passion. It is not an end in itself, but a medium for the expression of something greater than itself. Bernhardt without the emotions and glitter of the stage would have been unthinkable; but Sybil Thorndike's personality is independent of the footlights. You can imagine her in any other calling without doing any violence to the impression she gives. If she had devoted herself to the piano—as in her childhood seemed probable, for she was something of an infant musical prodigy —she would still have been the Sybil Thorndike we know.

This unprofessional habit of mind would seem to be a handicap in a calling that demands the complete surrender of personality to the emotion. The actress must be a reed shaken by the wind. Passion must be uncontrolled, and the fewer the normal restraints it has to suffer the wider and freer is its flight. It may be that those restraints will prevent Sybil Thorndike ever reaching quite the altitude of the fixed stars. But in another sense her individuality is the secret of her peculiar appeal. She hitches the drama to the general activities of life. It is not a thing apart without a conscience or an aim. It is an instrument for enriching the quality of life, and it is this sense that, behind the artist, there is the spirit of a crusader fighting less for a personal triumph than for an ideal of the stage that is the source of the interest she awakens in multitudes of minds ordinarily indifferent to the acted drama. It is as the St. Joan of the British stage that she leads her battalions to Leicester Square.

But in laying emphasis on this aspect of Sybil Thorndike's career, we must not immolate the actress on the altar of the reformer. She has a gospel, a very noble gospel, but it is a gospel that derives its impulse from her own genius for her art. Although we may withhold our assent to Dr. Alexander's comparison of Sybil Thorndike with Duse, we shall do so without regarding it as mere flattery. If there is anyone on the English stage who may be mentioned in such a connection without disrespect or irony, it is Miss Thorndike. If she is not the equal of the greatest she is of their company. She belongs to the great tradition of the tragic muse with as high an authority as any English actress since Mrs. Siddons.

Nature and art alike have equipped her for the rôle. She has not the august profile that Gainsborough and Reynolds have made us familiar with in the case of Siddons, but the broad brow, blue, candid, direct eyes, and angularity of feature are not unfitted for the tragic theme. Her figure is tall, straight and challenging, and her carriage has a sweep and imperiousness that give a sense of power. In the court scene in "Henry VIII." and in "The Medea" she communicates to the mind that feeling of physical extension that she has told us she experiences herself in intense moments. "I felt ten feet high that day," she said, speaking of her performance of "Lady Macbeth" in Paris; "and it is perhaps a remarkable fact that under great emotional stress I always feel enormously tall. It is a strange feeling: I seem to be on a higher plane, looking down on the audience from a vast height."

This spiritual exaltation is under the governance of a stern and instructed discipline. She has said of Duse that "she knew all the tricks and used none," and the remark illustrates the acute intelligence she brings to her art. On the stage, as in writing or in painting, what is left out is as important as, often more important than, what is left in. Stendhal's axiom that the adjective is the enemy of the noun has its counterpart in the superfluous gestures, overemphasis and facile tricks of the actor. Nothing remains more vividly in the mind in regard to Coquelin, probably the greatest comedy actor of all time, than the economy of his method. There was no word, or gesture or movement that was idle or irrelevant. Like Jane Austen's incomparable portrait of Mrs. Norris, every stroke told, and the impression left was of a finality, a repose, a flawless unity that dwells in the mind like a sonnet of Keats.

Sybil Thorndike does not reach this high level. Her voice at times shows a tendency to "go over the top"—less than it used, for, as I have said, she is always learning. It is not a voice of exceptional beauty, but it is extraordinarily efficient, and is managed with such skill that her whisper will reach to the back of the pit when the ordinary tones of most of her fellows sound as if they were muffled in wool. Much of her effect is due to this faculty of "getting home," and her attention to her "r's" should make Mr. St. John Ervine purr with delight.

I have spoken of Sybil Thorndike as a tragedy queen, and it is in that character that she finds the truest expression of her genius. She has told us that as a child—for she began her acting career in the nursery of the home of her father, Canon Thorndike of Rochester—her ambition was to play Hecuba and St. Joan. And when at last her ambition was fulfilled, and she had added Joan to Hecuba, she declared that she did not care if she ended in the workhouse. She has much to do that we shall demand of her before that final tragedy is accomplished, and it will be increasingly in the tragic vein, for she alone among living actresses has brought back the fine flower of that culture to the English stage. We have yet to see her in "Lady Macbeth," and now that she has shown that she can fill the most famous temple of folly in London nightly with grave audiences that hang upon her lips, we may assume that she has entered on the royal progress of her career.

But though she is the acknowledged tragedy queen of the English stage, it is not in tragedy alone that she has graduated and won fame. She has explored the whole gamut of her art since the days when she tried her 'prentice hand under the inspiring lead of Miss Horniman at Manchester, from whence she passed to the Old Vic. preparatory to storming the West End and planting her flag on the turrets of Leicester Square. And in this journey she played many a light-hearted rôle from the Fool in "Lear" to "Advertising April." In this long apprenticeship she had the good fortune to have a husband, Mr. Lewis T. Casson, who is a colleague in her art. "There are all the brains behind my fame," she says, pointing to him. "I just do what I am told." It has been one of the happiest partnerships of the stage; but I do not think "Queen Katherine" is quite so negligible off the stage as that. She has a practical intelligence not often associated with such conspicuous emotional gifts, and a disinterested passion for her profession which should do much to transform the stage.

She has no illusions about us. She thinks the English, as a nation, do not care for the theatre. They are interested in good plays rather than in good acting. In so far as there is a genuine passion for the serious drama it is found, not in the twelve-shilling seats, but in the five-and-ninepenny, and it is to the increase of the five-and-ninepenny public that she looks for a new impulse to the drama. But straddling across this prospect is the Apollyon of high theatre rents which limit the welcome to those whose enthusiasm for the fine things of the stage would rekindle its glories and inspire its actors. Those glories have been dimmed by the long run and specialisation. Actors and actresses have the spirit of their calling deadened within them by a damnable iteration —the same play for an infinity of nights until the spark in the bosom, if there ever was one, is dead. Against this intolerable stagnation Joan raises her banner. Her aim has been to march to the conquest of the Philistine West End to the brave music of the Old Vic. There the splendours of the drama chase each other across the stage, and the actors' souls are kept alive by ever-changing stimulus. When she has a theatre of her own, she has said, she will have three plays a week running. Her raid on Leicester Square, we may hope, is the signal of the accomplishment of her ambition.   It would be a lasting shame to London if so fine an actress and so vivid and stimulating a passion for the high things of the drama could not find a permanent home in the heart of our civilisation.

XXXIII. "Jix"

I MEAN no affront by and offer no apology for the title of
this article. When a man has achieved a national nickname
he has achieved much more than a Garter, or a baronetcy, or
a peerage. A man may have a Garter and be unknown to
the world; but to win a soubriquet by which everyone from
Land's End to John o' Groats knows you is to be famous.
A peerage may have no more significance than that you
have brewed good ale or have been a skilful toady. It may
be conferred by a hungry party organiser for a handsome
cheque to the party funds. But a nickname is the tribute of
the public. It is the voice of democracy acclaiming one of its
chief jesters or one of its favourite actors. It is a recognition of a certain quality of mind and character, a certain
breeziness and gaiety, oddness or fancifulness or even fool-
ishness, something that appeals to the humour of men rather
than the gravity of men. It is inconceivable that anyone
ever called Milton "Jack." It would have sounded almost
like sacrilege. But Shakespeare was "Will" to all his
friends. A nickname for Burke would have sounded as im-
proper as a ribald joke, but "Pam" and "Dizzy" fitted their
wearers like a glove, and there was once a popular King who
was known as "Tum-Tum." And the more you said "Tum-
Tum" the more you liked him, and the more popular he became.

And so with "Jix." Who invented that happy vocable I
do not know; but he was certainly a public benefactor. It
comes so trippingly from the tongue, has such an engaging

air of irresponsible levity that merely to say it gives you the feeling of a good joke. It has the flavour of the Mad Hatter. It takes you through the Looking Glass into Alice's Wonderland, where perhaps you may meet Humpty-Dumpty and Tweedledum and Tweedledee and, with exceptional good luck, the Walrus and the Carpenter walking hand-in-hand. It has a delicate aroma of Jinks—high-Jinks—but it is better than Jinks. In all the history of nicknames it seems to me quite the most triumphant. It would not, of course, be triumphant if it were not apposite. You could not think of Mr. Amery as "Jix." The mind reels at the thought of Mr. Chamberlain as "Jix." Even Mr. Baldwin could not "get away with it." He is Alice in Wonderland herself, or perhaps Mr. Toots, for nothing is really of any consequence, "no consequence whatever."

But Sir William Joynson Hicks wears the name as if he were born with it, exuded it from his soul, exhaled it on the ambient air. He comes into your midst, dapper, frock-coated, debonair, cheerfully self-complacent, as if all the riddles of life were simple things that he could unloose, "familiar as his garter." Things have got into a dreadful tangle, he seems to say pleasantly. Of course they oughtn't to have got into a tangle. They wouldn't have got into a tangle if I had been called in earlier. But there they are. And now, if you will sit quite still, we will put everything nice and tidy and comfy again. And he bustles about, purring to himself with the happy feeling that at last this foolish world has got into competent hands and that all its perplexities are going to be smoothed out. "It is all so simple," as they say in the advertisements. You do this, and that and the other. And—well—there you are. And it is because he is so likeable, and well-meaning, and has such a simple and touching faith in himself, that, however angry he may make us at times, we all have a sneaking liking for him, and find his quaint name fall pleasantly on our ears. His naïveté disarms us, and though he often speaks daggers he leaves us unafraid, for the more serious he becomes the less serious we feel.

He said not long ago, in addressing a gathering of Imperial Advertising delegates, that "I still wear the reactionary frock coat of the Victorian Tories." I doubt whether that sepulchral garment was ever the peculiar toga of Toryism. If it was, then I fear Sir William did not wear it in his youth, for when he first appeared upon the stage, as plain Mr. Hicks—the Joynson is an accretion from his marriage —he seems to have had painful tendencies of a Radical order and sat in the Highbury Parliament which met at the Highbury Athenæum in North London as Radical member for Peterborough. I do not drag this disreputable fact out of its native darkness to discredit him. We all have skeletons in our youthful cupboard. I have one of my own. I too sat in one of those local parliaments so popular in the early eighties, and I sat as a Tory for Plymouth. I mention this obscure fact only to assure Sir William that he is not alone in having had a wild and giddy youth.

And I refer to his own youth, too, because it throws light on a certain "streakiness" which is apparent in Sir William's Toryism. He is not really of the true cult. The purity of his robe is spotted with reminiscences of a Puritan origin. He came first into prominence as a crusading Evangelical, one of the band of stern warriors who gathered under the banner of Lady Wimborne to rout out the Romanizers in the Church of England, and the embers of that remote and forgotten crusade still glow in his soul. The Scarlet Woman still disturbs his slumbers, and periodically he awakes and thunders at the gates of recumbent bishops, bidding them to be up and doing. And then he is a teetotaller of the old ardent type who saw alcohol as "the devil in solution" and fought him as the Prince of Darkness. An anti-gambler, too, and a foe even of King Alcohol's sinister consort, My Lady Nicotine. He feels so strongly about that enchantress that he once appeared on the platform at the Queen's Hall, with Mrs. Bramwell Booth, to denounce the practice of smoking among women, and conjured up with deep emotion the spectacle of mothers blowing tobacco fumes into the innocent faces of their offspring.

I do not speak disrespectfully of these loyalties; but they make Sir William's Toryism equivocal and they perhaps explain the shrillness of his note. Being something of a Puritan in a non-Puritan camp, it is necessary to be a little more die-hard than the born Die-hard where Puritanism is not involved. And so we see the two currents bravely battling for expression. Now the Puritan note of challenge rings out clearly as in the old Highbury days, only to be muffled by a stentorian affirmation of the Diehard creed. He is subdued to what he works in, and his moral fervours are asphyxiated in the atmosphere he breathes. When he went to the Home Office he went with soul aflame to cleanse the social sewers. Drink, gambling, night clubs, all the brood of darkness should know that at last a real St. George was abroad in Merry England. But no blow fell. On each adventure he was quietly and painlessly disarmed, and he learned, what some of us had suspected, that Puritanism is not a strongly marked characteristic of Toryism and that it does not do to quarrel with one's bread and butter. Drink, after all, is the Gibraltar of Toryism, and even night clubs have their friends in the inner shrine of the party. And so Sir William went to a night club in the purity of his heart, gave it an irreproachable certificate and—no more of that. So with the other social ailments. He looked them straight in the face—and passed on.

But if on the moral side he is a little out of step with his party, and has to restrain his ardours, he more than redresses the balance of his political orthodoxy. Here he is always well ahead of the band, always waving the Union Jack with an engaging gesture of dauntless hardihood, always defying the hosts of Midian that envelop the gallant little land for which he will give the last drop of his blood. His rôle is that of the protector of this realm, this happy isle set in the silver sea, this England, and the Jehovah he worships is a tribal god made somewhat in his own image. He has no passion for the League of Nations, for in a League of Nations what room is there for a chosen people? "The League may do some good if it does not become too active," he says, "but it is not going to solve the difficulties of the world." In a word, let us clear our minds of cant. Let us follow the simple rule—

> The good old plan
> That they shall take who have the power
> And they shall keep who can.

And so with the subject peoples who have had the inestimable privilege of falling under our protection. Do not let it be supposed that it is for their benefit that Providence in its wisdom has extended to them this favour.

"We did not conquer India for the benefit of the Indians," he once said. "I know it is said at missionary meetings that we conquered India to raise the level of the Indians.

That is cant. We conquered India as the outlet for the goods of Great Britain. We conquered India by the sword and by the sword we should hold it. ("Shame.") Call shame if you like. I am stating facts. I am interested in missionary work in India, and have done much work of that kind, but I am not such a hypocrite as to say we hold India for the Indians. We hold it as the finest outlet for British goods in general, and for Lancashire cotton goods in particular."

It may be said in extenuation of this incredible utterance that he was speaking in Lancashire for Protection, and was anxious to assure the cotton trade that Tariff Reform would have no evil repercussion in India. But the levity of such a picture of our relation to India explains why Sir William is as great a thorn in the side of his own party as he is valuable to his opponents—why, in a word, he is "Jix." He overstates every case and overacts every situation. The more delicate and combustible the elements, the more reckless and incendiary his speech, as when speaking at Warrington in the most critical phase of the Ulster question, in 1913, he said, "The people of Ulster have behind them the Unionist party. Behind them is the God of Battles. In His name and their name I say to the Prime Minister 'Let your armies and your batteries fire! Fire if you dare! Fire and be damned!'" The soil of his mind is meagre and his tongue outruns his judgment. He has a thoughtless fluency of speech, and the suppressed enthusiasms of his Puritan upbringing find vent in a caricature of patriotism that makes him the easy prey to any wave of folly. It is much easier to cut a knot than to untie it, and he always takes the easy way. He is a Die-hard, not because he is a sanguinary man, but because to his childish and romantic vision no Englishman ever surrenders, right or wrong, to anything or anybody.

His mind responds instinctively to the short-sighted view and the popular expedient. He thinks, not as a statesman, but as a talkative man in a suburban train who has just read the headlines in his favourite paper. Since he cannot round up the brewers, he will round up the abominable alien, and if the Communists become troublesome his mind incontinently leaps to Fascism as the corrective, and he has to be reminded by his Prime Minister that this is a constitutional country, that it is the function of the Government, and not of Black Shirts to protect the community, and that a Mussolini is not wanted. If he ever should emerge, it will not be Sir William Joynson Hicks who will fill the part. He does not belong to the serious drama of affairs, but to the comedy stage, and his rôle has been allotted to him in the genial and festive name which the public has, not without affections as well as derision, bestowed upon him.

xxxiv. Robert Smillie

In THE presence of the crisis in the coal trade, it is natural to turn our attention to the remarkable man who may be said to have created the present mood and outlook of the miners. If there had been no Robert Smillie there would doubtless have been trouble in the mining world, for the elements of disruption and discontent have long been present in the industry, and were bound to come to the surface. But it was Robert Smillie who focussed the discontents, gave them shape and purpose, and inspired them with the spirit of a bold, uncompromising leadership. With the memorable strike of 1911, in which he was the dominating power on the miner's side, the industry entered on a period of domestic conflict the end of which is not yet in sight.

Until that time, the mild and benevolent sway of Thomas Burt had not been challenged. That fine and gracious spirit had for a generation represented the aims and aspirations of the miners. Those aims and aspirations had no revolutionary motive. They might almost be said to have no political motive. Burt was a product of the mid-Victorian movement, with its flavour of piety, its enthusiasm for knowledge, its Sunday Schools, its *Popular Educator*, its mechanics' institutes and its mutual improvement societies. It aimed at widening the basis of the Constitution, extending the individual liberties of men, and increasing the facilities of education for the children and the opportunities of life for the worker. But it accepted the economic structure of society, worked within that structure, and, in so far as it

276

sought the interests of a class, limited its aim to the improvement of conditions of labour and the removal of practical grievances and perils.

Robert Smillie changed the orientation of the mining world. He switched the thought of the movement into political channels. He gave it a revolutionary purpose, and set before it as an ultimate goal the subversion of the whole economic system. Other influences and other men were, of course, at work to effect the change, but it was Smillie who was the voice of rebellion, and it was his powerful personality that gave force and impetus to the motive. And even though he is no longer the nominal leader, it is his spirit and his outlook that prevail.

The secret of this domination is not obscure. It abides in a character of rare strength, tenacity, simplicity. "I am," he says, "a rebel against the present system of society." It does not sound a very sensational or novel declaration. Many men have said the same thing on the platform, and have meant it, but have found in practical life many reasons for compromising, accommodating, qualifying. Not necessarily selfish reasons only; but often wise reasons, the fruit, it may be, of a wider intelligence, a quicker appreciation of new aspects, a clearer understanding of the complexities of an ancient society.

But Smillie is a rebel all the time. He looks out on the Capitalistic society with a steady, relentless hostility that admits no compromise. Clear the abomination away: why cumbereth it the ground? is his attitude. Wages, conditions, hours of labour? What are these things but means to an end? In themselves they are good, but they are not the goal. They are only the weapon with which the citadel of Capital can be reduced and carried by storm. They are only the means by which the present system can be paralysed and destroyed and replaced by that sovereignty of the proletariat which will make all things new and fair. And the miners are the key to this beneficent revolution. Upon their activities the whole fabric rests. Knock away the pit props and the roof of Capitalism falls in, not in the mining world only, but over the whole arch of society.

In effecting this revolution, he is not opposed to the use of the Parliamentary weapon. He himself stood for Parliament seven times before he was elected for Morpeth, in 1923, and he says he wants to see Parliament converted from the club of the rich to the meeting-place of the proletariat; but the processes of Parliament are too slow, too encumbered by powerful interests and checks and balances. Direct action can alone force the crisis and bring the machine of Capitalism to a standstill. And behind all the controversies in the coal trade during the past fifteen years there has been this ultimate motive of social and economic overthrow.

It was this motive that inspired the idea of the Triple Alliance of which he was the engineer-in-chief. Had that terrific instrument functioned when the crisis came it might have brought the system with which Mr. Smillie is at war to the ground; but it did not function. It fell asunder, and Labour has ever since been struggling to find a common term between the revolutionary gospel of Mr. Smillie and the practical opportunism of Mr. Thomas. There is no such common term, for the one thinks only of the future goal and the other thinks only of the present objective.

There is no price upon his convictions, and neither personal ambition nor private interest deflects his purpose. He wields the power that always belongs to the man who wants nothing, asks nothing, and concedes nothing. What he was forty years ago, that he is to-day, and that he will remain to the end.   There is in him, as in Keir Hardie, whom he most resembles, an austere pride in the rejection of what other men clamour for.   In the great phrase of the Shunamite woman, he dwells among his own people.   He has not risen from his class, but is a miner, first, last and always, living in a "but-and-ben" stone-flagged cottage in the uplands of Lanarkshire, where—having migrated from Belfast, where he was born, and having spent some time in the shipyards of Glasgow—he began that life in the pit the memory of which has bitten deep into his mind and his heart.   He began as a hand pumper in Summerlee Colliery, Larkhall.   He says:

The work of keeping the water down was not exhausting, but as there were only two boys to attend to the pump during a continuous twenty-four hours, it meant that I was engaged alone, every day, Saturdays included, for twelve hours with no time off for meals, which I snatched as I could. This pump was situated a mile away from the pit bottom, and my mate and I took half an hour each way, so that our shift was really thirteen hours underground.   There was no official recognition of the fact that walking to and fro in the attitude of a half-shut clasp knife was really harder than our actual work.   Only those who have actually made such journeys, day in, day out, under the low dripping roofs of the galleries, can realise what this groping one's way to work means.   But the most trying experience of this part of my early life was the fortnightly vigil of twenty-four hours which I was doomed to keep.   Every Saturday one of the pumpers went on his shift at six p.m., and remained at his post until the same hour on Sunday.   This was done to alternate from day work to night work in turn.   Now as the miners spent Sunday above ground, I was, with the exception of a man in charge of the pumping engine a mile away, for twenty-four hours every fortnight *alone in the pit*.

It was from such a background of experience that Robert Smillie emerged on to the public stage, and it is from that experience that his conclusions about the diseases and the reme-

dies of society are drawn.   If he is a rebel, he may claim the
warrant from his own past.   He learned his lessons in a bitter
school, and it is always to those personal lessons that he re-
verts for the justification of himself and his opinions.   Thus,
speaking in the Morpeth division at the by-election at which
he was elected in 1923, he answered his own question as to
why he is a rebel against the present system of society.   He
said:

> One of your neighbours, the Duke of Northumberland, possesses
> 169,000 acres of land.   In 1913 he took £82,000 in royalty rents from
> the coal hewed in that county.   The Duke of Hamilton owns 56,000
> acres and draws £113,000 in royalty rents.   This man's predecessor was
> Duke of Hamilton when I was twenty-five years of age, working as a
> coal-cutter.   I was paid 10d. a ton and my master at the palace of
> Hamilton claimed as much as that for royalty rent.   I got 3s. 4d. for
> four tons and the Duke got 3s. 4d. from my four tons.   He had
> £120,000 in royalty rents at that time, and my fellow-hewers found it
> impossible to get food and clothing for their little ones.   When I found
> that the Duke had a minimum wage running into thousands of pounds,
> I could not believe that any God or Creator had foreordained any such
> state of affairs.   I found the men themselves were to blame and I have
> been a rebel against such a system ever since.

It may not be difficult to show that the remedy for such
flagrant wrongs in the social system does not require the
Nasmyth hammer of revolution to accomplish.   Even Mr.
Smillie would not deny that the labours of the Burts, the
Wilsons, and the Fenwicks, who worked through public
opinion and Parliamentary action, profoundly ameliorated
the conditions of the miner, and that the history of the nineteenth century was an unceasing record of enlightened reforms, political and industrial, of which the Hammonds's
great history of the Industrial Revolution is witness.

But it is not difficult either to understand the power of

appeal of a man who draws so directly, so freshly, and so simply upon his own funds of experience and translates his will into action so formidably. His gifts of speech are great. He talks with his heart, without tricks and without rhetoric. He is no demagogue. He does nothing for effect, but achieves it by the cold passion and intensity of his feeling and the hard, clear grip of his argument and his facts. He has something of Parnell's genius for enveloping himself in an atmosphere of detachment, can remain silent while others talk, firm while others waver, and at the end imposes his will by the force of personality. In the cut and thrust of negotiation, Mr. Thomas is more nimble, more full of feints and ambuscades; but it is admitted that the miners have never had a leader so skilful as Smillie is in stating their case, so resolute in purpose, or so capable of crossing swords with the most accomplished advocates of the employer. They have certainly never had a leader who in spite of the violence of his aims has commanded in a higher degree the respect of his opponents for the qualities of character. He can be brusque in manner and has a dour disdain that is no respecter of persons, but his intimate bearing is kindly and companionable, and behind the harsh, even wrathful, exterior there is tenderness and a good deal of sentiment.

He calls himself always, a little defiantly, an "agitator," a preacher of "divine discontent," and though, after many failures, he is in Parliament for so long as he cares to stay there, his gifts are neither Parliamentary nor executive. When Mr. Lloyd George, greatly daring, offered him the position of Food Controller, he wisely refused. "For what reason?" asked the Prime Minister. "Because," Mr. Smillie said, "I should demand plenary powers to deal in my own way with the food profiteers. Some I should be content to send to prison; others I should feel obliged to hang." But the real reason was the sense of his true vocation, and the love of his own freedom. He is the prophet of unrest, and a prophet of unrest in office would be as lamentable a spectacle as an eagle in a cage. He does well to cling to his herbs and his locusts, his wild honey, and his eyrie on the uplands of Lanarkshire.

xxxv. Lord Rothermere

"MR. PUNCH" once described the late Sir William Robertson Nicoll as "the most successful Christian of his time." In the sense that "Punch" meant, Lord Rothermere is the most successful journalist not merely of his own time but of all time. The sheets that issue from his presses morning, noon, and night, strew the land, thick as autumnal leaves in Vallombrosa. The primeval forests of Newfoundland turn to pulp at his word and become the myriad messengers of his decrees. Though we flee to the uttermost parts of the land we cannot escape his influence, and even in the deserts of Sahara or on the golden road to Samarkand, he will maintain speech with us. His riches outshine the wealth of Ormuz and of Ind. Probably no one in these islands ever accumulated so vast a fortune in so short a time as he has done.

The King has, at the inspiration of successive Ministers, showered titles on him, and during the war he was raised to great office without the formality of serving an apprenticeship to public life or the necessity of opening his mouth in Parliament. And he is still well on the sunny side of sixty. If in the "Punch" sense he is not the most successful man of his time I do not know where we shall look for him.

Nor is his success to be measured by his riches and his dignities alone. It is the success of power. The brewer or the contractor or the iron master may heap up as great a fortune without achieving power. But Lord Rothermere has a potentiality more commanding than that of any subject of the King. He can saturate the mind of the public with any idea that possesses him. He controls the raw material of public opinion. He can make millions of people read what he wishes them to read. He can suppress what he does not wish them to read. It is useless to deny this power. I have heard men as distinguished as Lord Oxford deny it; yet the career of Lord Oxford himself is conclusive witness to the fact. It was not the circumstances of the war that dethroned him, but the ceaseless refrain of "Wait and See" kept up in the Harmsworth Press that finally undermined his position. He did not cultivate the press and others did and he paid the penalty.

And for another example, turn to the story of the post-war years. Why has it taken eight years for Europe to begin to get out of the morass in which the war engulfed it? The main reason is the dominion which France and M. Poincaré established for so long over the policy of the Allies. During four years successive British Governments, headed in turn by Mr. Lloyd George, Mr. Bonar Law, and Mr. Baldwin, broke on the implacable rock of Poincarism and revenge. Again and again they sought to turn the tide of Allied action into peaceful channels and always they were defeated.

They were defeated because the most powerful instrument for forming public opinion in England was violently, ferociously, pro-Poincaré. It was more French than the French. Through his multitudinous organs, morning and evening, week-day and Sunday, London and provincial, Lord Rothermere mobilised British public opinion against the British Government, month after month, year after year, in the interests of the now miserably defunct policy of French Imperialism. He did more. Through his Paris organ he infected France and the Continent with the conviction that

the British people were not behind the British Government
and that Poincaré had only to stand fast in order to bring
this country to its knees. His daily invocation to France was
to go into the Ruhr and to adopt "drastic methods such as
Germany employed in France and Belgium during the war."
"Hats off to France!" was his triumphant "hallelujah" when
at last Poincaré plunged into the Ruhr and so bedeviled
Europe for three years more. Next to Poincaré, Lord
Rothermere was the chief architect of the most catastrophic
episode since the war. Indeed, but for his activities in London and in Paris, it is probable that there would not have
been any Ruhr adventure at all.

I repeat, therefore, that it is useless to deny the power of
Lord Rothermere. It is blind, blundering power; but it
has operated in the past, and, given those conditions of public
excitement in which mob passion stampedes governments, it
will operate again. It is the power not of a man but of a
machine. It is true that if we accepted the testimony of the
Daily Mail, we should have to regard Lord Rothermere as
a super-man. "He may be best described," said that organ
in one of its disinterested panegyrics of its proprietor, "as
one of those human dynamos who are content to hum in the
midst of vast enterprises, setting all their machinery going,
sending their fame out to the uttermost regions, and content
to remain themselves unheard, so long as their machines
work perfectly."

Far be it from me to deny that Lord Rothermere is "a
human dynamo." Indeed, he has something of the appearance that one would expect a human dynamo to have—its
massive bulk and its impassivity of countenance. But though
dynamos are excellent things for service, it is not customary
to leave them to run themselves. They need to be intelli-

gently inspired if they are not to run amuck. And it is the inspiration of the human dynamo that I distrust.

Perhaps, as an indication of the measure of his wisdom, I may recall his touching faith in that prophet of the war, Mr. Horatio Bottomley. In those days Mr. Bottomley was Lord Rothermere's "star" turn in the most popular of his Sunday picture papers. Sunday by Sunday a Bottomley encyclical fell upon the ears of an expectant world. (It seems that he did not pen his own encyclicals; but these illustrious men rarely do: they supply the signature.) Sometimes it proclaimed a "non-stop to Berlin," sometimes with hand upon its heart (a rival Sunday paper having "taken to religion") it suddenly announced the reconciliation of Mr. Bottomley and his Creator. But in spite of the fervour of the prophet, the Government remained obstinately indifferent to the importance of engaging him to finish the war. Lord Rothermere's patience was at last exhausted, and thus he wrote in the *Sunday Pictorial* of July 25, 1915:

> Although we are not short of leaders of men we do not sufficiently employ them. Take the case of Mr. Horatio Bottomley, whose tonicsome utterances in this journal give inspiration and comfort to the most lugubrious souls. Mr. Bottomley exercises an enormous influence with his pen and voice. Are recruits wanted? He gets them. Is there a strike to settle? He can pour oil on troubled waters. Is there a cause to plead? He pleads it successfully. . . . Yet his great talents are most exercised "unofficially." He is a force in the State. His services should be utilised more and more by the Government.

So much for the wisdom of this potentate of public opinion in regard to men. Let us glance at an example of his steadiness of mind in regard to measures. If there is one question on which even the humblest of us might be assumed to have a considered conviction it is that of Free Trade and

Protection, about which we have been talking off and on for twenty years. When Mr. Baldwin made his memorable plunge into Protection in November, 1923, Lord Rothermere's *Evening News,* in its lunch edition, announced:

An article by Lord Rothermere, "My Plea for Tariffs," will appear in next Sunday's *Sunday Pictorial.*

It was a momentous declaration. It meant that the whole might of the most powerful press in the land would be thrown into the election on the side of Mr. Baldwin. But then something happened. Perhaps Lord Rothermere met his dear friend and rival Lord Beaverbrook and talked it over. Perhaps they agreed that it was more important to teach Mr. Baldwin that he could not afford to snub those who had been accustomed to have Prime Ministers feed out of their hand than it was to have Protection. In any case, in the 6:30 edition of the *Evening News* the same day the notice was altered thus:

An article by Lord Rothermere, "Should Free Trade have Another Chance?" will appear in next Sunday's *Sunday Pictorial.*

Thus between morning and afternoon Lord Rothermere reversed the whole argument of his papers on the most vital and most discussed domestic issue of the time. He improved on the record of his brother, the late Lord North-cliffe, who went to Chamberlain's meeting at Glasgow, in 1903, breathing fire and slaughter against the "Stomach Tax" and was so impressed by the meeting that he declared for the Stomach Tax next morning. All of which goes to show that these human dynamos may be trifles light as air in that large world of ideas where they wander so forlornly without any guidance but the momentary impulse.

But it is not necessary to test Lord Rothermere's intellectual fitness to be Chief Adviser to the British people by these things. He has been in office. We have seen the human dynamo in action on the grand stage. Why and how he became Air Minister is in itself one of the comedies of the war. It was a time when the Harmsworth brothers were at the meridian. They had the ear of the mob, and if Ministers did not obey them or make terms with them they set the mob at their heels and they had to go. One day the world was startled by the publication of a letter to the Prime Minister, Mr. Lloyd George, from Lord Northcliffe declining after the manner of Cæsar, the offer of the throne at the Air Ministry. No one was so much startled as Lord Cowdray, the Air Minister himself, who had not been informed that his throne was vacant. Of course, it became vacant then, for Lord Cowdray was not the sort of person to take the affront with meekness. Fortunately, as the hymn says, "the way appears." Lord Northcliffe was not the only Harmsworth. Brother Harold was getting impatient—— But perhaps the sequel can best be told by the following advertisements in the public press:

Friday, Nov. 2, 1917.

Buy Sunday's issue of the *Sunday Pictorial* for a remarkable article in which the writer with great force and clearness critically examines our methods of conducting the war, entitled

THE TOO LATE GOVERNMENT

By James Lumsden, editor of the great North of England newspaper, the *Leeds Mercury* [then also owned by Lord Rothermere]. . . . The writer, quoting the memorable criticism of our First War Government, applies the fatal words Too Late with equally telling effect to the Government of which Mr. Lloyd George is the head to-day.

Nov. 17 (*a fortnight later*).

Buy to-morrow's *Sunday Pictorial* . . . for a striking article in which the writer deals clearly and outspokenly with the political crisis, entitled

MR. LLOYD GEORGE THE ONLY MAN

By G. H. Lethem, editor of the *Daily Record* [also then owned by Lord Rothermere]. . . . The writer explains in this powerful article why Mr. Lloyd George is the "Only man to whom the Allies must look," etc.

From the Times, Nov. 27, 1917 (*a week later*).

LORD ROTHERMERE'S APPOINTMENT

It is officially announced that the King has been pleased to approve the appointment of Lord Rothermere to be President of the Air Council.

It is a pretty comedy which will repay careful study. It will help to illuminate not only Lord Rothermere, but the whole problem that centres in him, his power over public opinion and the relation of a certain type of politician with the press. It is enough here to say that his stay at the Air Ministry was brief, and memorable only for the modest suggestion that the British Museum should be disembowelled to provide an office for him. When he resigned on the eve of being called upon to make his maiden speech in the House of Lords in defence of his policy, the waters of public life closed over him with an indifference that was hardly respectful to a human dynamo.

But to do him justice Lord Rothermere would not claim to be a statesman or a journalist. His brother had a romantic flair for the sensational side of journalism. He knew better than any newspaper man of his own or any time how to give the public ginger "hot in the mouth," and being unencumbered by any philosophy of government, and charged with an imperious egotism that took no account of odds, he splashed through life with a resounding tread. But Lord Rothermere has nothing of this powerful, if undisciplined, contact with affairs. He is a financier who applies the Midas touch to the ponderable things of life. If it was Northcliffe's flair for sensational journalism that made the *Daily Mail* a portent, it was Rothermere's business gifts that reaped the harvest of the adventure. He built up the vast network of systems that, with its interlockings, alliances, and subsidiaries has changed the whole face, structure, and spirit of modern journalism. It was he who made the momentous discovery that the public like a paper with "pictures stuck in anyhow and hardly any words at all." When Alfred Harmsworth started the *Daily Mirror* as a woman's daily and found that women did not want a "daily" devoted to their sex, Harold Harmsworth took the *Mirror* to himself and found that what the world of women and men alike was hungering for was "pictures." And from that centre his financial evolutions radiated out in ever-widening circles, incorporating the *Daily-Mail* system, plums from the Hulton system which he bought and disposed of with profits on a regal scale, and shares in the Beaverbrook system.

The whole structure of finance recalls the House that Jack Built. The *Daily Mirror* controls the *Sunday Pictorial;* together they control the Daily.-Mail Trust; the Daily-Mail Trust owns 53 1/3 per cent of the deferred shares of the Associated Newspapers, Ltd., which owns *Daily Mail, Evening News, Weekly Despatch, Overseas Daily Mail,* and I know not what else. Then the *Daily Mirror* and *Sunday Pictorial* control the *Daily Sketch* and the *Sunday Herald* and the Empire Paper Mills. "The only simple part of the story," as the financial expert of *The Nation* observes in unravelling these mysteries, "is that Lord Rothermere controls the whole lot by controlling the *Daily Mirror*. With the minimum of personal risk—merely by owning more than half the 700,000 £1 ordinary shares in Daily Mirror Newspapers, Ltd.—Lord Rothermere now controls five newspaper companies, with a combined share and loan capital of £7,355,437, valued on the Stock Exchange at £24,000,000. The public put up the big money and Lord Rothermere kept control."

Before such an achievement in finance, the only attitude is one of respectful abasement. Before the implications of the achievement we may reasonably entertain other feelings. If these gigantic operations had related to the manufacture of soap or railways or iron and steel or cotton goods or even whisky there would be no room for concern, and Lord Rothermere's rudimentary enthusiasm for economy, especially economy in popular education, his enthusiasm for Mussolini, and his ardent advocacy of M. Poincaré would leave us indifferent. But his activities are related to the manufacture of public opinion, and it is in virtue of that entirely accidental by-product of his financial genius that he is important. He is not a personality of significance, but he is a power of immense significance. In himself he is—in spite of many amiable traits of public benevolence—negligible. As the master of the greatest machine of publicity the world has ever seen, he is a sort of Fourth Estate of the Realm. The possibility of the association of such power with so unschooled and irresponsible a direction is not the least disquieting problem of democracy.

xxxvi. Sir James Barrie

I DO NOT know whether it is customary for pilgrims from afar, in their search for the homes and haunts of famous men, to turn out of the bustle and noise of the Strand into the calm of Adelphi Terrace, where the spirit of Adam still lingers like a perfume from the past. But it is tolerably certain that in future times no curious visitor to London will fail to go to the quiet little street with its dozen houses that goes by the name of Robert Street, where the two most illustrious playwrights of this generation lived opposite each other, and where J. M. Barrie—the future will happily forget that he was a baronet—threw plum-stones at Bernard Shaw's windows whenever he saw that his rival had got a dinner party on.

Shaw denied the plum-stones. He even denied that he ever had dinner parties. But I am a poor judge of posterity if, in such a conflict of testimony, it does not prefer to believe Barrie's tale rather than Shaw's denial. It will know the very window from which Barrie took aim, and it will probably go to Christie's to buy the plum-stones he threw. The plum-stones will become a part of the great Barrie legend which will perplex the historian.

For Barrie is not so much a man as a myth, a fable, a fairy tale, a midsummer night's dream, a creation of moonbeams, a beneficient sprite peering from behind bushes in Kensington Gardens, and disappearing in the arch of a rainbow. The personality of his friend and neighbour across the way is as emphatic as a time-table; but Barrie is as shy

as a fawn, as fleeting as a vision. Shaw's name is defiantly
blazoned in a brass plate at No. 10 Adelphi Terrace; but
no directory, no telephone book, will disclose the secret of
the dweller on the other side of the street. If you want
him you must inquire for him at Kirriemuir (which is pronounced Thrums), and Kirriemuir is a long way off. And
even at Kirriemuir you would probably not get on his trail,
for he fogs the scent of his movements with the cunning of
a creature of the woods.

And when at last you have run him to earth, he may still
elude you by the impalpable garment of silence with which
he envelops himself. When Mr. Frohman went to discuss
with him the production of "The Little Minister," he tells
us that "during the two hours I was there he did not utter
more than twenty sentences, and only two of these related
to 'The Little Minister.' They were exactly alike and con-
sisted of two words, 'Quite right.'" The stories of such
experiences are numberless. It is not a silence of hostility or
surliness or scorn. It certainly does not give the impression
of the silence of pride, or spiritual aloofness. It is as though
the faculty of speech will only respond to a certain touch,
a note, a hint that releases the genial current of the soul.
Then it is that one enjoys as delicate a feast of good talk as
this generation has to offer.

I was the fortunate instrument on one occasion to strike the
rock of his silence with the appropriate wand. I joined a
group of friends in which he was seated, and made some
remark, I think about cricket, which interested him, and
thenceforth for an hour he held the company by the demure
drolleries of fancy and memory, related with that rather
wistful melancholy that gives flavour to his fun. He im-
provises as he talks, with an uproarious playfulness with

fact and possibility that has a disarming air of truthfulness, guaranteed by the sad gravity of the face and the low, slow tones of voice, as of one seeking to avoid the suspicion of exaggeration. I recall especially among his cricket stories the description of Mr. Birrell at the wicket waving his broken bat and crying aloud, "Send me some more bats," and a riotous fancy about a famous ball that he himself bowled which was so slow that the batsman hit at it twice before it reached him, and was just too late with his third stroke, which was in progress when the tired ball, with its last exhausted effort, touched the stumps and removed the bail. When he had gone one of the company turned to me and said, "It is fortunate you joined us. We have had Barrie to lunch and we had sat with him half an hour after lunch and until your remark unloosed his tongue he had not uttered a word."

He has the rare art, both on the stage and off, of making us sad and merry at the same time, of releasing the opposite emotions and touching our laughter with the pity of things and our sorrow with the fun of things. Perhaps it is not true to speak of it as an art. There is art in it, of course; perhaps even artifice. Stevenson, who was no bad judge of the artifices of art, scented it from the beginning. "But Barrie is a beauty," he wrote to Henry James, in 1892. ". . . Stuff in that young man; but he must see and not be too funny. Genius in him; but there's a journalist ever at his elbow—there's the risk. What a page is the glove business in the 'Window'! Knocks a man flat." The years have not invalidated the criticism. Barrie's consummate mastery over the instrument of human emotion is never quite free from the sense of the audience. His fancy plays with our feelings a little consciously and deliberately, and he lacks the great passion of creative imagination which sweeps the mind clear of the realm of limelight and sentiment.

But though he has art and perhaps artifice, they are not false to his nature. They may strain the emotion, but they do not violate it. His attitude to life is that of a half-sorrowful, half-playful revolt against the hard facts of existence. The child comes into the world trailing clouds of glory from afar and doomed to see that glory "fade into the light of common day." The wonder passes, the rainbow loses its magic, the vision splendid dies away. Most of us accept the eclipse and settle down, happily or unhappily, to the realities and activities of a matter-of-fact world. We leave the Golden Age behind, and are so busy with our buyings and sellings, our ambitions and our schemes, our loves and our hates, that we forget that we once dwelt in Arcady, where dreams were true and beautiful visions plentiful. But Barrie refuses to forget Arcady. He will not surrender the Golden Age. He moves on the journey with reverted eyes, forever trying to recapture and hold the glow and glory of youth. Like his great countryman, his song is to the refrain of "Over the Seas to Skye":

> Give me the sea, give me the sky,
> Give me the sun that shone;
> Give me the eyes, give me the soul,
> Give me the lad that is gone.

It is this yearning for the irrevocable, this passion to keep the glamour and wonder of the child vision fresh and unsullied amid the coarse contacts of the disillusioning world that is the secret of his pathos and of the poignancy of his appeal. For in the heart of the most worldly of us there is still a reminiscence of Arcady, still a faint echo of the lad that is gone.

This motive runs like a golden thread through all the web of his work. It is implicit everywhere, and culminates in the exquisite fancy of "Peter Pan," which has made Barrie the Pied Piper to the children of all lands and of all ages. The story of his life is woven into that masterpiece. It was, as he has told us, when a boy at the Dumfries Academy that he climbed the school wall and entered the realm of dreams where Peter was truly born, and it was long after, when fame and success had come to him, that, walking in that paradise of childhood at Kensington Gardens, he made the acquaintance of a family of children who revived the impulse to give his childish fancy a local habitation and a name. Those children—the offspring of Arthur Llewellyn Davies and his wife, a daughter of du Maurier, the artist— lost both their parents soon afterwards, and Barrie adopted them, only to lose the elder boy in the first year of the war and the younger in a bathing accident at Oxford.

But Barrie would not have won his unprecedented empire over the emotions of his time if his sentimentalism had not been irradiated by a humour as fresh, sparkling, and inexhaustible as any in our literary annals. He attributes this glorious and irresponsible levity to the unruly half of himself, McConnachie by name, who does the writing. "I," he says, "am the half that is dour and practical and canny; he is the fanciful half. My desire is to be the family solicitor, standing firm on my hearth rug among the harsh realities of the office furniture, while he prefers to fly about on one wing." It is McConnachie, we may assume, who throws the plum-stones at Bernard Shaw's window in the Adelphi, and keeps up the revels of childhood, while the melancholy Barrie looks on and laments the evanescence of youth. And it was the indomitable spirit of McConnachie which brought him through his great adventure, when, a timid youth from the North, pausing on his way at Nottingham to learn the craft of journalism, he descended on London. "The greatest glory that has ever come to me," he says, "was to be swallowed up in London, not knowing a soul, with no means of subsistence, and the fun of working till the stars went out. To have known anyone would have spoilt it. I didn't even quite know the language. I rang for my boots and they thought I said a glass of water, so I drank the water and worked on."

I am not sure that even yet they might not bring him water when he asked for his boots. And I am sure that if they brought it he would drink it. For, famous, betitled—alas!—and beloved as no writer of our tongue since Dickens has been beloved, he still remains the shy, Doric-speaking, elvish spirit that came to town forty odd years ago. In the interval he has had a career of success unparalleled in the records of literature. From the day he bought his first top-hat and went to see Frederick Greenwood at the old *St. James's Gazette* he has caught the ear and possessed the heart of the public. His rewards have been munificent beyond all precedent. No man in any country in any time who has used the pen as a means of livelihood has found it so rich a medium. It may be that his fame has outstripped even his high deserts. There can hardly be any doubt that it is so in the case of his novels, for who to-day takes down "The Little Minister" or reads "Sentimental Tommy"? When they appeared they overshadowed, in contemporary judgment, the masterpieces of Hardy, but seen beside them to-day one marvels that the popular mood of the moment could make so grotesque a valuation.

For the plain truth is that Barrie had not the sense of form or the sustained power of imagination that the novel demands. His genius is fanciful and episodic. It needs the movement, the lighting, the colour, the swiftness, the illusion of the stage to give it coherence and momentum, and it is by his contributions to the stage that his work will live. Even here there will be much winnowing out by time. But from the mass of plays with which he has delighted his generation, it is safe to say that two of his ventures at least will sail the theatrical seas till they run dry. "Peter Pan" has all the characters of an immortal, and it is not easy to conceive a time when "The Admirable Crichton" will not be treasured as one of the deathless things of the drama. It may be that other fruits of his art will survive the tooth of time; but in these two plays assuredly are enshrined a rare and beautiful genius that is imperishable. He is an enviable man who goes down to posterity with such gifts of gracious tenderness and sweetness, of laughter and tears. And we may rejoice that we have been privileged to share posterity's luck, and to see Barrie play "hide and seek with the angels." Long may he live to look sadly on while McConnachie flings plum-stones at Bernard Shaw's windows in the Adelphi.

xxxvii. Mr. "Tim" Healy

MORE accurately, of course, it should be His Excellency Timothy Michael Healy, Governor-General of the Irish Free State; but there are some men too rich in the qualities of plain, unadorned nature to be disguised by dignities, and "Tim" Healy would still be "Tim" Healy though he were made Mikado of Japan or the Grand Lama of Thibet. Bottom is still Bottom even though he be "translated." And what a "translation" is this which has converted the stormy petrel of the past into the tenant of the Viceregal Lodge, and the solemn head of an Irish Kingdom. The European earthquake which has worked such miracles, placing an old army pensioner from Hanover in the seat of the Kaiser, a hunted refugee from Switzerland in the seat of the Tsar, and making a blacksmith's son the dictator of Italy, has done nothing more strange than this, and few things more gratifying.

It has been done not without sacrifice. The House of Commons will never again be the thrilling place it was when the Irish brigade sat a solid phalanx, defiant and irreconcilable, below the gangway, a grim, resentful cloud hanging over the Parliamentary sky, flashing with sudden lightnings and reverberating with ceaseless thunders. What memorable figures there were in that phalanx—the "Chief," pale, silent, secret, his hat over his eyes, his arms folded across his breast, a symbol of implacable revolt; John Redmond, spacious, generous, eloquent; the stately Dillon; the frenzied Obrien; the odd, grotesque Biggar; the gay and chivalrous

William Redmond, the trumpet-tongued Devlin, the brilliant Tom Kettle and many another. All have vanished, save the genial "Tay Pay," who, as Father of the House, lingers on like a reminiscence of an epoch that has become "one with Nineveh and Tyre."

And in all that phalanx there was no more devastating presence than that of "Tim" Healy. For a generation he was *l'enfant terrible* of Parliament, the prince of guerilla warriors, fighting for Ireland, but fighting still more for his own inscrutable ends; flashing through the lists with a tongue that smote like a sword, solitary, defiant, whimsical, incalculable, sad and merry in the same breath, a strange, haunting figure of unrest and indignation, in which all the pathos and all the comedy and all the savageries of Ireland seemed to find expression. What memories his name awakens in those who have been familiar with the House of Commons since, little more than a lad, picked out by the keen eye of Parnell, he first entered the Chamber! How often and with what expectation have we seen him rise from the corner seat below the gangway, his hands clasped behind his back, his quaint, peasant figure swaying forward, his eyes gleaming through the glasses that sat so uneasily on his nose, gleaming with passion and mischief and malice and wit, all under the control of an incomparable serenity. And as he rose, every door opening and the Chamber filling with a magical suddenness, as it only fills when the great artist is on the stage.

And what an artist he was! Not an orator of the "proud, full sail" of Redmond or the declamatory energy of Devlin. He spoke quietly, dreamily, as if communing with himself, with a touch of aloofness, a certain monkishness as of one who had come from a monastery, bringing with him the atmosphere of strange and ghostly things. And out of this reverie, in which the voice of the prophet and the cadence of the poet and the dreamer were curiously mingled, there would leap some withering phrase that stabbed like death. Woe to the man who crossed swords with that terrible blade. There was no tongue so swift and so bitter. "When the cat's away," said Chamberlain, on one occasion, commenting on the absence of Gladstone, "the mice will play." "And the rats," said "Tim," with cold incisiveness, as if he were helping the speaker out of his forgetfulness. "The question is, who is to be the master?" said Parnell in the historic struggle in Committee Room XV. "The question is, who is to be the mistress?" hissed the voice of Tiger Tim. He was the master of all moods. The soft, almost crooning accents, had the pathos of incommunicable things, and he could melt the House to tears, as in the famous "Dark Rosaleen" speech, or awe it to silence as in that sombre utterance on the Boer War, when, with the daylight fading in the Chamber, and the slow sentences falling on the ear like strokes of fate, he, the loneliest figure in the House, with every man's hand against him and his hand against every man's, held friend and foe spellbound as if they saw visibly the writing of doom upon the walls.

His impudence was sublime, enveloped in a seriousness, a gravity, that made it gorgeous comedy. Who that heard it will forget the *tour de force* by which he turned the whole current of a debate from Uganda to Ireland. The subject of discussion was a grant for the Uganda railway. The Irishmen, following their custom, had sought to turn the theme to the advantage of their own distressful country. How different was this generosity from the parsimony towards Ireland. "Order, order," said the Speaker. Enough of this irrelevance. Then "Tim" rises sadly, slowly, in his place. What now? Is he going to question the ruling, defy it, flout it? No, he leaves such coarse fare to others. His art is subtler, more difficult to combat. "I rise as a native of Uganda. There will be joy throughout the length and breadth of that beautiful country at this grant from England towards her prosperity." He speaks with fluent ease of the conditions of Uganda, naming this place and that, Bally-this and Bally-that, with calm matter-of-factness. Members sit up as they see the whole question of Ireland, that interminable, that inexhaustible question, being served up to them again under the disguise of an Uganda allegory. They look at the Speaker, but his silence confesses defeat. They look at the unrevealing face of "Tim," pursuing the colossal jest without a hint of levity, and then they give themselves up to the enjoyment of the fun, and when the joke has been carried through unfalteringly to its close, they break into cheers for the impish wit that has out-manœuvred them.

I think of him in association with another figure in the House, with whom he has superficially little in common. But it is that likeness to Lord Hugh Cecil which gives us the key to "Tim" Healy's baffling and fascinating mind. He and Lord Hugh are the only Parliamentarians since Gladstone who have brought the sense of spiritual things on to the floor of the House of Commons. They both spoke with the air of men who had a commission which was not entirely of this world, and who came into the House from the sanctuary. One felt that if "Tim" had come garbed in a monkish robe and with a rope round his waist, he would have been in character. You would not have been surprised to know that there was a hair shirt under his garments, and that that forward tilt of the body and that fixed gaze as he walked were due to the uncomfortable fact that he had pebbles in his boots. Through all the vicissitudes of his stormy life, the one constant thread is the religious motive. He is a frank obscurantist, a fourteenth-century monk born out of due time, and he assails the scientists, with their "microbes and monkeys," with a scorn as unbridled as Mr. Chesterton's and a naïveté as childlike as W. J. Bryan's. Take a recent speech of his on "Why the Catholic Church is Hated." Speaking of evolution, he said:

> Such teaching leads straight to paganism, and it is because the Catholic Church says so and says so boldly, that she is hated. . . . These so-called philosophers and scientists are mere bubble blowers. There is no greater humbug than the so-called scientist of modern times. . . . One fellow at Oxford lately said he had discovered the beginning of life. They could not start the hind leg of a flea. . . . This monkey business was started because it struck deliberately at the existence of the human soul. And it is because these men know that these so-called philosophies are part of the devil's apparatus that they are so continuously and assiduously propagating them, and for that reason the Church is continuously denying them, and incurring thereby the hatred of these philosophical nincompoops. The only thing I can see that this free thought gives is the right to loose living and loose thinking. They may box the compass of unbelief in any way they please, they may decorate it with the pretences of human liberty, but in the end it comes down to nothing else than the license to defraud one's neighbour or one's neighbour's wife.

It takes one's breath away; but it is important to remember that this is not only the authentic "Tim," but that it is also the authentic Ireland—a country with a civilisation so different from ours as to be not merely in a different hemisphere but in another and a far off century. "Tim's" passion for Ireland is for the Ireland of the saints and the legends. I do not think it was the political association with England that outraged him; but the spiritual association— the feeling that the faith and morals of the country were contaminated by our godlessness.

It was this spiritual motive that made him the most implacable and ferocious enemy of Parnell after that great man's exposure. Parnell had discovered the genius of the young railway clerk who had come from Bantry to Newcastle, had made him his private secretary, and started him on the career which opened to him the path of success in journalism, in Parliament, and at the bar. But Parnell was outlawed by the Church, and Mr. Healy pursued him with the fury of a Crusader or a Texas "fundamentalist." There was in addition, no doubt, a certain perverse and impish quality that contributed to the vendetta. He was congenitally unable to keep in step with anybody, long, a trait that gave point to his remark in the House one night that "there are two united parties in this House: I am one of them."

He has always been like that, a lonely, unquiet spirit, with an ungovernable tongue that falls on everyone in turn like a whiplash across the face. He was the most uncomfortable bed-fellow even the Irish Party ever had, and his quarrels left him at last friendless and isolated. His cruelty to that great gentleman, John Redmond, would be unforgiveable if we did not remember that he is at heart the primitive peasant of Ireland, and his savage insults from the platform to "Kitty O'Shea" can only be condoned on the same consideration. He was horsewhipped for those insults and repeated them the same night, for, whatever graces of public conduct he lacks, his courage is dauntless.

It is said that he is always pained by the discovery that he has given pain. This is not difficult to believe when one meets this singularly gifted man in private and falls under the spell of his kindly voice and persuasive talk. I do not know a more companionable man, or one who can make the hours fly on swifter wing. The play of his mind is warm and childlike, but the brooding sadness that envelops it gives a depth and emotion to his talk, a sort of cloistral quietude, that is curiously appealing. Education in the formal sense he has little of. He once told the House that he could not spell, could not parse a sentence, and did not know the rule of three. But his understanding is capacious, he is widely read in French and German literature, the range of his intellectual interests is infinitely various, and he will put as much fervour into a subject like spelling reform as he used to put into the story of "Dark Rosaleen," or into the woes of his client. His personal friendships, unlike his political friendships, are many and unexclusive, and in spite of his monkishness he is an uncommonly astute business man. He has more than a sneaking affection for the English, and is not afraid to laugh at his countrymen. "How did the English conquer and enslave us and oppress us?" he said not long ago. "By a very simple plan. They gave it out that we were a very clever people and that they were a stupid people. Now we ar-r-ren't and they are."

After his stormy life he has become the tenant of the Viceregal Lodge, and no more representative Irishman could fill the great office he holds. He has mellowed with the years, the old savageries are forgotten, and out in Phœnix Park we may see him, a peasant among a peasant people, walking with body thrust forward, hands clasped behind his back, and eyes fixed ahead as if he is looking for something he has lost—a pleasant figure that has strayed out of a passionate tragedy and is sunning himself beneath the calmer skies that overspread "Dark Rosaleen." Even the scientists may forgive him as they laugh at his mediæval obscurantism.